FIANNA FÁIL, IRISH REPUBLICANISM AND THE NORTHERN IRELAND TROUBLES 1968–2005

25/2/13

FIANNA FÁIL,
Irish Republicanism
and the
Northern Ireland Troubles
1968–2005

CATHERINE O'DONNELL

IRISH ACADEMIC PRESS
DUBLIN • PORTLAND, OR

First published in 2007 by
IRISH ACADEMIC PRESS
44 Northumberland Road, Dublin 4, Ireland

and in the United States of America by
IRISH ACADEMIC PRESS
c/o ISBS, Suite 300, 920 NE 58th Avenue
Portland, Oregon 97213-3786

© 2007 by Catherine O'Donnell

WEBSITE: www.iap.ie

British Library Cataloguing in Publication Data
An entry can be found on request

ISBN 978 0 7165 3360 3 (cloth)
ISBN 978 0 7165 2859 3 (paper)

Library of Congress Cataloging-in-Publication Data
An entry can be found on request

Printed by Antony Rowe Ltd., Chippenham, Wiltshire

Contents

Acknowledgements

The completion of a major research project such as the publication of a book is dependent upon the kindness and generosity of many. Firstly, my thanks go to Professor Richard English and Dr Margaret O'Callaghan for their support, encouragement and the kind assistance that they continue to give to me. I would also like to thank the Head of the School of Politics, International Studies and Philosophy, Queen's University, Belfast, Shane O'Neill, for providing me with access to funds under the Research and Travel Award scheme, which enabled me to make a number of research trips to Dublin. I am enormously grateful to Professor Mary Daly for her support and guidance in her role as mentor during my time as Government of Ireland Post-Doctoral Fellow at the Humanities Institute of Ireland, University College, Dublin. I wish also to express my appreciation to the Irish Research Council for the Humanities and Social Sciences for funding my post-doctoral fellowship at UCD.

I would like to thank the staff at the libraries in Queen's University, Belfast and University College, Dublin. The staff at both the Northern Ireland Political Collection at the Linenhall Library, Belfast and the Newspaper Library, Belfast provided me with much appreciated assistance. I am grateful to the staff at the National Archives in Dublin for their help. I also wish to thank the staff at the Archives Department at University College, Dublin for their help when I was accessing the Fianna Fáil archives. Particular thanks go to the staff at the Buncrana Community Library, Co. Donegal, for acquiring numerous books for me.

The book has been enriched through the material obtained in the course of a number of interviews. I would like to thank both those who took the time to talk to me and those in the offices of the interviewees who organized that time. I would also like to thank Frank Millar at the The Irish Times for his assistance in sourcing the cover image.

Very special thanks go to many great friends and family members who have made getting to the end of this project possible; Bredge

Doherty, Karen Doherty and Eleanor Scott for their support and for providing me with accommodation on many research trips to Dublin; very special thanks to Christopher Farrington; to Paul McIvor and Finbarr McCluskey for their hospitality and friendship; thanks also to Sarah Lowndes and Ismael Al Hinti for words of encouragement when they were needed most; Christopher Farrington, Jane McConkey, Peter McLaughlin and Kieran Rankin for their proofreading skills and useful comments. Most importantly, I want to thank my family, in particular my father and my sisters Julie and Madeline and my brothers Dominick, Brian and Paul. I am grateful to my nieces, Nicole and Ciara, for some of the lighter moments. Finally, in her absence, this book is dedicated to the memory of my mother.

Abbreviations

AIA	Anglo-Irish Agreement
APNI	Alliance Party of Northern Ireland
AP/RN	An Phoblacht/Republican News
CSJ	Campaign for Social Justice
DHAC	Derry Housing Action Committee
DUP	Democratic Unionist Party, otherwise known as the UDUP (Ulster Democratic Unionist Party)
EEC	European Economic Community
EU	European Union
FARC	Fuerzas Armandas Revolutionaries de Colombia (Revolutionary Forces of Colombia)
GAA	Gaelic Athletic Association
IICD	International Independent Commission on Decommissioning
IMC	Independent Monitoring Commission
IRA	Irish Republican Army
MLA	Member of Legislative Assembly
MEP	Member of European Parliament
MP	Member of Parliament
NICRA	Northern Ireland Civil Rights Association
O/C	Officer in Command
PDs	Progressive Democrats
PSNI	Police Service of Northern Ireland
PUP	Progressive Unionist Party

RTÉ	Radio Telifís Éireann
RUC	Royal Ulster Constabulary
SDLP	Social Democratic and Labour Party
TD	Teachta Dála (member of the Dáil)
TUAS	Tactical Use of Armed Struggle/Totally Unarmed Struggle
UDA	Ulster Defence Association
UDP	Ulster Democratic Party
UFF	Ulster Freedom Fighters
UKUP	United Kingdom Unionist Party
UN	United Nations
USA/US	United States of America
UVF	Ulster Volunteer Force
UUC	Ulster Unionist Council
UUP	Ulster Unionist Party

Preface

In Conor Lenihan's view there are two points upon which the electorate judges the competency of a party in the Republic of Ireland: management of the economy and management of problems relating to Northern Ireland. Lenihan, the Minister of State at the Department of Foreign Affairs, argued that the issue of Northern Ireland is hugely important in elections in the Republic because 'it's a benchmark of competence, how well you manage the Northern Ireland situation defines whether you become respected and the public allow you to become the government party'.[1] Arguments by Fianna Fáil that it is the most competent party on the issue of Northern Ireland are most obvious in the course of the peace process since the 1990s. However, Fianna Fáil candidates also argued in the course of the 1972 general election that their party was most capable of dealing with security issues relating to Northern Ireland and was more committed than Fine Gael and Labour to ensuring that violence did not cross the border. Speeches during that election campaign by Fianna Fáil members including the Minister for Foreign Affairs, Brian Lenihan, and the Minister for Defence, Gerry Cronin, highlighted the competency of the Lynch government on security and stressed the lack of agreement within the proposed Fine Gael–Labour coalition on the issue.[2] In 1982, a Fianna Fáil election canvass manual compared its record on Northern Ireland with that of the Fine Gael–Labour coalition. It highlighted what it called the coalition's support for the unionist position and advocacy of a constitutional crusade that '[distracted] attention from real issues'. In contrast, a Fianna Fáil government promised to retain Articles Two and Three of the Irish Constitution and, most importantly, had proven to have put an actual initiative at Anglo-Irish level in place.[3]

Correspondence from constituency workers to Fianna Fáil headquarters during the 1987 general election illustrates that attitudes relating to the importance of the Northern Ireland issue varied across constituencies. For example, reports from the Dublin South West constituency stressed that the issues of social welfare, education and unemployment dominated. Similarly, it was reported that Northern Ireland was not an issue in Offaly. In contrast, reports from Laois and Monaghan highlighted the importance of the Northern Ireland issue and complained about Charles Haughey's poor performance on Northern Ireland in a recent television debate with Garret FitzGerald. A constituency report from Meath outlined exactly what was needed: '... A strong forthright approach by Mr Haughey is called for.' In addition the report stated: 'The Northern Ireland issue must be removed immediately if possible i.e. it should be incapulated [sic] in a simple formula so far as this is popular, either an acknowledgement that we agree or disagree, Yes or No.' It went on to report that constituency workers were facing extreme difficulties since it was impossible to put the party's message across on Northern Ireland. They called on Haughey to make a statement and to clear up misunderstandings.[4]

Sections of the electorate may not view Northern Ireland as the leading issue but nonetheless insist that the government party or parties display a level of competence on the issue through the implementation of a clear policy. Within Fianna Fáil's support base some sections care more about Northern Ireland than others. However, as a whole Fianna Fáil supporters demand a clear and strong position on Northern Ireland so that questions do not arise as to what the party's policy may be. The fact that Fine Gael had a very clear position on Northern Ireland in the 1980s threatened Fianna Fáil and it was for this reason that, in the absence of a simple but forthright and lucid policy, Fianna Fáil was seen to be lacking. The nature of that policy has generally been dictated by the section of the party which has a more obvious interest in the issue: the republican wing of the party.

For the republican wing Northern Ireland is clearly important and the fact that the objective of reunification was stated as the first and most important goal for the party illustrates the significance of the issue at ideological and policy levels. In electoral terms Northern Ireland necessitates an intelligible and productive approach so as to assure the electorate of competency and it is at this level that parties compete with one another. This is an important point because both parties have a common objective on the North: securing reunification. Thus, since the parties cannot compete on the long-term goal of reunification, it is rather competency in dealing with the situation on a short-term basis that matters. This was the case during the 1972 general election, it was the issue at the centre of competition between Haughey and FitzGerald on Northern Ireland in the 1980s and can be seen in Fianna Fáil's pronouncements that Fine Gael cannot be trusted with the peace process, given the collapse of the IRA ceasefire during a Fine Gael led government in 1996 (see Chapters Four and Five). The 1987 constituency report from Meath referred to above also called on the party leader to make 'a stirring and rousing speech' so as to lift the spirits of party workers. If Haughey could give a strong speech on Northern Ireland then this would boost the party's morale. This is exactly what the peace process has meant for the party; it has enabled it to argue that it is the best party to manage Northern Ireland, and this has improved its morale and electoral standing.

Despite Northern Ireland's integral position in electoral politics in the Republic and its centrality to Fianna Fáil since its formation in 1926, a substantial analysis of that party's language and policy on Northern Ireland since the outbreak of the Troubles has not been attempted until now. This book does just that. It draws upon new archival, newspaper and interview material and provides a systematic and coherent delineation of Fianna Fáil's response to the outbreak of the Northern Ireland Troubles in 1968 and its subsequent policy formation and language on Northern Ireland. The Introduction provides an outline of Eamon de Valera's ideological legacy as well as the precedents that he established both in terms of policies in relation to Northern Ireland and in the arena of Anglo-Irish relations. This historical context sets out the extent to which de Valera succeeded in constructing a republican orthodoxy within the party and the state itself. The rest of the book will analyze the extent to which Fianna Fáil's rhetoric and ideology have been altered since the late 1960s. A recurring factor that has both contributed to and stalled this process of change relates to the party's need to defend that orthodoxy from alternative, more strident forms of republicanism, either from within, or external to, the party. The book will highlight how this threat to Fianna Fáil's form of republicanism has determined its choice of rhetoric and policy. The changing nature of this threat affected the position adopted by the party on Northern Ireland at the end of the twentieth century and in the early years of the twenty-first century.

It is important to explain both the distinction and the relationship between Fianna Fáil's policy formation and language and its ideology. The distinction between policy formation and ideology will be shown to be crucial in justifying the concessions made by the party in the course of the peace process. This distinction will become clear in the chapter on Bertie Ahern. Historically, the party's ideology has been at odds with its policy on Northern Ireland. This is most adequately exemplified by Clare O'Halloran's description of the contradiction between Fianna Fáil's ideological commitment to unity and its partitionist policies.[5] The party cared more about its ideology than about the fact that this was contradicted by the policies it adopted.

Understanding Fianna Fáil policy and rhetoric throughout the Troubles is more complicated. Throughout the Troubles the party maintained an ideology that was committed to unity and the integrity of the nation, but within that ideology contradictions like those referred to by O'Halloran can be identified. For example, if the party's policy on unification, which sought to persuade the British government to support such an outcome, was successful, it would no doubt have proved counterproductive, since it overlooked unionist objections to unity. Nevertheless the overall objective of unification has remained a constant for the party. In contrast, the party's day-to-day policy and choice of language has been dictated by context. The language and policy adopted by Jack Lynch was very much dictated by the outbreak of the Troubles, IRA violence and the continued impasse at Anglo-Irish level. Haughey's use of anti-partitionist language was determined by the context of competition with FitzGerald, the politicization of Sinn Féin and his position in power or in opposition. For Albert Reynolds and, in particular, Bertie Ahern, the absence of anti-partitionist language is explained by the context of peace and the peace process more generally. The absence of anti-partitionist language does not mean that Reynolds and Ahern hold different interpretations of unionists and the Northern Ireland problem from that of their predecessors. They both maintain an ideological commitment to, and belief in, a united Ireland. Thus it is necessary to make a distinction between policy and language and ideology.

The distinction between ideology and policy is central to understanding Fianna Fáil's position on Northern Ireland and the party's acceptance of the Good Friday Agreement, but in the case of the peace process it is the interaction between the two that is most significant. Fianna Fáil's role within the peace process is distinctive in that its policy involved addressing ideological issues of self-determination and consent. Hence the peace process represents a period in which it is more effective to think in terms of the relationship between Fianna Fáil's policy and ideology. It is in this sense that ideological concepts dominate the study of Fianna Fáil's policy formation throughout the peace process. The peace process involved reconciling the ideological commitment to unity and the integrity of the nation with a policy and language that gave practical recognition to

Northern Ireland, so as to enable the abandonment of anti-partition-ist rhetoric. Achieving this reconciliation entailed an amalgamation of self-determination and consent, but the ideological adherence to unity remained intact through the maintenance of the integrity of the nation.

Two basic principles have guided Fianna Fáil policy on Northern Ireland since the outbreak of the Troubles. The first is the natural affinity felt towards the nationalist community in Northern Ireland on the part of Fianna Fáil, as a republican party, and the Irish government in general. The second is the belief that the problem lay with IRA violence and it was within the capabilities of the Irish government, because of that affinity with northern nationalists, to do something to bring this to an end. These two principles, which have guided Fianna Fáil's approach to Northern Ireland, provide continuity in policy from Lynch to Ahern.

Chapter One assesses Jack Lynch's record on Northern Ireland. It shows that, while Lynch consistently rejected force in bringing about a united Ireland and supported a process of conciliation with unionists, he adopted a traditional republican position on Northern Ireland. He put the goal of unification at the centre of his government's policy on Northern Ireland. Lynch unsuccessfully attempted to undermine claims of legitimacy by the IRA by seeking to secure a declaration from the British government of its interest in unity.

Chapter Two looks at the impact of the growing strength of Sinn Féin in both the North and the South on Fianna Fáil's rhetoric and policy on Northern Ireland during Charles Haughey's period of leadership. The chapter argues that the decision by Haughey to open contacts with Sinn Féin in 1988 was an important proactive and independent judgement on his part and one which developed into a *rapprochement* between the two parties. This relationship became the central driving force behind the peace process. Securing Sinn Féin's place in politics and at the negotiation table became the main objective of Fianna Fáil's Northern Ireland policy in the 1990s. It is in this way that Fianna Fáil policy on Northern Ireland from the late 1980s and throughout the peace process was directed by its relationship with Sinn Féin.

Chapters Two and Three distinguish between the peace process and the process which was previously in place under the Anglo-Irish Agreement of 1985. The book emphatically challenges the literature that has tended to accept that there is an inevitable linkage between the two; that the peace process that developed was the inevitable outcome of the Anglo-Irish Agreement. Chapter Two also looks at the implications of the 1988 talks between Fianna Fáil and Sinn Féin from an ideological perspective, the implications for the notion of self-determination and the principle of consent. It sets out the importance of the decision to introduce the concept of self-determination for the entire peace process.

Chapter Three examines Albert Reynolds' contribution to the peace process and, in particular, his views relating to the centrality of the establishment of a pan-nationalist alliance. It examines the significance of this pan-nationalist association as well as with commitments made by Reynolds on behalf of the Irish government to the IRA's decision to call a ceasefire in 1994. The inability of successive Fianna Fáil governments to engage in a reappraisal of unionism will be demonstrated and it will also be revealed that the party did not recognize the need for such a reassessment as central to the search for peace. Chapters Three and Four will illustrate that Fianna Fáil found its approach in conflict with its successive coalition partners, the Progressive Democrats (PDs) and Labour, on this issue. The tension between Fianna Fáil's efforts towards the establishment of a pan-nationalist front and the belief held, in particular, by the Labour leader, Dick Spring, that the Irish government must embrace unionist concerns is seen throughout the entire peace process of the 1990s. It will be demonstrated that Anglo-Irish relations suffered from Reynolds' interpretation of his government's role in finding a solution to the Troubles and this will challenge the view that good relations between the two governments resulted from the Anglo-Irish Agreement and sponsored the peace process. Instead, it is argued that relations strong enough to produce a joint approach only materialized during the Ahern–Blair administrations.

It is Bertie Ahern's contribution to the peace process that is addressed in Chapter Four. The chapter covers both his party's time in opposition and his first term in office that saw the Irish government's participation in the negotiations which produced the Good Friday Agreement in 1998. The account presented of Fianna Fáil's language relating to Northern Ireland while in opposition provides an insight into the principles which were at the core of the party's perception of the peace process and of the Irish government's responsibilities to the republican movement through the pan-nationalist front. Indeed, the very centrality of the pan-nationalist front is illustrated through the criticisms made by Fianna Fáil of the Rainbow Coalition's handling of the peace process. Once again, the importance of this alliance is emphasized when the IRA ceasefire collapsed in 1996. The change of government in Dublin in 1997 witnessed a rejuvenation of the peace process and also entailed a change of approach from Fianna Fáil, now in power once again. The negotiating process necessitated a shift away from a concentration on getting republicans to the table to keeping all parties involved. It is at this stage that both governments become 'joint-guarantors' of the process and subsequently of the Good Friday Agreement.

It is clear then that the book concentrates on the leaders of Fianna Fáil rather than on debates internal to the party. The reason for this relates to the way in which the party's position on Northern Ireland has tended to be directed by its leader and by those who held the confidence of the leader. The book also emphasizes the relationship between Fianna Fáil and Sinn Féin throughout the 1980s, 1990s and into the twenty-first century; a relationship which took place initially only at elite level, without the knowledge of the wider party.

As well as assessing the role of the Irish government under Fianna Fáil in the peace process of the 1990s, the book also aims at providing a view of the peace process as experienced by the Republic of Ireland. Hence views of opposition parties, journalists and other commentators are included throughout, so that the role of Fianna Fáil is not provided in isolation from the opinions of others. A narrative of the attitudinal changes and altering governmental approaches associated with the peace process is included. The continued use of public debates throughout the book is intended to ensure that the account of the relationship between two political parties (Fianna Fáil and Sinn Féin) and its centrality to the peace process is presented with reference to the perceptions of the other political parties and political commentators of that relationship. This also has the purpose of engaging with both the assumptions and the criticisms of the peace process (this is most clear in Chapter Five).

The use of debates taking place externally to the party illustrates the point at which Fianna Fáil engaged with these debates from the early 1990s onwards as a result of the party's commitment to the peace process, which involved dialogue with the Social Democratic and Labour Party (SDLP) and Sinn Féin. It will become clear that, despite an apparent acceptance of the principle of consent by Lynch and Haughey, these leaders failed to engage the party with a wider debate on Northern Ireland. Such debates[6] posed many challenges to traditional Irish republicanism. Despite such challenges, Fianna Fáil only seriously began to debate the principle of consent, national self-determination and changes to Articles Two and Three in the late 1980s and 1990s, when the party's relationship with Sinn Féin changed in such a way as to enable the possibility of change (see Chapters Two–Four). Fianna Fáil began to address the issues of self-determination and consent at this point, and this reflects the fact that the party's function within the peace process has been determined by its willingness to facilitate Sinn Féin's desire to embrace constitutional politics.

A noticeable feature of the Republic's experience of the peace process has been the level of consensus that it has produced. Noel Treacy, Minister of State at the Department of An Taoiseach, identified the level of 'open consensus' about Northern Ireland as one of the major implications of the Good Friday Agreement and the peace process.[7] That consensus has eliminated debate on Northern Ireland and the peace process itself. The peace process has necessitated a blanket acceptance of the principles underpinning that process. This was achieved in the years immediately after the Good Friday Agreement but has been periodically broken at times of general elections and seriously threatened by recent crises in the peace process.

The fifth and final chapter moves away from the concentration on the Fianna Fáil leadership and develops further the use of public political debate. The chapter focuses upon a debate which took place prior to the 2002 general election as a means of both assessing the peace process itself and the relationship which was central to it: that between Fianna Fáil and Sinn Féin. The academic literature has analyzed the peace process in terms of the players involved, the institutions produced, or the ideological repercussions of the Good Friday Agreement. What is now needed is an examination of the process itself. Chapter Five does this through the prism of a number of newspaper columnists writing in the main broadsheets in the Republic, who have consistently highlighted the inadequacies of the peace process. The final task of the book is to assess the extent to which the controversies relating to IRA criminality affected Fianna Fáil's approach to the peace process in 2005.

The strength of the book is thus multi-faceted; not only does it amount to a study of the factors which have influenced Fianna Fáil's Northern policy during the period 1968–2005, it also enables an understanding of how the party has developed and redefined its understanding of republicanism throughout this period. In addition, the book provides a comprehensive explanation of the forces which have directed the peace process in nationalist Ireland. Most significantly, it details the extent to which the role of the Irish government in the search for a solution for Northern Ireland has altered from the time when Fianna Fáil first came to formulate policy on the area in 1968, when its desire to participate was denied, to the Good Friday Agreement, when its involvement has been central to the entire nature of the process. A fundamental premise upon which this book is based is a view of the politics of both Northern Ireland and the Republic of Ireland as interdependent. The book concentrates upon the relationship between Fianna Fáil and the exponents of a more extreme republicanism and, in the case of the peace process, between Fianna Fáil and Sinn Féin. The book does not deny that there were other influences, particularly that of the SDLP and John Hume. While the book illustrates this point, it is the significant part which Sinn Féin has played in determining Fianna Fáil policy and its role in the peace process which is given prominence. Irish republicanism in the Republic cannot be understood without reference to the position of northern republicanism. The impact of the Arms Crisis of 1970 and the peace process of the 1990s validate such an approach. The book demonstrates the huge part which the conflict within republicanism has played in determining how the Irish state has developed both its brand of republicanism and its approach to Northern Ireland.

NOTES

1. Interview with Conor Lenihan, 16th Nov. 2005. Tom Kitt, the Government Chief Whip, has also identified the issues of the North and the economy as the two central priorities for Fianna Fáil: Interview with Tom Kitt 12 Jan. 2006.
2. See material relating to the 1972 general election in the Fianna Fáil Archives, University College, Dublin, P176/842.
3. Canvass Manual, general election 1982, Fianna Fáil Archives, P176/847.
4. Meath Constituency Report, 14th Feb. 1987, Fianna Fáil Archives, P176/851.
5. O'Halloran, C. *Partition and Limits of Irish Nationalism: An ideology under stress* (Dublin: Gill and Macmillan, 1987), p 27.
6. See works such as O'Brien, C.C. *States of Ireland* (London: Hutchinson & Co. publishers, 1972); FitzGerald, G. *Towards a New Ireland* (Dublin: Gill and Macmillan, 1972). Also see Boyce, D.G. and O'Day, A. (eds), *The making of modern Irish history: Revisionism and the revisionist controversy* (London and New York: Routledge, 1996); Brady, C. (ed), *Interpreting Irish History: The debate on historical revisionism* (Dublin: Irish Academic Press, 1994) for more on general revisionist debates and the issues at their core.
7. Interview with Noel Treacy 1 Dec. 2005.

The North in the South: The Irish State and Partition 1921–68

Despite its internal factionalism, Irish republicanism has been a defining feature not only of the modern Irish state but also of that state's relationship with Northern Ireland. The 1921 Anglo-Irish Treaty had the effect of underlining 'the profound differences among the Republicans, which had been comparatively hidden during the 1919–21 period'.[1] These divisions came to characterize the development of republican thought in subsequent generations. As a result, republicanism has been difficult to define adequately. Those who have attempted to provide such a definition have highlighted the differing forms which republicanism has taken. Tom Garvin has outlined a number of tenets that he claimed have been central to Irish republicanism. He has argued that, while it had favoured 'political democracy, representative institutions, and human rights', at its core it has been an 'insurrectionist anti-British nationalism'.[2] Thus, for Garvin, republicanism represents a combination of fundamentalist Catholicism and separatist nationalism which has produced 'a series of moralistic political movements often of impressive organisational effectiveness, intellectual forcefulness and political sophistication'.[3] In addition, Bill Kissane has argued that republicans have viewed themselves as the 'guardians of that community's highest values and aspirations', and has labelled this as an identification with the 'public band' tradition.[4] Paul Arthur has added to these elements. He has argued that republicanism is based upon 'a profound sense of piety, a deep sense of history and of grievance, and an essential sense of the contemporaneousness of the past. It is a narrative of dispossession overlaid by a fundamental religiosity secularised by a doctrine of manifest destiny'.[5] Kevin Bean has also referred to the way in which the past has been a central guiding force for republicanism. He has claimed that republicanism can be

viewed as 'eclectic and pragmatic'.[6] Viewing republicanism as eclectic
is useful in this context. It is the level of diversity within Irish republicanism stemming from the split in 1921 that has ensured continued
division and which came to define the 'internal cleavages within Irish
nationalism'.[7] Thus John Coakley has described the progression of
Irish republicanism: 'Much of Irish political history in the twentieth
century was conditioned by the evolution of Sinn Féin and by the suc-
cession of divisions within the movement that were occasioned, in the
eyes of the radical side, by the fact that a section of the party leadership was engaged in unprincipled compromise for short-term political
gains'.[8]

It is in this context of division that Eamon de Valera's[9] bid to build
a broad spectrum of support for his republican party and movement
must be understood. In aiming to ensure that his party was not open
to the allegation of a 'sell-out', its ideology was invariably dependent
upon a strong nationalist rhetoric. Dunphy describes how Fianna Fáil
'succeeded in establishing its intellectual, moral, and cultural leadership'[10] and Prager has claimed that Fianna Fáil's ability to 'successfully bridge[d] the two political–cultural worlds – the world of cos-
mopolitan, secular, democratic institutions and the world of roman-
tic, traditional, and religious commitments' – was central to the
party's dominance.[11] Fanning has explained that Fianna Fáil's ability
to gain such dominance was due to its willingness to employ the
'green card' and, as a result, republicanism acquired a central role for
the party.[12] This introduction aims at setting out the way in which de
Valera and Fianna Fáil constructed a particular brand of republicanism that came to underpin the centrality of the party in Irish political
culture. It will provide an insight into the orthodoxy of Fianna Fáil's
republican thought, which became the dominant influence on Irish
life from the 1930s onwards. The study of de Valera is essential to
understanding not only the entire ethos which permeated Irish society and politics for many decades even after his formal departure from
politics but also the context within which partition has been viewed
and approached by Fianna Fáil right up to the Good Friday
Agreement in 1998. De Valera set the boundaries for Irish nationalism and placed an emphasis on the advancement of sovereignty coupled with a rhetorical concentration on partition. The extent to which
de Valera's successor, Sean Lemass,[13] altered the republican basis of
the party is also examined and this provides a more immediate context for the intellectual standpoint of Fianna Fáil at the outbreak of
the Northern Ireland crisis in 1968. It is essential to provide such a

historical analysis of Fianna Fáil's position on Northern Ireland and partition prior to the outbreak of the Troubles in order to appreciate the level and nature of the challenge posed to Fianna Fáil ideology by the Northern Ireland Troubles.

CONSTRUCTING AN ORTHODOXY

De Valera's quest to mould the republican movement began in the aftermath of the 1916 Rising, continued in the years following the Treaty in 1921 and culminated in the foundation of Fianna Fáil: The Republican Party, in 1926. While de Valera's brand of republicanism drew inspiration from the post-1916 Rising era and claimed to be continuing in the pursuit of the same goals, John Regan has identified an earlier process whereby the legacy of 1916 was modified in the years prior to the Treaty settlement in 1921. According to Regan, de Valera set about advancing 'the objective ... of securing the militarist-republicans' support for a settlement which would compromise the republic'.[14] But de Valera's attempts to persuade republicans to accept the inevitability of compromise were hampered by political circumstances. The period following the 1916 Rising was influenced by the legacy of the extremist language of the 1916 Rising leader, Patrick Pearse, and his fellow volunteers, who felt that anyone accepting less than the full republican dream for Ireland was less than Irish. This represented an obstacle to de Valera's plan to de-radicalize republicanism, but he did this by, in David Fitzpatrick's words, 'mould[ing] Irish republicanism into something the Easter martyrs would surely have distrusted; a vast, open, oddly respectable populist movement'.[15] Fitzpatrick explains that de Valera managed to 'turn the Easter tradition on its head' by 'the clear separation of the political, military and governmental facets of the republic'.[16] His attempts to win support for a compromise reflected de Valera's realization that the republican goal of a united, separatist republic would not be conceded by Britain: 'It was made clear during the negotiations that there could be no question of recognition of an Irish republic. Irish membership of the Commonwealth and allegiance to the crown at its head was a *sine qua non* of the talks.'[17]

So, while de Valera was to reject the Treaty 'on the grounds that it envisaged less than a unitary, separatist republic',[18] this disguised the fact that he had already accepted the impossibility of achieving this. The very existence of his *rapprochement* formula of external association[19] proved it. In fact he had (in this period) been 'responsible for much of the small print in Sinn Féin's attempt to meet the conflicting requirements of their own supporters, the British government and the Ulster Unionists'.[20] De Valera's opposition to the Treaty was not merely a matter of principle but one explained by issues relating to leadership, power and republican loyalty. The fact that the Treaty was signed without his knowledge or consent meant that he was naturally hostile to it. De Valera had accepted the need for a compromise, but the 1921 Treaty was not his compromise.[21] The issue of leadership was an important factor: by signing the Treaty in de Valera's absence, the plenipotentiaries undermined his leadership. Lee has stressed that 'unity on his side was his [de Valera's] over-riding objective'.[22] As a result, it was important for de Valera to attempt to keep republicans such as Austin Stack, not yet reconciled to the notion of compromise, on board.[23] The diary of de Valera's secretary, Kathleen O'Connell, refers to his efforts prior to the signing of the Treaty to bring '[Cathal] Brugha and Stack along the road of external association'.[24] However, the fact that de Valera's Document No. 2 did not find support among the opponents of the Treaty, mainly because it did not give absolute independence to Ireland and granted Ulster autonomy, reflected the gulf between the pro- and anti-Treatyites.[25] De Valera was reluctant to cause a split in the republican movement and miscalculated the likelihood of defeat at cabinet level and subsequently in the Dáil. De Valera's crusade in the years prior to the Treaty had not been fully successful and, although he had acceded to the need for compromise, he remained loyal to the extremist element within the movement, in a bid to avert a split.

Another important point in explaining de Valera's rejection of the Treaty is the distinction that he drew between recognizing partition and being a party to it. He sought to maintain the moral high ground on the issue of partition but also wished to be relieved of any responsibility with regard to the signing of any document that would sanction partition. This point was underlined in de Valera's response to the Boundary Commission in 1925, when he attacked the Free State government for having been party to the official sanctioning of partition: 'If we are too weak to prevent this outrage from being committed against us – if it can be perpetrated with impunity for the moment – who will say that we are so weak that we can be compelled to give it a sanction of our consent?'[26] In a further statement on the Boundary Commission he elaborated on this by saying: 'We may have to bow our heads for a time to the enforced partition of our country by a foreign power, but the sanction of our consent that partition can never have.'[27] T. Ryle Dwyer has summed up the position adopted by de Valera on partition: 'in short, he was ready to accept Northern Ireland's right to secede but was really anxious to give the public impression that he was not formally acknowledging what he was in fact accepting'.[28] While rejecting Dwyer's assertion that de Valera conceded the right of the unionist population to opt out of the Irish nation, the distinction between acknowledging the reality of partition and being party to it remained central to Fianna Fáil's approach to Northern Ireland after his departure from politics. By rejecting partition Fianna Fáil has been able to exploit the use of anti-partitionist language, and this is why de Valera placed the re-unification of the country at the centre of his brand of Irish republicanism. As Prager explains, republicanism was central to Fianna Fáil since it enabled the party to gain wider support for its movement into constitutional politics: 'By walking gingerly between Republican conceptions and Free State institutions, the party proved to this population that the democratic structures could represent, via Fianna Fáil, their interests as well.'[29]

PARTITION AS A TACTICAL DEVICE

Thus, de Valera's position relied upon drawing a distinction between acknowledging the reality of, in the republican mindset, a British enforced partition and sanctioning it. This distinction was crucial in enabling de Valera and his party, Fianna Fáil, to draw upon its opposition to partition as a tactical device in negotiations with the British and in ensuring the maintenance of the party's electoral strength. De Valera was vocal in his demand for self-determination for the Irish people between 1917 and 1921. He claimed that 'the people of Ireland constitute one distinct and separate nation, ethnically, historically and tested by every standard of political science; entitled, therefore, to self-determination'.[30] He refused to accept the compromise involved in the 1921 Treaty and the 1925 Boundary Commission and this enabled his party to claim later that it had not sanctioned the limits that these imposed upon the exercise of self-determination. De Valera first adopted a practical and tactical approach to the Ulster problem on his return from America in 1920 in the aftermath of the Government of Ireland Act. His position on Ulster during the negotiations is summed up by Lee and Ó Tuathaigh as follows:

Obviously, nationalist Ireland was not prepared to accept the justice of the permanence of this partition. But for the moment,
nothing could be done to reverse the development. What was
open to question, to struggle and bargain for, was the kind of
state which would operate for nationalist Ireland, and it was for
this that the War of Independence was fought.[31]

The northern issue was not a priority for de Valera and it featured little in his correspondence with the British Prime Minister, David Lloyd
George, prior to the Treaty negotiations.[32] The right of 'constituencies' in the north-east of Ireland to be ruled by a parliament as set out
in the 1920 Government of Ireland Act was conceded by de Valera in
October 1921.[33] Nevertheless, de Valera planned to use the Ulster
question as a mechanism of tactical leverage in the pursuit of independence in the form of external association for the twenty-six counties. According to Lee and Ó Tuathaigh, 'the heart of the matter
seemed to be how far would the British be prepared (or forced) to go
in respect of the status and sovereignty of the twenty-six-county
state?'[34] They argued that de Valera took the view that 'even a sub-
stantively strengthened version of dominion status could only be considered if the North would come into an all Ireland settlement.
Otherwise, a twenty-six county state must be a republic'.[35] This was to
form the crux of de Valera's preparations for the Treaty negotiations.
    At the Sinn Féin Árd Fheis on 28 October 1921, de Valera outlined
that he would 'be willing to suggest to the Irish people to give up a
good deal in order to have an Ireland that could look to the future
without anticipating distracting internal problems'. He went on to rule
out the possibility of conceding the oath, in an attempt to prevent partition by declaring: 'Whatever concessions, therefore, our representatives at present in London may feel constrained to offer – an Oath of
Allegiance will not be one of them'.[36] However, he envisaged that the
Ulster question could be used as a tactical device in the course of the
Treaty negotiations. In short, it was as follows: 'Significantly when de
Valera was advising the Treaty negotiators on how to proceed if the
settlement offered was unsatisfactory, he said they should break on
Ulster. There would be odium attaching to whichever party broke off
the talks: Ulster would be an acceptable excuse.'[37] It is not surprising
then that partition was not a major issue in the Treaty split and subsequent Civil War.[38] During the Treaty debate de Valera referred to it as
'a *fait accompli* that had to be faced'.[39] He outlined his view on the
clauses in the Treaty relating to Ulster during a private session of the

Dáil on 15 December 1921, in which he accepted them almost word for word, subject to a declaration that no section of the population had the right to opt out of the nation.[40] De Valera's Document No 2 referred to the issue of Ulster as follows:

> That, whilst refusing to admit the right of any part of Ireland to be excluded from the supreme authority of the Parliament of Ireland, or that the relations between the Parliament of Ireland and any subordinate Legislature in Ireland can be a matter for treaty with a government outside Ireland, nevertheless, in sincere regard for internal peace, and in order to make manifest our desire not to bring force or coercion to bear upon any substantial part of the Province of Ulster, whose inhabitants may now be unwilling to accept the national authority, we are prepared to grant to that portion of Ulster which is defined as Northern Ireland in the British Government of Ireland Act of 1920 privileges and safeguards not less substantial than those provided for in the Articles of Agreement for a Treaty between Great Britain and Ireland signed in London on 6 December 1921.[41]

This was to become a sacred principle within the Fianna Fáil doctrine in relation to partition. De Valera and, subsequently, Fianna Fáil rejected the use of force as a means of bringing Ulster unionists under the rule of an all-Ireland parliament, but he also rejected the right of the unionist community to opt out of the Irish nation. This is crucial in understanding the limits of Fianna Fáil's ability to engage in the search for a solution for the Northern Ireland problem: central to Fianna Fáil's republicanism is the definition of the nation as encompassing the entire island. The challenge facing Fianna Fáil in the latter decades of the twentieth century was to reconcile this with the reality of partition and the ethnic divisions on the island.

In the aftermath of the Civil War, de Valera successfully altered the terms of the debate relating to partition in order to place it at the centre of his new party's ideology. In his speech to the Sinn Féin Árd Fheis in 1925 de Valera revealed that republicans were willing to grant local autonomy 'to all those areas in the North' which could 'prove they had a majority' but they 'never contemplated giving their sanction to the cutting off of any portion from Ireland' and claimed that 'in justice' the Ulster unionists 'could not ask for anything more'.[42] Also, and more interestingly, he went on to say that, while 'they did not like it', Sinn Féin was prepared to tolerate an external association with the British Empire as a further gesture to the North. De Valera claimed that this 'was a great concession for national Ireland'.[43] De Valera presented this as a concession to Ulster, but in fact it signified his use, once again, of Ulster as a bargaining tool. Firstly, he had not objected to the clauses on Ulster and, more specifically, those on the Boundary Commission in the Treaty; he was now presenting it as though he had. Secondly, he did not have an offer of external association from Britain; this was in fact the best he had hoped to achieve in 1921. He now attempted to make it look as though he would accept it to appease the Ulster unionists and sell it as a mechanism to save the country from partition. In reality, external association was his objective and not the ending of partition. If external association was accepted by Britain this would amount to a gain rather than a concession. This marks the beginning of a more blatant emphasis on partition for tactical and propaganda purposes and to justify his stance during the Civil War. This is an approach that de Valera was to utilize throughout his long political career.

Dunphy has pointed out the extent to which Fianna Fáil's rise in popularity from the 1930s onwards was due to its ability to provide 'concrete policy proposals which enjoyed widespread popularity – for example economic protectionism' – and has demonstrated the tendency of the party to combine this with nationalist rhetoric.[44] According to Dunphy, de Valera's success was due to his party's appeal to the lower middle classes in society in a manner that enabled the party to 'articulate the interests of the social forces which it represented in such a way as to identify them with the interests of the nation'.[45] The party's mixture of nationalism and Catholicism ensured support from the Catholic hierarchy.[46] Fianna Fáil's talent in claiming to be representative of the interests of the nation, together with its concentration on the injustices of partition, allowed de Valera to counter the apparent threat which republicanism itself posed to the very existence of the state. The exploitation of anti-partitionist language can be explained in this light, it was also a mechanism to maintain unanimity within the republican constituency. It provided a buffer against criticism from radical republicanism and was aimed at de-legitimizing the IRA. After he became Taoiseach, de Valera was able to claim that his party had a coherent approach for accomplishing unity, and this was used to justify his harsh treatment of the IRA, which included the introduction of the Offences Against the State Act in 1939 and his refusal to accede to demands of IRA members who were imprisoned under this legislation when they engaged in a series of hunger strikes from the 1930s onwards.[47] While de Valera displayed a degree of political pragmatism which distinguished him from radical republicanism and was increasingly irritated with the IRA,[48] republican rhetoric was central to Fianna Fáil's success. Thus, de Valera's involvement in constitutional politics resulted in a somewhat uneasy mixture of fervent republican doctrine and a desire to maintain and guard the state from the threat intrinsic to the principles espoused by non-Fianna Fáil republicanism.

IDEOLOGICAL CONTRADICTIONS: SOVEREIGNTY VERSUS UNITY

While de Valera continued to equate his party with the interests of the whole Irish nation, Fianna Fáil's position within the southern state inherently meant an acceptance by the party of a compromise to the ethos of 1916. Bowman describes the contradictions which were to define de Valera's political career:

> The rest [from 1921] of his long career was devoted to reconciling, on the one hand, the aspiration to an independent, sovereign, separatist republic for the entire island of Ireland, with, on the other, his appreciation that, strategically, Irish defence was inseparable from that of Britain, and in the north east of the island, a local majority was determined to resist Irish unity on the nationalists' terms.[49]

Since his priority lay with protecting the twenty-six-county state, what developed can be termed 'a twenty-six-county state nationalism'. The manner in which de Valera inculcated a Catholic and Gaelic republicanism committed to national unity, as espoused in the 1937 Constitution, into Irish society and politics became the foundation of Fianna Fáil's position within the state. Inevitably the complexities of Fianna Fáil's position within the state and the reality of the two states on the island necessitated the formulation of a contradictory ideology giving priority to conflicting emotions.[50] The strong rhetorical endorsement of the cause of unity conflicted with the consolidation of a homogenous Catholic identity which paradoxically limited this republicanism to the twenty-six counties. De Valera strove to protect the established twenty-six-county state, not just by exerting the sovereignty of that state at international level through neutrality in World War II, but also from the threat of dissident republicans. This highlights the fact that the Fianna Fáil party has historically been more concerned to ensure that an ideological commitment to unity is maintained than to attempt to adopt a policy that could achieve this end.[51]

Central to de Valera's policies was exerting the state's independence in the arena of Anglo-Irish relations and, as Kennedy demonstrates, this approach did not entail the construction of favourable relations or links with Northern Ireland.[52] At the inaugural meeting of the new party, Fianna Fáil: The Republican Party, on 26 May 1926, de Valera announced the party's plan 'to sever the Free State's constitutional ties with Britain "one by one until the full internal sovereignty of the twenty-six counties was established beyond question". Then, he said, "the position would be reached in which the solution of the problems of successfully bringing in the North could be confidently undertaken".'[53] This was the instigation of a plan to exert the sovereignty of the twenty-six counties, in the hope that the solution to partition would present itself and would be aided by the strong constitutional position of the Irish Free State. This is later seen in his efforts to amend the 1922 Free State Constitution in the 1930s, the 1937 Constitution, the Economic War (1932–8) and his stance of neutrality during the Second World War. Speaking in the Dáil in 1939, de Valera outlined the reasoning behind the decision to maintain a neutral stance during the Second World War: 'We believe that no other position would be accepted by the majority of our people as long as the present position [partition] exists.'[54] De Valera sought to achieve a constitutional position whereby 'the proclaiming of the Republic may involve no more than a ceremony that formal confirmation of a status already attained'.[55] Unfortunately the outcome of this approach was to widen the already broad gap between North and South. Joseph Lee has argued that de Valera's approaches, not just to neutrality, suffered a lack of

> ...understanding of the technical links between various aspects of policy, failing to see the implications of policies (as distinct from politics) in one field for policies in others ... He never related his social vision of an arcadian utopia or his cultural vision of a Gaelic Ireland to his political vision of a united Ireland. His dream of the frugal fare of the small farm held no place for the Shankill or even for the Falls.[56]

Neutrality, for example, 'did much to emphasise the consciousness of sovereignty',[57] as did the Constitution of 1937, but both had serious implications for partition. Basil Chubb has identified within the 1937

Constitution 'a set of objectives aimed at by de Valera, Fianna Fáil and many, perhaps most, Irish people that were in fact contradictory and even mutually exclusive. To look for a Gaelic, Catholic, 32 county Republic was to ask for the impossible given the presence of northern unionists'.[58] Yet de Valera continuously equated 'Irish' with 'Catholic' both in his choice of language and in his constitutional provisions.[59] The deliberate snub to Stormont inherent in de Valera's provision in the 1937 Constitution for regional government, which he envisaged as subordinate to the Dáil, further alienated the northern unionists and entrenched the divisions North and South.[60] Charles Townshend has correctly underlined the fact that 'the combination of Catholic social values and the territorial claim to the whole island (enshrined in the 1937 Constitution) cemented the alienation of the northern Protestant Unionists, so that the very success of the nation-building process ensured the frustration of the desire for unification'.[61] De Valera's constitutional changes of the 1930s further confirmed unionist interpretations. Unionists viewed the provisions relating to the Irish language, the Catholic Church and the prohibition of divorce as evidence of the southern state's willingness to ignore minority rights.[62] The close ties that developed between Church and state meant there was 'a certain intimacy about Irish society where clerical and political institutions were interlocked'.[63] The confessional nature of de Valera's government further alienated the ideal of unity, which in Laffan's words was 'based on geographical or historical images rather than on political realities'.[64] 'The continued rhetorical concern for national unity and unionist sentiment', in Lee's analysis, 'seems curious in view of the fact that the constitution contained numerous clauses bound to be repugnant to any self-respecting Protestant'.[65] Article 2 laid claim to the entire island of Ireland as encompassing the national territory, while Articles 41 and 44, respectively, banned divorce and upheld the special position of the Catholic Church in the state. The Constitution also upheld the belief that true sovereignty could only be exercised under God.[66] Whyte has said that, even though it was not as Catholic as it might have been and reflected the position of the two main parties of the state, de Valera's Constitution represented a desire to protect Catholic values and promote favourable relations between the state and the Catholic Church.[67]

However, de Valera did attempt to recognize the position of other churches in the state.[68] Lyons has also defended Article 44 as representing 'no more than ... the actual situation in the Irish Free State' and claims that 'the broad toleration revealed by these clauses' was

designed 'to reassure the minority within the twenty-six counties and
also to convince doubting Protestants in the six counties that Home
Rule had not, after all, meant Rome rule'.[69] Lyons also argued that the
fact that de Valera did not declare the state to be a republic was evidence of a recognition that this would be 'anathema to the men of the
North' and therefore provided an opening to future reunification,[70]
although Pádraig O'Malley has pointed out that this recognition did
not prohibit de Valera and his party from voting in favour of the 1948
Bill removing Éire from the Commonwealth and declaring the state
to be a republic.[71] It is true that a number of elements of the
Constitution would suggest that de Valera recognized the limits
brought by the existence of Northern Ireland but this acknowledgement was not reflected in the type of society he advocated. This coincided with another central feature of Fianna Fáil's approach to
Northern Ireland: the persistence of an incoherent stance and inadequate understanding of the unionist community that populates the
north-east of the island. The general inability of Irish republicans to
comprehend the complexities of unionism relates to the central position which imperialism has assumed within the republican mindset.
The tendency to view Britain's intentions towards Ireland in the twentieth century as based upon imperialism, the belief that Britain represented the only real obstacle to unity, and the perception of the unionist community as 'little more than a malleable creature of British policy' allowed republicans to avoid any serious consideration of unionism.[72] Thus Clare O'Halloran has concluded that traditional assumptions relating to unionism have remained a constant element in the
thinking of the Irish state, its leaders and people.[73] De Valera's understanding of the Ulster problem was lacking due to an over-riding sim-
plification of the problem in his thinking. Dwyer provides a further
illustration on this point: 'De Valera, as president of the Irish
Republic, revealed a rather shallow perception of the depth of the
Ulster problem, which he seemed to think could be resolved by a combination of economic incentives and economic pressure'.[74]

Fanning has argued that northern policy emanated from a memorandum circulated by Ernest Blythe, a northern Protestant and member of the Provisional government's committee responsible for the
consideration of issues relating in Ulster in 1922. He advocated a policy of recognition of, and cooperation with, Northern Ireland. This,
according to Fanning, represented the instigation of a policy of 'non-
violent, constitutional northern policy pursued by the successive governments of independent Ireland until the present day'.[75] While

Fianna Fáil policy can correctly be depicted as non-violent, the party did not do enough to promote co-operation and understanding and instead relied upon fervent nationalism. This explains why Peter Mair has claimed that 'Irish politics is about nationalism; the appeal for an end to partition and the bringing together of North and South into a united 32 county republic'. The existence of the Irish state has been defined in relation to partition, but this has not meant a clear commitment to ending partition.[76] This account of de Valera's contribution to Irish politics underlined the fact that it was he who defined the manner in which nationalism would be central to politics in Ireland. The dichotomy between the quest for sovereignty and the desire for unity at the core of de Valera's ideology is explained by the need to balance the exigencies of the southern state and to ensure that the party was not open to criticisms on the national question.[77] It also formed part of the party's quest to maintain its place as a central force in Irish political and social life.

SEÁN LEMASS: 'AN ERA OF RADICAL CHANGE'?

The challenge facing the Fianna Fáil party when de Valera left office in 1959 was to reconcile his legacy, firstly, with Lemass' realization that the inward-looking ideology could not realize the potential of the state and, secondly and most significantly, with the reality of the situation in Northern Ireland from 1968 onwards. The de Valera era institutionalized what O'Halloran termed the 'co-existence of irredentism-in-theory with partitionism-in-practice'.[78] The question as to whether Lemass evoked a radical departure from the ethos of de Valera is subject to debate. There is a perception that the subsequent period under the guidance of Seán Lemass amounted to an 'era of radical change'.[79] For example, Laffan has argued that the Lemass era 'symbolized a new mood in his realization that the best way to undermine the border was to talk about it less and to concentrate on making the Republic a more attractive place to live in'.[80] In addition, Ruane and Todd have claimed that from the 1960s onwards the Irish state espoused 'a less intense nationalism' and, as a result of the Republic's ability to advance its independence, Anglo-Irish relations had improved by the end of Lemass' term in office.[81]

That Lemass might adopt an approach distinctive from that of de Valera's was hinted at many years previous to his becoming Taoiseach. Brian Farrell's short biography of Seán Lemass emphasizes his role in

the foundation of Fianna Fáil through encouraging a split within Sinn
Féin and persuading de Valera to form a new party. Lemass' objection
to the Sinn Féin party rested on its tendency towards inaction: 'Of
what use are ideals if they do not spur us to action? Action alone will
justify our faith.'[82] It is within the context of such an ethos that
Lemass has been judged, and hence the belief exists that he oversaw
the transition away 'from protectionism ... in favour of more open
competition and planned economy'.[83] While Raymond James
Raymond has challenged the image of Lemass which has 'portrayed
[him] as the progressive architect of the modern Irish economy' and
has instead claimed the planning for Lemass and Whitaker's economic expansion had 'come from de Valera', which can be traced back to
1942,[84] he does argue that the idea of the preservation of full employ-
ment is 'entirely attributable' to Lemass. This, he claims, generated
'the most far-reaching debate on Irish economic policy since the
foundation of the state'.[85] For Lyons it is irrelevant whether the new
economic expansion plans originated from de Valera or not, since 'the
responsibility of implementing it fell squarely upon Mr Lemass'.[86] He
has described him as 'intelligent, pragmatic, with almost an instinctive
understanding of economic problems', and affirms that 'it is no mere
exercise in public relations which links his name indissolubly with the
forward policy of these years'. Farrell certainly concurs that Lemass
made a powerful contribution to the state and the nation: '... a man
more concerned to stimulate changes yet to be achieved than to pro-
claim the transition from the era of de Valera to the world of Lemass
already accomplished; a man trying to create rather than just reflect a
community consensus; a man unsure of the acceptability of his image
of Ireland to his contemporaries'.[87]

The debate as to whether it was de Valera or Lemass who was
responsible for new economic policies of the 1960s is not entirely
irrelevant to the question of partition, since the previously espoused
economic protectionism was a remnant of the Sinn Féin ethos – 'ourselves alone'. Nevertheless the aim here is to assess whether Lemass'
meetings with the Northern Ireland Prime Minister, Captain Terence
O'Neill, reflected a wider intellectual shift on Northern Ireland within his administration. Henry Patterson has rightly referred to the fact
that many academics have perceived Lemass' first term and his first
meeting with O'Neill as reflecting an era 'in which the philosophies
and political priorities of both states in Ireland were transformed'.[88]
Stephen Collins, in his study of the Fianna Fáil party, has stressed the
significance of the Lemass era as deriving from the fact that his

deputies were not 'inculcated with the same values and sense of commitment that animated their elders ... brought no civil war baggage with them and were content to follow the Lemass policy of a peaceful approach to the Northern problem and all that it entailed for politics in the South'.[89] Keogh has also described the Lemass–O'Neill meetings as evidence of the Irish government's 'attempt to place North–South relations on a functional basis' and as the consequence of Lemass' recognition that the Ulster question required the building of favourable relations with the northern state.[90] Patterson has, however, challenged this view and points to the language utilized by Lemass as reminiscent of de Valera's rhetoric.[91] Patterson suggests that Lemass' more progressive ideas in relation to 'the growth of a practical system of co-operation between the two areas in advance of any political arrangement' were overshadowed by his adherence to traditional republican language in his call for a united Ireland with a republican form of government.[92] Writing elsewhere in conjunction with Paul Bew and Paul Teague, Patterson has demonstrated how the label 'technocratic anti-partitionism'...

> only partially reflects the complexity of his [Lemass'] position. For while he was vigorously pursuing closer forms of co-operation with the North in a range of areas, he was also publicly making clear his desire for a political settlement in which London would play the role of catalyst by publicly declaring that it favoured an end to partition through the coming together of North and South.[93]

Patterson and Bew have maintained that 'Lemass has justifiably been praised for his initiative in meeting Terence O'Neill, the Northern Irish premier, in 1965. He offered a generous definition of Irish unity: "unity means first that – bringing the people together. It is not a matter of territorial acquisition".' However, they argue that 'Lemass contributed absolutely no new ideas in the Republic to the "debate" about the North'.[94]

Horgan has illustrated that, while Lemass' advocacy of a federal system was reminiscent of de Valera's language, his emphasis on the principle of consent was a significant development.[95] Lemass accepted that 'a climate of harmony and agreement' must be a prerequisite to national unity rather than a symptom of it.[96] Farrell has acknowledged the twin influences relevant to Lemass' approach; his 'starting point was a fervent nationalism', but one which was coupled with the recognition that 'efforts to coerce or compel the Unionists into a united Ireland were futile'. His attempts to harbour useful cross-border links must therefore be viewed as his attempts to 'advance on the Cold War mentality of traditional anti-partition propaganda'.[97] Nevertheless, Lemass, as leader of Fianna Fáil, recognized for the first time the existence of a parliament in Northern Ireland which commanded the support of the majority there.[98] He once again accepted *de facto* recognition of Northern Ireland through his subsequent meetings with Terence O'Neill.[99] So, while it may have been fair for Bew and Patterson to conclude that Lemass' rhetoric differed little from that of de Valera and that debate on Northern Ireland was not advanced, it is the pro-active nature of Lemass' approach that emphasizes the departure from de Valera's preference for rhetoric on its own. The undertaking to establish favourable North–South relations represented an acceptance of the shortcomings in the previous non-recognition attitude and thus the symbolic importance of the meetings was very real. In addition, the records of the meetings held on the Northern Ireland side show that a lot of progress was being made in the area of North–South co-operation and that this continued into the early years of Jack Lynch's administration.[100] However, any progress which might have resulted from the continuation of Lemass' approach and attempts at better North–South relations was ultimately undone by the onset of the Troubles in Northern Ireland in 1968. In a context of peace and apparently improved relations within Northern Ireland, Lemass' use of anti-partitionist language had fewer negative implications than was the case for Lynch from 1968 onwards. The Troubles in Northern Ireland highlighted the dangers associated with the use, by the Irish government, of anti-partitionist rhetoric. Fianna Fáil's response to the crisis that resulted from the violence in Northern Ireland is assessed in Chapter One. The following decades witnessed the continued appeal of irredentism and the willingness of the southern state to manipulate the progression of republicanism in order to protect the southern state, and this manifested in the Arms Trial of Jack Lynch's first term in office.

NOTES

1. English, R. *Ernie O'Malley: IRA Intellectual* (Oxford: Clarendon Press, 1998), p. 83.
2. Garvin, T. *1922: The Birth of Irish Democracy* (Dublin: Gill and Macmillan, 1996), p. 11.

3. Garvin, T. 'Patriots and Republicans: An Irish evolution', in W. Crotty and D.E. Schmitt (eds), *Ireland and the Politics of Change* (London and New York: Longman, 1998), p. 145.
4. Kissane, B. *Explaining Irish Democracy* (Dublin: University College, Dublin Press, 2002), p. 18.
5. Arthur, P. 'The Transformation of Republicanism', in J. Coakley (ed), *Changing Shades of Orange and Green: Redefining the Union and the Nation in Contemporary Ireland* (Dublin: University College, Dublin Press, 2002), p. 89.
6. Bean, K. 'Defining Republicanism: Shifting discourses of new nationalism and post-republicanism', in M. Elliott (ed), *The Long Road to Peace in Northern Ireland. Peace Lectures from the Institute of Irish Studies at Liverpool University* (Liverpool: Liverpool University Press, 2002), p. 132.
7. O'Duffy, B. 'British and Irish Conflict Regulation from Sunningdale to Belfast Part I: Tracing the status of contesting sovereigns, 1968–1974', *Nations and Nationalism*, 5, 4 (1999), p. 525.
8. Coakley, J. 'Conclusion: New strains of unionism and nationalism', in Coakley (ed), *Changing Shades of Orange and Green*, p. 133.
9. Eamon de Valera: Irish Volunteer commandant at Easter Rising 1916; elected as Sinn Féin MP and President of Sinn Féin in 1917; opposed the Anglo-Irish Treaty in 1921; elected as Sinn Féin TD in 1923; founded Fianna Fáil in 1926; led Fianna Fáil into government in 1932; Taoiseach 1937–48, 1951–4,1957–9; President of Ireland 1959–73.
10. Dunphy, R. *The Making of Fianna Fáil Power in Ireland, 1923–1948* (Oxford: Clarendon Press, 1995), p. viii.
11. Prager, J. *Building Democracy in Ireland: Political order and cultural integration in a newly independent nation* (Cambridge: Cambridge University Press, 1986), p. 194.
12. Fanning, R. *Independent Ireland* (Dublin: Helicon, 1983), p. 100. While public opinion in the Republic has become ambivalent to ending partition, voters have continued to view Northern Ireland as an important issue for government: see Marsh, M. and Sinnott, R. 'The Voters: Stability and change', in M. Gallagher and M. Laver (eds), *How Ireland Voted 1992* (Dublin: Folens and the Political Studies Association of Ireland Press, 1993), p. 99. Similarly, the desire for unity has remained constant: see Hayes, B.C. and McAllister, I. 'British and Irish Public Opinion Towards the Northern Ireland Problem', *Irish Political Studies*, 11 (1996), p. 77. For a discussion of the commitment to the achievement of unity, see Cox, W.H. 'Who wants a united Ireland?', *Government and Opposition*, 20, 1 (Winter 1985).
13. Seán Lemass: Irish Volunteer involved in Easter Rising 1916; member of anti-Treaty IRA 1922–3; elected as Sinn Féin TD in 1924; founding member of Fianna Fáil in 1926; Tánaiste 1945–8, 1951–4, 1957–9; Taoiseach 1959–66.
14. Regan, J.M. *The Irish Counter-Revolution 1921–1936: Treatyite politics and the settlement in Independent Ireland* (Dublin: Gill and Macmillan, 1999), p. 5.
15. Fitzpatrick, D. 'De Valera in 1917: The undoing of the Easter Rising', in J. O'Carroll and J.A. Murphy (eds), *De Valera and his Times* (Cork: Cork University Press, 1983), p. 103.
16. Fitzpatrick, 'De Valera in 1917', p. 105.
17. Hopkinson, M. *Green Against Green: The Irish Civil War* (Dublin: Gill and Macmillan, 1988), p. 19. Also see Lee, J.J. *Ireland 1912–1985: Politics and society* (Cambridge: Cambridge University Press, 1989), p. 48.
18. Bowman, *De Valera and the Ulster Question* (Oxford: Clarendon Press, 1982), p. 60.
19. This formula would ensure Irish sovereignty in internal matters with Ireland remaining associated with the Crown in external affairs; see Lee, *Ireland 1912–1985*, p. 48.
20. Bowman, *De Valera*, p. 60.
21. Fanning, *Independent Ireland*, p. 3. It is worth noting the level of confusion which surrounded the status of the plenipotentiaries. Dorothy MacArdle has maintained that de Valera was clear that the plenipotentiaries must consult the Dáil before signing any agreement: MacArdle, D. *The Irish Republic* (London: Victor Gollancz Ltd, 1938), pp. 548–9. Yet, according to Lyons, the relevant provision passed by the cabinet suggested the delegates had power to sign an agreement and the demand that the delegates must not sign without the Dáil's agreement was given independently by de Valera: see Lyons, F.S.L. *Ireland since the Famine* (London: Fontana Press, 1985), pp. 429–30.
22. Lee, *Ireland 1912–1985*, p. 49.
23. The only cabinet members to reject the Treaty were de Valera, Cathal Brugha and Austin

Stack. Longford, Earl of and O'Neill, T.P. *Eamon de Valera* (Dublin: Gill and Macmillan, 1970), p. 169.

24. As quoted in Longford and O'Neill, *Eamon de Valera*, p. 170.
25. Townshend, C. *Political Violence in Ireland: Government and resistance since 1848* (Oxford: Clarendon Press, 1983), p. 364.
26. De Valera, 6 Dec. 1925 in Moynihan, M. *Speeches and Statements by Eamon de Valera 1918–73* (Dublin: Gill and Macmillan, 1980), p. 123.
27. De Valera, 6 Dec. 1925 in Moynihan, *Speeches and Statements by Eamon de Valera 1918–73*, p. 123.
28. Dwyer, T.R. 'Eamon de Valera and the Partition Question', in O'Carroll and Murphy (eds), *De Valera and his Times*, p. 77.
29. Prager, *Building Democracy in Ireland*, p. 197.
30. As quoted in Fitzpatrick, D. *The Two Irelands 1912–1939* (Oxford: Oxford University Press, 1998), p. 28.
31. Lee, J.J. and Ó Tuathaigh, G. *The Age of de Valera* (Dublin: Ward River Press in association with RTÉ, 1982), p. 39.
32. Laffan, M. *The Partition of Ireland, 1911–1925* (Dundalk: Dundalgan, Historical Association of Ireland, 1994), pp. 74, 78.
33. MacArdle, *The Irish Republic*, pp. 563–4.
34. Lee and Ó Tuathaigh, *The Age of de Valera*, p. 51.
35. Lee and Ó Tuathaigh, *The Age of de Valera*, p. 39. Also see Dwyer, T.R. *Michael Collins and the Treaty: His differences with de Valera* (Dublin and Cork: The Mercier Press, 1981), p. 76.
36. De Valera, 28 Oct. 1921 in Moynihan, *Speeches and Statements by Eamon de Valera 1918–73*, p. 74.
37. Edwards, O.D. *Eamon De Valera: Political portraits* (Cardiff: GRC Books, 1987), p. 102.
38. Lee and Ó Tuathaigh, *The Age of de Valera*, p 52; Fanning, *Independent Ireland*, p. 24.
39. Dáil Éireann Private Session, Dec. 15 1921, in Moynihan, *Speeches and Statements by Eamon de Valera 1918–73*, pp. 85–6.
40. See Dwyer, *Michael Collins and the Treaty*, p. 77.
41. The Alternative to the Treaty 'Document No. 2' by Eamon De Valera, Fianna Fáil Archives, University College, Dublin, P176/944. The clauses relating to Ulster in the first draft of Document No. 2, as presented to the Dáil in Dec. 1921, differed from the version circulated in Jan. 1922. See Bowman, *De Valera*, pp. 66–9.
42. Bowman, *De Valera*, p. 86.
43. Bowman, *De Valera*, p. 86.
44. Dunphy, *The Making of Fianna Fáil Power in Ireland*, p. 8. Prager has also pointed out that Fianna Fáil combined 'public policy and cultural vision' by 'linking the rhetoric of national independence to specific policy debates', Prager, *Building Democracy in Ireland*, p. 205.
45. Dunphy, *The Making of Fianna Fáil Power in Ireland*, p. 48.
46. Hanley, B. *The IRA 1926–36* (Dublin: Four Courts Press, 2002), pp. 68, 70.
47. For an account of relations between the IRA and Fianna Fáil in the 1930s see Hanley, *The IRA 1926–36*, chapters 6–7.
48. Townshend, *Political Violence in Ireland*, p. 378.
49. Bowman, *De Valera*, p. 3.
50. It is appreciated that Northern Ireland does not have the characteristics of a state. However, for ease of usage the book refers to the existence of two states on the island. It also highlights the fact that Northern Ireland is not under the jurisdiction of the Republic.
51. Fianna Fáil's emphasis on an ideological commitment to unity and the integrity of the nation even where its policy gives practical recognition to the existence of Northern Ireland is again central to the party's acceptance of the Good Friday Agreement in 1998. This point is highlighted in Chapter Four and again in the Conclusion.
52. Kennedy, M. *Division and Consensus: The politics of cross-border relations in Ireland, 1925–1969* (Dublin: Institute of Public Administration, 2000), p. 43. For a study of North–South relations from a northern perspective, see Kennedy, D. *The Widening Gulf: Northern attitudes to the independent Irish state, 1919–49* (Belfast: The Blackstaff Press), 1988.
53. Dwyer, 'Eamon de Valera and the Partition Question', p. 79.
54. Quoted in Murphy, J.A. *Ireland in the Twentieth Century* (Dublin: Gill and Macmillan,

1981), p. 100.
55. As quoted in Longford and O'Neill, *Eamon de Valera*, p. 289.
56. Lee, *Ireland 1912–1985*, p. 337.
57. Murphy, *Ireland in the Twentieth Century*, p. 107.
58. Chubb, B. *The Politics of the Irish Constitution* (Dublin: Institute of Public Administration, 1991), p. 16.
59. Lyons, F.S.L. *Culture and Anarchy in Ireland 1890–1939* (Oxford: Clarendon Press, 1979), p. 152.
60. Kennedy, *Division and Consensus*, p. 58. Article 28A of the Constitution deals with local government and Article 15.2.2 refers to the creation of legislative bodies subordinate to the Oireachtas (Dáil and Seanad).
61. Townshend, C. *Ireland: The Twentieth Century* (London: Arnold, 1998), p. 147.
62. Kennedy, *The Widening Gulf*, pp. 148, 160–1, 173–4.
63. Keogh, D. *The Vatican, The Bishops and Irish Politics, 1919–39* (Cambridge: Cambridge University Press, 1986), p. 201. Keogh's book provides a discussion of the manner in which the Catholic Church impacted upon de Valera's government in the period under study: see Chapters 6 and 7.
64. Laffan, *The Partition of Ireland*, p. 116.
65. Lee, *Ireland 1912–1985*, p. 203.
66. Lyons, *Ireland since the Famine*, p. 538.
67. Whyte, J.H. *Church and State in Modern Ireland, 1923–1970* (Dublin: Gill and Macmillan, 1971), p. 61.
68. Longford and O'Neill, *Eamon de Valera*, p. 297.
69. Lyons, *Ireland since the Famine*, p. 547.
70. Lyons, *Ireland since the Famine*, p. 539.
71. O'Malley, P. *The Uncivil Wars* (Belfast: The Blackstaff Press, 1983), p. 70.
72. Bourke, R. *Peace in Ireland: The war of ideas* (London: Pimlico, 2003), pp. 29, 119.
73. O'Halloran, C. *Partition and Limits of Irish Nationalism: An ideology under stress* (Dublin: Gill and Macmillan, 1987), see in particular Chapter 2.
74. Dwyer, 'Eamon de Valera and the Partition Question', p. 75.
75. Fanning, *Independent Ireland*, p. 35.
76. Mair, P. 'Breaking the Nationalist Mould: The Irish Republic and the Anglo-Irish Agreement', in P. Teague (ed), *Beyond the Rhetoric: Politics, economics and social policy in Northern Ireland* (London: Lawrence and Wishart, 1987), p. 82.
77. Boyce, D.G. '"Can anyone here imagine": Southern Irish political parties and the Northern Ireland problem', in B. Barton and P.J. Roche, *The Northern Ireland Question: Myth and reality* (Aldershot: Ashgate, 1991), p. 175.
78. O'Halloran, *Partition and the Limits of Irish Nationalism*, p. 27.
79. Keogh, D. *Twentieth Century Ireland: Nation and state* (Dublin: Gill and Macmillan, 1994), p. 245.
80. Laffan, *The Partition of Ireland*, pp. 122–3.
81. Ruane, J. and Todd, J. 'Irish Nationalism and the Conflict in Northern Ireland', in D. Millar (ed), *Rethinking Northern Ireland* (London and New York: Longman, 1998), p. 61.
82. As quoted in Farrell, B. *Seán Lemass* (Dublin: Gill and Macmillan, 1991), pp. 14–15.
83. Keogh, *Twentieth Century Ireland*, p. 245.
84. Raymond, R.J., 'De Valera, Lemass and Irish Economic Development 1933–1948', in O'Carroll and Murphy (eds), *De Valera and his Times*, p. 116.
85. Raymond, 'De Valera, Lemass and Irish Economic Development 1933–1948', p. 131.
86. Lyons, *Ireland since the Famine*, p. 584.
87. Farrell, *Seán Lemass*, p. 100.
88. Patterson, H. 'Seán Lemass and the Ulster Question, 1959–1965', *Journal of Contemporary History*, 34, 1 (1999), p. 145.
89. Collins, S. *The Power Game: Ireland under Fianna Fáil* (Dublin: The O'Brien Press, 2001), pp. 7–8.
90. Keogh, *Twentieth Century Ireland*, p. 287.
91. Patterson, 'Seán Lemass and the Ulster Question, 1959–1965', p. 146.
92. Patterson, 'Seán Lemass and the Ulster Question, 1959–1965', pp. 151–2.
93. Bew, P., Patterson, H. and Teague, P. *Between War and Peace: The political future of Northern Ireland* (London: Wishart and Lawrence, 1997), p. 21.

94. Bew, P. and Patterson, H. *Seán Lemass and the Making of Modern Ireland 1945–66* (Dublin: Gill and Macmillan, 1982), p. 11.
95. Horgan, J. *Seán Lemass: The enigmatic patriot* (Dublin: Gill and Macmillan, 1997), p. 287.
96. Horgan, *Seán Lemass,* pp. 256–7.
97. Farrell, *Seán Lemass,* p. 114.
98. Patterson, 'Seán Lemass and the Ulster Question, 1959–1965', pp. 152–3.
99. O'Malley, *The Uncivil Wars,* p. 72.
100. Public Records Office of Northern Ireland, File No. CAB/9U/5/2 'Meetings with the Prime Minister of the Irish Republic'.

CHAPTER ONE

Jack Lynch and the Failure of Conciliation 1968–79

INTRODUCTION

It is generally agreed that the response of Jack Lynch's[1] government to the outbreak of the Northern Ireland Troubles was seriously lacking.[2] This is perhaps unsurprising given the general neglect of Northern Ireland by successive Irish governments in the years and decades before it was forced to respond to the Troubles in 1968.[3] The tendency towards crisis management and non-intervention was also mirrored by British government policy-making.[4] Keogh has described the overall competence of the Lynch administration as 'very poor on the Northern question' and he quotes a former Fianna Fáil backbencher, John Moher, who has recorded the lack of debate on the subject within the parliamentary party in the 1950s and 1960s.[5] Despite continued support for reunification among the political parties and the public in the Republic, both had become accustomed to partition. The tendency towards non-involvement and the emotiveness of the issue were shown in the response by the Republic to the outbreak of the conflict in Northern Ireland. The Troubles in Northern Ireland had a huge impact on southern nationalists. This has been described by Ruane and Todd: 'The outbreak of the conflict in 1969 was contradictory in its effects. On the one hand it made southerners much more aware of the experience and aspirations of northern Catholics; on the other hand it revealed the difficulties each had in understanding and empathising with the other.'[6]

As a result, the early years of the Troubles in Northern Ireland proved to be the most controversial period in the history of the Irish state since the Civil War in 1922–3. The Irish government's response has tended to be surrounded by secrecy and misunderstandings and this is compounded by the inclination to assess Lynch's record on Northern Ireland within a narrow study of the Arms Crisis of 1970.[7] The distinction between Lynch's consistent belief that the unionist community should not be forced into a united Ireland and the involvement of some of his cabinet in the illegal importation of arms for use by the IRA in Northern Ireland is clear. Yet his devotion to a policy based on conciliation with unionists is blurred by his continued use of anti-partitionist language. While the Arms Crisis is an essential event in explaining Lynch's approach in 1969–70, it is necessary to look beyond this to understand fully the factors which eventually led to the failure of his attempts to harbour a policy of friendship and conciliation. Thus, this chapter examines Lynch's northern policy by paying attention to the dynamics of Fianna Fáil politics, events in both parts of Ireland and Anglo-Irish relations in order to explain the failure of his conciliatory approach. The chapter utilizes archival material relating to meetings between British and Irish officials and shows the significance of the failure at this level to Lynch's overall approach. In addition, the archives demonstrate a sense of inadequacy and lack of direction as a result of growing IRA violence after the 1969 IRA split.

JACK LYNCH AND THE NORTHERN IRELAND TROUBLES

It is necessary to make two observations about the general context of Lynch's response to the Troubles. The first relates to the position adopted by the British government in response to the Irish government's attempts to influence its policy on Northern Ireland. While there was a realization at some level of the need to involve the Irish government in the search for a solution for Northern Ireland, this did not impact significantly on British government policy regarding Northern Ireland in this period.[8] In a meeting at the Irish Embassy in London on Friday, 1 August 1969, the Secretary of State for Foreign and Commonwealth Affairs, Michael Stewart, told the Irish Minster for Foreign Affairs, Patrick Hillery, that 'responsibility for this area rests with the Stormont and London governments, and not with your government'. On the issue of possible future reforms in Northern Ireland, Stewart adhered to the same line: 'I must say to you [Hillery] that there is a limit to the extent to which we can discuss with outsiders – even our nearest neighbours – this internal matter.'[9] The British Prime Minister, Harold Wilson, made the same point to the

Taoiseach, Jack Lynch, when they met in November 1968. Wilson is recorded as saying that the matters discussed by the two leaders, while of concern to the British government, remained within the jurisdiction of Northern Ireland.[10] This reasoning was presented again to Hillery in what seems to have been a heated discussion with Lord Chalfont, Minister of State, who was at the time in charge of the Foreign and Commonwealth Office, at a meeting in London on 15 August 1969. Dr Hillery presented the Irish government's proposal for either a joint British–Irish or United Nations peacekeeping force for Northern Ireland. Lord Chalfont stressed that questions relating to Northern Ireland are to be dealt with by the UK government on the basis that it is an 'internal matter' and reminded the Irish delegation that 'the maintenance of law and order in the UK is primarily our concern. This responsibility is exercised in concert with the government of Northern Ireland.'[11] In these early years of the Troubles the British government, at least in discussions with Irish government officials, defended the Northern Ireland government's right to maintain responsibility for its own security.

Richard Crossman, the Secretary of State for Social Services, confirmed that in 1969 Hillery was 'reminded that the Northern Irish Troubles were an internal affair of the United Kingdom, of no concern to the Republic', when he visited the Foreign and Commonwealth Office on 15 August 1969.[12] The leader of the Conservative Party, Edward Heath, also expressed concern 'about what he described as the interference of "Eire" in the situation there (Northern Ireland). "Eire" had had no right to interfere in the affairs of a part of the United Kingdom.'[13] In August 1971, Heath, now as British Prime Minister, again outlined in a telegram to Jack Lynch that he had no right to 'attempt to interfere in the affairs of the United Kingdom'.[14] Lynch's ability to exert pressure on the British government to act on Northern Ireland must be judged in this context. Nonetheless, Anglo-Irish relations in this period can only have suffered from Lynch's constant statements that 'the basic cause of the situation in Northern Ireland was partition'.[15] The Irish government's inability to change the British government's position on its involvement was significant again in 1971–2 and much later in 1979 (see below).

Secondly, politics internal to the Republic affected Lynch's Northern Ireland policy. Lynch resisted opportunities to consult with the opposition parties and the Nationalist Party in the North when forming government policy on Northern Ireland. Brendan Corish, the

Labour Party leader, urged Lynch to recall the Dáil in August 1969 to discuss an appropriate response to the worsening situation in Northern Ireland. The Taoiseach replied that while the 'government are seriously concerned ... we do not feel that it is necessary to recall the Dáil to discuss the matter'.[16] Corish again pressed Lynch on this matter when he visited the Taoiseach's office on 15 August 1969.[17] The Fine Gael leader, Liam Cosgrave, also suggested the establishment of an All-Party Committee of the Dáil on Northern Ireland affairs. Lynch replied that this would be 'an inappropriate arrangement' and that 'the Government do not consider that it would be wise to provide Dáil time for a debate on the subject at the present time'.[18] The Taoiseach also turned down a proposal from the Nationalist Party in February 1970 to 'have a combined committee set up consisting of members of the Government in the Republic and members of the Nationalist Party to keep the situation in the Six counties under constant review', on the advice that it would 'antagonise other important elements in the opposition'. The Minister for External Affairs advised the Taoiseach to wait and see the outcome of movements underway towards the foundation of another nationalist party[19] by Gerry Fitt, John Hume,[20] Ivan Cooper, Paddy O'Hanlon, Austin Currie[21] and Thomas Gormley.[22]

THE ARMS CRISIS 1970

As has already been noted, discussions of Lynch's record on Northern Ireland in the early years of the Troubles have tended to concentrate on the Arms Crisis of 1970. This is because the Arms Crisis presents many questions about the commitment of Lynch's government to the peaceful and conciliatory approach it publicly espoused. It is also a perfect illustration of the indecisiveness and lack of leadership offered by Lynch on the subject of Northern Ireland. Lynch had been selected as a compromise choice for the leadership of Fianna Fáil in 1966 and the factions present during that leadership contest are shown again in the Arms Crisis in 1970, when the outbreak of hostilities in Northern Ireland presented Lynch's adversaries within the party with a perfect opportunity to challenge his leadership. Opinion is divided as to at what point Lynch became aware of the activities of Neil Blaney,[23] Charles Haughey[24] and the Minister for Defence, Jim Gibbons. While Arnold has sought to demonstrate that Lynch did not know of the attempts to import arms,[25] Justin O'Brien has provided a compelling and convincing case that Lynch did become aware of the plot earlier than admitted.[26] Whether or not he was aware of it, it is agreed that his handling of the affair amounted to 'one of the most startling abdications of leadership in the history of the southern state'.[27] The important point about the Arms Crisis is that it must be seen within the context of Lynch's failure to act as a strong advocate of a policy that categorically precluded any violent involvement in Northern Ireland by the Irish government as well as his failure to exert control over Northern Ireland policy.

Bruce Arnold has rejected criticism of Lynch and argued that he was very lucid in his support for the principle of consent[28] and that nothing in his speeches prior to the Arms Crisis could have been interpreted as lending legitimacy to the actions of Blaney and Haughey:

> It [spending state money on buying arms] would have been totally against government policy as adumbrated then and later by Lynch. Any government statements at the time, including those that referred to aid for those in the North who were under attack, were statements about government policy and not about the actions or responsibilities of the committee.[29]

However, it is not easy to accept Arnolds's assertion that Lynch did not give encouragement to the republican ethos espoused by Blaney, given the nature of the language used by the Taoiseach. While Lynch made it clear in a speech, delivered in Tralee in County Kerry, that 'we have no intention of using force to realise this desire [reunification]'[30], anti-partitionism was a continuing theme in his speeches. In the course of his presidential address to the Fianna Fáil Árd Fheis in January 1969, Lynch concentrated on the need for reform, human rights and the need to end discrimination in Northern Ireland. He went on to explain that such a concentration did not distract from the overall objective of unity:

> We want to see all the people of Northern Ireland living in peace and harmony together just as we want to live in peace and harmony with them. Good neighbourliness should, we believe, have no boundaries. But let nobody be under any illusion that these sentiments or our efforts to promote good relations between North and South or our sincere desire to see the vital reforms, to which I have referred, speedily implemented – let nobody be under the illusion that all this in any way indicates the abandonment by us of our just claim that the historic unity of this island be restored.[31]

Internal reforms in Northern Ireland would not prejudice the quest for unity. In making that point Lynch aligned himself with the many resolutions submitted at the Árd Fheis reaffirming the party's continued 'adherence to the ideal of unity, free and Gaelic'.[32] The following month Lynch responded to a speech made by Blaney in which he called for the end of partition and the establishment of a federal united Ireland by stating that Blaney's position 'accord[ed] fully with government policy'.[33] This response came despite the fact that the Northern Ireland leader, Terence O'Neill, had issued a statement which expressed the view that:

> any government in the Republic genuinely interested in friendly relations with Northern Ireland should think twice about the wisdom of retaining this party hatchet-man who has done so much to disrupt those relations. His intrusions into our affairs are, I repeat, an impertinence and wholly unacceptable to the government and the majority of the people of Northern Ireland.[34]

In October 1968, Lynch stressed that the people of Ireland knew that the disturbances and riots witnessed in Northern Ireland at that time had their origins in partition: 'partition is the first and foremost root cause. And partition arose out of British policy'.[35] His address to the Anglo-Irish Parliamentary Group a couple of weeks later expressed the same view that 'the clashes in the streets of Derry are an expression of the evils which partition has brought in its train'.[36] At his meeting with the British Prime Minister, Harold Wilson, Lynch is recorded as '... pointing out that the basic cause of the situation in Northern Ireland was partition'.[37] Asked if he believed that an end to partition was the only solution to the Troubles in Northern Ireland, Lynch replied: 'In the long run, I believe that it is the best possible solution, and I think in the context of the right of self-determination for Nations like Ireland that it is the just and inevitable solution.'[38] Challenged by an interviewer on whether it was wise to place emphasis on partition rather than a need to address civil rights issues in Northern Ireland considering the reaction from Captain O'Neill, Lynch maintained that: 'Partition is, as I said before, the basic problem. I think the human rights position will have to be resolved as well, and I hope that in the wake of the Derry incidents there will be a greater realisation in the north of Ireland for the necessity to give fundamental human rights to all citizens in that territory.'[39] This traditional interpretation of partition, which declined even to refer to Northern Ireland as such, was

presented despite Lynch's claim that 'my government and its predecessors [aim to] promote the reunification of Ireland by fostering a
spirit of brotherhood among all sections of the Irish people'.[40] When
Lynch stressed that his government's approach was designed to show
that 'unity can be founded on tolerance and goodwill and to achieve
the maximum possible measures of co-operation in practical matters
of public concern between the two areas into which Ireland is now
divided',[41] he gave only a limited commitment to this less aggressive
approach, given his continued use of anti-partitionist rhetoric in public, in meetings with British officials, and especially in his endorsement of Blaney's stance.

Contrary to a further claim made by Arnold that Lynch agreed with
Eddie McAteer of the Nationalist Party and Gerry Fitt of Republican
Labour that he would concentrate on reforms within Northern
Ireland, Lynch appears to have ignored such pleas when adopting such
an anti-partitionist stance. Arnold claims that at a meeting between
Lynch, McAteer and Fitt on 9 October 1968, the Taoiseach agreed to
adopt a new stance and call for reform within Northern Ireland. He
claims that Lynch disguised this agreement through the continued use
of traditional republican language. Thus, according to Arnold, Jack
Lynch's reaction from mid-October 1968 was 'based almost exclusively on maintaining the pressure for reforms and saying nothing that
might worsen [North–South] relations'.[42] If there was an agreement
between the Taoiseach and representatives of northern nationalism to
this effect, there was little evidence of a new approach in Lynch's
meetings with British and Northern officials and politicians. In successive meetings between Irish and British officials, the Irish government
was asked to refrain from making provocative statements on Northern
Ireland. In reply to Lynch's argument that the Troubles witnessed in
Northern Ireland in the late 1960s originated from partition, Harold
Wilson 'expressed the view that "banging of the drum" would only
make conditions worse than they were and would be of little help to
the Taoiseach's co-religionists'.[43] A more direct plea was made to the
Irish Minister for External Affairs, Patrick Hillery, by Lord Chalfont of
the Foreign and Commonwealth Office, who called on the Irish government to be '... decisive. What is needed now is studied moderation
and not reflection of irrational feelings: To damp [sic] down and control them so as to make irrational action impossible.' Lord Chalfont
also alleged that 'the situation is being made subject to considerable
provocation' by some of the actions taken by the Irish government,
including the decision to set up military hospitals at the border.[44] In

August 1969, Lynch met with a Nationalist deputation during which
Austin Currie urged the Taoiseach that:

> any announcements I [Lynch] would make in relation to what
> we were doing should highlight the word 'protection' for the
> Catholic population. I gave them an indication of our attitude to
> the people of the North generally, that we regarded them all as
> Irishmen (with a view to long-term settlement of the national
> problem) and that he could rest assured that we were particular-
> ly anxious about the situation of the Catholic population.[45]

Clearly some ten months into the alleged agreement, which Arnold
refers to, northern nationalists were still attempting to impress upon
the Lynch government the need to refrain from using language which
would aggravate an already 'explosive' situation.[46]

So rather than remain committed to a friendly approach which
would stress reform, as suggested by the Nationalist Party, Lynch
moved to protect the government's position from outside influence
and proceeded to give control of the government's Northern Ireland
policy to the republican wing of the Fianna Fáil party at a cabinet
meeting on 16 August 1969. A Government Sub-Committee for the
Relief of Distress in Northern Ireland was established and its members
included Blaney and Haughey. While Haughey, the Minister for
Finance, had remained silent on Northern Ireland, Blaney had been
outspoken on the issue. The fact that Lynch had stated that unity
would not be achieved by force did not matter once government policy was abdicated to the republican wing of the party. The cabinet
minutes from that meeting record the following decision:

> That the sum of money – the amount and the channel of dis-
> bursement of which would be determined by the Minister for
> Finance – should be made available from the Exchequer to pro-
> vide aid for the victims of the current unrest in the six counties
> and ... that machinery should be established with the object of
> maintaining permanent liaison with opinion in the six counties.[47]

Rather than adopt an approach which was conscious of North–South
relations, the first meeting which met in August 1969 to consider the
situation in Northern Ireland reached two decisions: to 'authorise the
mobilisation of the first line reserve of the Defence Forces so as to
ensure that they will be in readiness for participation in peace-keeping

operations' and that the Minister for External Affairs would inform the British government that the Irish government would be seeking the appointment of a United Nations peace keeping force to Northern Ireland.[48] The government addressed the second of the above aims, to bring the case of Northern Ireland before the United Nations immediately. Patrick Hillery circulated a memo entitled 'Bringing the situation in the North of Ireland before the UN'. The stated aim of 'such an approach would be the attempt to ventilate the question in that forum and the attendant publicity'.[49] This did bring the intended publicity but, as had been anticipated by the Irish government, these attempts to drum up support for action on Northern Ireland had no success at the UN.

In a press release on 16 August 1969, it was made clear what function the defence forces were to serve:

> The Taoiseach emphasised the concern of the government for peaceful conditions in the six counties. The actions of the government are directed to that end … five Field hospitals and two refugee Camps have been established by the Army as a practical and humane act … the mobilisation of the Defence Forces First Line Reserve had been authorised so that sufficient forces will be available for peace-keeping and domestic duties.[50]

Lynch's repeated statements that government policy was 'peaceful' appear to suggest that the subsequent actions taken by Blaney and Haughey were contrary to the Taoiseach's approach. However, Lynch's subsequent decisions raise questions about his willingness or ability to enforce such a peaceful approach. His mistake was twofold. First, he allowed Blaney and Haughey, who sought to gain control of the party by exploiting the crisis, to have effective control of government policy on Northern Ireland from the 16 August 1969 and second, he failed to resist pressure from the republican section in his party, which resulted in the Taoiseach's emotive speech (below) which suggested immediate action and which drew immediate responses in Northern Ireland. This more affirmative language that suggested a proactive approach showed that the government was not endorsing the earlier pragmatism outlined in a memorandum of March 1969 written by Hugh McCann of the Department of External Affairs:

> On the question of civil rights and current political developments in the Six Counties, it is considered that our policy should

continue to be one of restraint, with as little active involvement
as possible and the less said the better. The reasoning behind this
policy is simply that there is nothing at this stage that we could
do to improve the situation in the North: on the contrary, any
suggestion of outside pressure or interference, particularly by us,
would only play into the hands of the Northern extremists.[51]

At the cabinet meeting on 13 August it was agreed that Lynch would
make a statement on the continued violence in the North to be broadcast on television and radio at 9 pm. In that speech Lynch said:

> The Irish Government can no longer stand by and see innocent
> people injured and perhaps worse. It is obvious that the RUC is no
> longer accepted as an impartial police force. Neither would the
> deployment of British troops be acceptable nor would they be like-
> ly to restore peaceful conditions, certainly not in the long term.[52]

It did not matter that Lynch set out the UN path as the immediate
route in dealing with the problem, since he continued: 'Recognising,
however, that the re-unification of the national territory can provide
the only permanent solution for the problem, it is our intention to
request the British Government to enter into early negotiations with
the Irish Government to review the present constitutional position of
the Six Counties of Northern Ireland.'[53] The political division of the
Department of External Affairs took care, in the preparation of the
speech, neither to attack British inaction explicitly nor to commit the
Irish government to seek a meeting with the British Prime Minister.
However, it was easy for members of the government such as Blaney
and Haughey to use Lynch's language and the cabinet decisions as justification for direct action and for effectively giving the Government
Sub-Committee for the Relief of Distress in Northern Ireland licence
to procure arms for northern nationalists. The decision to broadcast
the above speech was taken for 'maximum effect'.[54] This meant that
the message promising action was the only one heard, to the detri-
ment of his subsequent statement reiterating the government's commitment to peaceful means.

Arnold has argued that Lynch's postulation in favour of positive
action towards ending partition was simply the result of pressure
from the republican wing within his party. The divisions in the party,
according to Arnold, forced Lynch to take a public position which
was at odds with the 'real issues and intentions of the Government of

the South, as well as its interpretation of the problems of Northern Ireland, with statements which catered for strongly held, if ignorant, sentiments within the Fianna Fáil party'.[55] If this is in fact representative of Lynch's true thinking on the issue, the decisions reached at the cabinet meeting in that week dealt a severe blow to the alternative approach referred to by Arnold. However, there is little evidence to support Arnold's claim that Lynch held anything other than a traditional republican interpretation of the problems in Northern Ireland. This is clearly illustrated by the position which he adopted at meetings at Anglo-Irish level even after Blaney, Haughey and Kevin Boland had left office. Lynch may have genuinely wished to reach some form of conciliation with unionists by peaceful means but he did not see that this conflicted with a consistent insistence that unity must be at the end of the road of any process proposed for Northern Ireland.

There is no doubt that Lynch allowed his judgement to be influenced by his desire to assuage demands made by deputies such as Blaney and Boland. His pledge that 'my concentration at this juncture on fundamental political and social rights in no way derogates from the right of the Irish people as a whole to the unity of Ireland'[56] reflected this. The Taoiseach's failure to exert a conciliatory approach in a more convincing manner, his continued indecisiveness together with the absence of a firm control of the party on his part allowed Blaney and others to take control of northern policy. This, together with the refusal by the British government to accept that the Irish government had a right to be involved with the process of finding a solution for Northern Ireland (this will be seen more clearly in the next section), caused Lynch to appear ambivalent towards violence and ultimately removed any possibility that a conciliatory policy might succeed. While the continued impasse in Anglo-Irish relations is one reason why such a conciliatory approach did not prevail, Lynch's own policy of reunification suggests it would not have succeeded anyway. His consistent rejection of force was most likely viewed with scepticism by unionists, given his endorsement of Blaney in 1969, his decision to give responsibility for Northern Ireland policy to the republican wing of his party, his emotive response to the Troubles, which must have appeared to unionists to threaten all-out war, and his continued anti-partitionist statements in public and in meetings with British officials.

Lynch's subsequent decision to expel Blaney and Haughey from office did confirm his belief that a united Ireland could not and should not be brought about by violent means. It was also a belated move to assert control over the party and policy on Northern Ireland.

It did not, however, mean that Lynch was rejecting the republicanism of the party. He went on to put in place a policy on Northern Ireland that had, at its core, the objective of a united Ireland to be brought about by first of all convincing the British government that this was the best solution to the problem and then by securing a declaration by the British government of its intent to express its interest in a united Ireland. This is the first time in the history of the party that it put in place a proactive plan towards unity. Lynch's expulsion of those involved in the Arms Crisis and his continued condemnation of IRA violence has disguised his strong advocacy of a policy of unification through negotiation with the British government, which, in essence, meant ignoring the wishes of the unionist community.

UNITY AS THE ULTIMATE SOLUTION:
NORTHERN IRELAND POLICY IN THE POST-1970 ARMS CRISIS PERIOD

Lynch sought to persuade the British government to adopt a policy of unification, which he thought would make the unionist community accept unity. Then a process of conciliation with unionists would commence as a necessary precursor to unity. From a unionist perspective, this is objectionable on a number of grounds. However, Lynch strongly rejected the use of force as a legitimate mechanism in the quest for a united Ireland. In an address broadcast on RTÉ, the Taoiseach declared that 'in this island there is no solution to be found to our disagreements by shooting each other. There is no real invader here'.[57] In the course of his address to the United Nations General Assembly, marking the twenty-fifth Anniversary of the United Nations, Lynch expressed confidence that, 'when this [peace and justice in Northern Ireland] is achieved, the Irish people, North and South, will themselves put an end to ignoble relics of ancient disagreements and create the conditions which will fully restore the Irish nation, in all its diversity and cultural richness'.[58] He visualized this eventuality, when 'one day that community (in the North), long since Irish as it knows itself to be, will see that their future lies with us, that we have a desire to persuade them for the good of all Ireland to see this and no desire to destroy their values'.[59]

There are a number of other sources which underline the commitment of the Lynch administration to a new and conciliatory approach to Northern Ireland. Staunton, for example, quotes a document drafted by the then Tánaiste, Erskine Childers, and circulated to the cabinet on 29 August 1969, which conceded that the divergent economic growth in both parts of the island was an obstacle to unity and advocated the extension of the Lemass–O'Neill initiative with the aim of improving trade relations. In addition, Childers advocated the acceptance of the principle of consent, constitutional change and the removal of denominational legislation.[60] Another document produced mainly by Ken Whitaker entitled 'The Constitutional Position of Northern Ireland' and received by Lynch in November 1969 outlined both the legal claim in favour of the union as well as the moral claim for reunification. It recommended that force should not be revived in the pursuit of unification since it would only 'accentuate rather than remove the problem [and] would not be militarily successful'.[61] The report advocated 'A policy of Friendship', asserting that: 'The only successful policy is likely to be our most recent one of achieving unity by friendship and co-operation by being prepared to accept a future structural set-up between the two parts of Ireland which would allay Northern Ireland's fears and safeguard her interests. This is the course which is now accepted.'[62]

As evidence of his rejection of violence, Lynch took a stringent stance in his condemnation of IRA activities throughout 1971, when the Provisional IRA's campaign of violence and rioting continued. In March 1971 he was interviewed on a BBC programme, 'Panorama', in the course of which he declared the IRA an illegal organization and pledged 'to take action against them'. He confirmed that his government was contemplating the introduction of internment but hoped this would not be necessary.[63] He also denounced IRA activities since they 'only retard the movement towards reconciliation'.[64] In October of that year Lynch announced that measures were being taken to limit RTÉ coverage of events in Northern Ireland in an effort to protect both the interests of the public and the security of the state. Alluding to 'interviews with men who openly advocate violence and who unashamedly have claimed responsibility for bombings and killings' he presented the case that 'propagandising of these activities on our TV screens is highly dangerous in the present situation in the North, it is prejudicial to the maintenance of peace and to the ultimate reunification of our country'.[65] Addressing what was described as a 'hostile crowd' a month later,[66] Lynch defined 'republicanism' as his party understood it: 'Fianna Fáil is a republican party – that is a party which advocates government based on the free choice of the people. The corollary to this is that it has not and does not recognise the right of any group to dissociate itself from the majority, or to opt out of the

Irish community.'[67] He challenged the IRA; he said it lacked the mandate that his government had and pledged not to 'let the IRA or anyone take it from us – they are an illegal organisation'. In a question that drew no response from the crowd assembled at the Donagh O'Malley Fianna Fáil Cumann (local branch), Lynch asked: 'we are all Irish people and the million non-Catholics in the North are our Irish people. If we had military resources to take over the North by physical force are we going to drive these million people into the sea?'[68] He continued to make this point. In an interview in November 1971, Lynch accused the IRA of 'postponing that day (of reunification) ... when we talk about reunification we are not just talking about reunification of territories we are talking about reunification of the people and I am suggesting that the activities of the IRA are driving the people further and further apart'.[69]

However, at an Anglo-Irish level Lynch refused to contemplate a security-based approach to Northern Ireland. He reiterated his support for a political settlement that would eventually lead to reunification, despite rejecting the use of force and accepting that the unionist population could not be coerced into such an arrangement. He had already intimated that 'federation would be acceptable for a limited period, leading ultimately to complete unification' but that this would be an interim step and would be established on the basis that a Council of Ireland would be created with the potential 'to deal with mutual problems and make recommendations in certain limited areas for the respective governments to implement'.[70] In September 1971 Lynch's government stepped up its campaign to persuade the British government to consider such an eventual outcome. A two-day conference at Chequers scheduled for early September 1971 was much anticipated. The Irish delegation clearly expected a lot from the conference. It was reported that 'some proposals for internal changes in the North's constitution will be discussed'.[71] It was also envisaged that the meetings would lead to a series of such conferences on the North.[72]

The briefings supplied to Lynch in advance of his meeting with the British Prime Minister, Edward Heath, in September 1971 emphasized the centrality of the objective of unity. Under the heading 'What the Taoiseach should ask for', three points were outlined. The first was that 'the unionist monopoly of power must disappear', and secondly 'the British government should indicate publicly that it is in favour of Irish reunification by agreement'. The third requirement was an All-Ireland Council. In addition, the Taoiseach was, if pushed in the meeting with Heath, by way of a reply to provide the justification that: 'IRA activity is the product of the unsatisfactory situation in the North and the first priority is to examine political means of remedying that situation. When these are agreed then it is time to talk about dealing with the IRA, the support for which within the North would, in any event, diminish when solutions are in sight.'[73] This was in direct contrast to his public utterances on this particular subject where he had condemned IRA violence. These briefings provided the basis for Lynch's stance during his meeting with Heath. At that meeting Lynch stressed that 'partition was imposed and its existence always constituted a threat of violence because of the efforts to maintain Unionists in power'. He also emphasized that everybody in the Irish Republic was dedicated to unification and that his approach was to bring about unity by peaceful means.[74] Lynch went on to say that 'the IRA is a by-product of that situation (where the majority continued in power in Northern Ireland)' and, if the British Prime Minister 'could find it possible to state that the unification of Ireland would have to be the ultimate solution and gave an assurance of interest in working towards this end, this would be enormously helpful at the present time'.[75]

It is clear that the Irish government and Lynch were of the view that, if the British government were to move towards a policy of Irish unification, then the reasons for the IRA would cease to exist. According to Lynch, support for the IRA could be diminished if a political initiative was put in place and the British government were to agree to the release of all internees, the establishment of a commission to administer the area and to hold a quadripartite meeting between the two governments, the Northern Ireland Prime Minister, Brian Faulkner, and representatives of the nationalist community. Lynch also defended the right of the minority in Northern Ireland to aspire to a united Ireland and called on the British government to provide some initiative to ensure that the situation did not worsen. Lynch told Heath that he had wanted to be able to leave the talks and announce a British initiative that recognized Irish unity. He could not announce an initiative that did not represent an advance, since it became clear in the course of the talks that the British government did not intend to include the Irish government in the planned talks initiative. Lynch made no progress at that meeting towards his objective of obtaining British government agreement on the necessity of constitutional change towards unity.[76]

After the meeting the Taoiseach verified that Heath had rejected his proposal of a quadripartite meeting involving representatives from both governments and the nationalist and unionist leaders from Northern Ireland on the basis that the Irish government did not have a right to be involved in such discussions. Lynch explained his judgement that the type of government that had been in place in Northern Ireland amounted to 'an unnatural position'. However, he accepted as 'legitimate' the British government's argument that reunification cannot take place without the agreement (consent) of the majority in Northern Ireland.[77] The Taoiseach also responded positively to questions relating to constitutional change:

> I have said that we are prepared to give thought to these articles [Two and Three] and these legislative enactments to see in what way we could arrange them so as to satisfy all points of view … certainly my government and the people I represent would be willing to examine all these matters to see in what way we can make it possible for the Northern majority to live in peace with us.[78]

Having made such a gesture in the aftermath of his unproductive meeting with Heath, Lynch hoped much progress could be made at his subsequent meeting in London, this time with Heath and Brian Faulkner. Speaking in September 1971, before leaving for that tri-partite meeting, the Taoiseach predicted 'no limit to what we will discuss' and emphasised that 'Irish unity is central to the whole problem and real and lasting unity can be achieved only through peaceful means and by agreement. This will always be to the forefront in the talks I will have.'[79] It was also envisaged that the meetings would lead to a series of such conferences on the North.[80] Lynch made such statements despite the fact that the British government had made it clear in pre-meeting communications that the talks would not deal with specifics and the announcement of the Taoiseach's visit to London would emphasize that the aim was to hold discussions on a number of issues which 'will not involve constitutional negotiations'.[81] Lynch stressed to Heath that his policy remained unchanged. Reunification remained his central objective. He could not depart from this policy. While condemning the IRA, Lynch again argued that IRA violence was a result of the situation in the North. In a later exchange with Brian Faulkner, Lynch said that he would like to expand North–South economic co-operation with 'reunification in mind'. He defended the decision by the SDLP not to enter discussions until internment ended and argued that a new system of government was needed in Northern Ireland before the SDLP could be convinced that unionist rule would not return.[82]

Given the differing attitudes towards the meetings, it is not surprising that the statement issued on behalf of the three participants to the talks reflected the fact that little agreement was reached: 'each of us remains committed to his publicly stated position on the constitutional status of Northern Ireland.'[83] Lynch travelled to London again in December 1971 to meet with Heath. He referred to the Irish government 'losing control of the developments in the North'. In a general discussion relating to security and extradition, the Taoiseach expressed no real 'inhibition' about the latter. On the issue of reunification, Lynch endorsed a recent address given by Heath's predecessor, Harold Wilson, favouring British support for unification, and proposed the following:

> [I]f the British people could be encouraged to think that re-unification is the only ultimate solution and if this idea could be more positively supported by the British government, then the unionists in the North might tend to fall into line; if the grip of the unionists could be loosened, then the Dublin government might find it easier to move in their direction.[84]

This idea that the British government should become a persuader of unity had now become the bottom line for the Irish government in negotiations with the British government. Not only did this exemplify a lack of understanding of the intensity of the unionist desire to remain within the United Kingdom, but also exemplified the polarization of the British and Irish standpoints. Later that day the Taoiseach addressed the Parliamentary Press Gallery Group in the House of Commons. He once again communicated his belief that: 'It would take nothing away from the honour of Britain or the rights of the majority in the North if the British government were to declare their interest in encouraging the unity of Ireland, by agreement, in independence and in a harmonious relationship between the two islands.'[85]

Despite continued failure at Anglo-Irish level, Lynch remained undeterred from his aim to convince the British government to adopt a policy of supporting Irish reunification. In January 1972 he tried a somewhat different approach when the British Ambassador called on him. Lynch told the ambassador that he and his ministers had been refraining from talk on partition so as not to prejudice a political initiative that they expected the British government to announce. Despite refraining from public references to unity, the objective remained the same. Lynch told the ambassador that: 'If Heath could go a little further (on the issue of unity) and say they would facilitate and support any moves in this direction it would probably ease the intransigence of the Unionists. Instead there had been a repetition of the guarantee in the 1949 (Ireland) Act.'[86] Lynch's willingness to resist public anti-partitionist utterances while still advocating a policy of unity at a political level was most likely aimed at extracting the best possible political initiative from the British government, which would be advantageous to the nationalist community in Northern Ireland.

At a meeting between Eamonn Gallagher of the Department of Foreign Affairs and Cecil King in London later in the same month, Gallagher was specific about what kind of initiative the Irish government expected from the British government. Firstly, security would be transferred from Stormont to Westminster and the British government would announce its interest in restoring unity in Ireland. This was to be done without mind to any potential Protestant backlash in Northern Ireland.[87] In April 1972, Hillery met with Sir Alec Douglas Home, the Secretary of State for Foreign and Commonwealth Affairs. At that meeting the Minister for Foreign Affairs was adamant about the need for an initiative leading to unity. He told Douglas Home that the Taoiseach could not give a lead to or support an initiative that he did not believe had 'the solution of a united Ireland at the end of road'. He argued that what was needed now was 'assurances to the minority that there is no further need for the gunmen and that important political initiatives leading to a united Ireland are on the way'. He reiterated that the 'Taoiseach would at least have to be able to say that a united Ireland in independence and peace is in the offing. He could not say this unless he believed it to be true', and 'an indication by Britain that it would be in the interest of both countries to have a united Ireland could greatly strengthen the Taoiseach's position in the lead he could take at this time'. Similar points were made by the Minister of Foreign Affairs and Hugh McCann of the Department for Foreign Affairs at their meeting with William Whitelaw later that day.[88]

Domestic and Anglo-Irish Pressures: Understanding Policy on Northern Ireland in the post-Arms Crisis period

The 'new anti-British line' adopted by the Irish government identified from late 1971 onwards had, according to *The Irish Times*, won Lynch the support of the republican camp within the Fianna Fáil parliamen-

tary party and precipitated a complete standoff in Anglo-Irish relations.[89] Gaining support from the republican wing was needed, given
that there had been a number of dissatisfied members of the party who
had openly challenged Lynch's policy on Northern Ireland. The
announcement by Dr Bill Loughnane, the Fianna Fáil TD for
Clare–Galway, of his intention to resign his seat was much more significant in light of Seán Sherwin's defection from the party to join
Aontacht Éireann, the new party established by the former Fianna Fáil
minister, Kevin Boland.[90] Boland's new party had been launched in mid-
September 1971 with the aim of being, not an off-shoot of Fianna Fáil,
but rather 'a new and truly Republican party – to cut down the rotten
tree that Fianna Fáil has become and to replace it with a new growth
firmly rooted in the old tradition of nationhood'.[91] Neil Blaney also put
pressure on Lynch to deliver something from the talks at Chequers. He
continued to claim that Lynch's position on Northern Ireland was not
reflective of the ideals which formed the basis of the party. Blaney's
position within the party therefore depended on a successful outcome
to the talks: 'What is needed at this stage, very vitally from Britain is a
declaration of their intention to get out … any dealing that condones
partition is contrary entirely to my views and I believe to the views of
the principles of the party to which I belong, Fianna Fáil.'[92]

But it was not just the less moderate voices within his party that
Lynch had to deal with, since growing IRA activity in the Republic was
reaching the stage where 'a head on collision between the authorities
here and the IRA' was predicted.[93] The IRA regarded suggestions that
internment might have to be enforced in the Republic as having the
potential to 'bring about a very ugly situation as we would resist it
forcibly both within and without the internment camps'.[94] Lynch's government was also criticized about its failure to help counter continued
IRA violence in Northern Ireland. Not only was Lynch quizzed on the
matter in the Dáil,[95] but members of the Northern Ireland Parliament
explicitly accused Lynch's government of 'not only giving shelter to
terrorists by its tongue-in-cheek comments about their villainy [but of]
giving them encouragement by the ineffectiveness of its steps to stop
their activities'.[96] John Taylor, the then Northern Ireland Minister of
State at the Ministry of Home Affairs, questioned the Republic's commitment to combating the IRA: 'It certainly is a cause of puzzlement
that very much larger numbers, both of military and police, cannot be
drafted from the quieter areas of the Republic to the Border.'[97] Public
opinion was clearly mixed. An IRA spokesman pointed to 'considerable anti-republican activity'[98] despite the fact that the *Connacht*

Tribune reported that 'the public accepts [the] IRA within limits'.[99] The Taoiseach's office received numerous letters from the public calling for a firmer stance on the IRA and questioning his abandonment of a policy of reconciliation pursued in the initial stages of the Troubles.[100]

A strong line on unity during meetings with the British Prime Minister was necessary to offer assurances to those more republican-minded people within the party, but it was also adopted at the behest of John Hume and the SDLP. The association with Hume and the SDLP had strengthened and this relationship provides another explanation for Lynch's continued references to unity when meeting with Heath and Faulkner. Hume suggested that the Taoiseach should ask the British Prime Minister to outline the objections to reunification in order to 'enable an offensive position to be adopted by ourselves [Irish government] and the Northern opposition; to get objections on the record; to have the objections listed so that remedies could be put forward to deal with them by ourselves [Irish government] and by the Northern opposition'.[101] George Colley, the Minister for Finance, highlighted that this would enable the Irish government to 'say afterwards that the question of unity was discussed'.[102] Lynch's previous speeches would suggest that he was already aware what the objections to reunification were, but it does not appear that Colley dissented from the suggestion. It is perhaps unfortunate that these suggestions were presented to Lynch as the Taoiseach's position became noticeably tougher. He refuted Heath's statement that his government could not adopt a position favouring unity since that would mean 'usurping the right of the choice of the people of Northern Ireland' and urged the British government to enact the 'wishes of the British and the Irish peoples in their great majority' who supported unity.[103] Lynch was in effect proposing to bypass the wishes of the majority in Northern Ireland.

Lynch's use of anti-partitionist language on the Anglo-Irish stage seriously exacerbated the situation but many obstacles already existed at this level. Lynch may have offered 'any concession to the North that might relieve the present situation' but progress was never likely. The British government showed reticence when discussing future inter-governmental meetings[104] and continued to deny the Irish government's right of involvement. Indeed, the outcome of a British House of Commons debate on Northern Ireland was to endorse tripartite discussions (excluding the Irish government) as the way forward.[105] Bew, Patterson and Teague refer to the British government's refusal to accept the Republic of Ireland as an independent state and, more importantly, as a state with a valid input on Northern Ireland.[106]

The authors reveal how this attitude was particularly true of Wilson, but there is definite evidence that it prevailed into Heath's administration. In addition, the British government's approach was reliant upon the success of the moderate policy of Terence O'Neill and subsequently James Chichester-Clark, as is shown by Richard Crossman's diaries. Crossman states that the government was anxious not to alienate the majority Protestant government and thus be forced to rule Northern Ireland as a colony.[107] Throughout 1969 the British government refused to meet with Lynch on the basis that it might, according to Fanning, 'de-stabilise Chichester-Clark's government', and this had the effect of weakening Lynch's position within his party.[108] The same consideration applied after the Arms Crisis and Lynch's retreat to anti-partitionist rhetoric caused a complete impasse in Anglo-Irish relations.

Lynch's decision to argue that IRA violence was the result of an unsatisfactory situation in Northern Ireland was aimed at persuading the British government that a security based approach was inadequate. It was also intended to avoid committing the Irish government to any action on the IRA in the South which would have been politically difficult, given public sympathy in the Republic for the northern minority. It was also consistent with his argument that constitutional change was needed as part of a solution to the violence in Northern Ireland. Presenting a policy of unification to the British Prime Minister was aimed at extracting an initiative from the British government sufficient enough both to satisfy the demands of his party and the public and to undermine the claims of legitimacy made by the IRA. His stance was an attempt to demonstrate that political mechanisms could yield practical advantage and thus remove the support for the IRA within Northern Ireland. It was for this reason that he also sought recognition from the British government that the Irish government had a right to be involved in working out a solution to the Northern Ireland Troubles.

Thus, the adoption of a policy of unification was tactical but it also represented an expression of the republicanism of Lynch, Fianna Fáil and the Irish government at that time. Lynch clearly believed in a united Ireland as the solution to the Northern Ireland problem and also that the British government ought to facilitate this. This was based wrongly upon the belief that the British government might adopt such a policy and upon a particularly poor understanding of unionism, as alluded to by the British Ambassador to Ireland at the time, Sir John Peck.[109] The lack of understanding for the unionist case was unfortunately at the heart of Lynch's policy. This is seen in Lynch's statement

above that unionists 'long since Irish' could be persuaded into a united Ireland. Similarly, while Whitaker's 1969 report on unity, referred
to above, recognized that Protestants in Northern Ireland would take
issue with the ban on divorce and legislation relating to censorship, it
concluded that the main obstacle to reunification related to the economic capacity of the southern state.[110] It was such misunderstandings
about unionism that saw Lynch place a commitment to reunification
fundamental to his policy. Thus he demanded that the British government adopt a policy of restoring Irish unity against the wishes of
unionists and this ruined any chances of a successful conciliatory policy. Lynch did not succeed in convincing the British government to
involve the Irish government and, by demanding that which he could
never achieve, Lynch failed in his quest to undermine support for the
IRA. As he was unable to prove that the political arena could yield
results from the British government, Lynch's failure reinforced the
beliefs of those who had supported IRA violence. Had Lynch not concentrated on unity he may have been able to convince the British government that he had something practical to contribute to talks on
improving the situation within Northern Ireland. Instead, the refusal
by the British government in the early 1970s to allow Lynch a role in
efforts to find a solution to the Troubles in Northern Ireland severely
undermined his position. Lynch's concentration on reunification, his
demands for something from the British government that was never
likely to be forthcoming and his subsequent lack of success at an
Anglo-Irish level all contributed to the failure of a conciliatory policy.

FIANNA FÁIL NORTHERN IRELAND POLICY 1973–9

Lynch's commitment to a peaceful and benevolent approach was
eclipsed at a number of different junctures as a result of his insistence
on unity as the only possible long-term solution for Northern Ireland.
His response to the initiative undertaken by the Fine Gael-led government, which resulted in the Sunningdale Communiqué in 1973,
again reflected his adherence to a conciliatory approach and a lasting
commitment to the objective of unity. Speaking in the Dáil as leader
of the opposition[111] in 1973 on the announcement of the establishment of a power-sharing administration in Northern Ireland, which
was to involve the Unionist Party, the SDLP and the Alliance Party,
Lynch welcomed the development and stated that:

We wish the members of these bodies well in their efforts to work for all the people of Northern Ireland ... our immediate priority is to bring about peace with justice in the North and so to bring to an end violence and suffering ... all my efforts while I was Taoiseach in all the consultations I had with successive British Prime Ministers and other representatives of the British Government were directed towards this end.[112]

He continued to give his complete support to a process involving a power-sharing 'partnership' within Northern Ireland, linked to a Council of Ireland 'based on mutual respect and tolerance which will allow all Irishmen to co-operate in maintaining peace on this island and to work for the economic prosperity of all its people'.[113] But Lynch's approach was very firmly based upon the belief that such institutions would be interim and that the ultimate goal must be Irish national unity. He later attacked the Fine Gael Taoiseach, Liam Cosgrave, for implying that the level of violence and lack of political progress in Northern Ireland had affected the desire for unity. According to Lynch:

To imply, however, that we should cease – and I assert there was that implication – to aspire to a united Ireland by peaceful means in co-operation, understanding and justice because of violence is, in itself, a concession to those who pursue that violence. I am certain that the people in this part of Ireland do not want to abandon that aspiration. Above all, they do not want to abandon the minority in the North to the kind of life, the kind of subjection and domination they have suffered there for over 50 years. If that were the case, the minority in the North could hardly be blamed if they saw no way out of their dilemma other than to turn to the men of violence.[114]

Lynch raised concerns about reports that the government was contemplating a new approach to Northern Ireland which would entail modifying the state's territorial claim over the North. He reiterated his claim made in 1971 that the British government ought to encourage the idea of Irish unity as the final solution and also claimed that 'repeated assurances' given to the northern majority were simply resulting in 'those who were being re-assured [becoming] more obstinate and demanding'.[115] While Lynch was consistent in advocating a movement away from militant republicanism, he was not prepared to abandon the republican ideal of unity nor was he capable of engaging at any stage, whether in power or opposition, with a reassessment of unionism. Acceptance of the principle of consent in a real and meaningful manner necessitated a reappraisal of such notions. Speaking of loyalists, Lynch contended:

> Most of all they are loyal to themselves and to the idea that only they are entitled to rule what they call 'Ulster'. The issue then is not so much the preservation of the link with Britain as the maintenance of power by a particular group over part of this island in perpetuity ... the *raison d'être* of whose members is domination and deprivation of their neighbours, a society whose intransigence is motivated and cemented ... by the depth of hatred of their neighbours because of their religious beliefs.[116]

Lynch's inability to convince the British government that the Irish government had a right to be involved in the search for a political rather than a security based solution to the problems facing Northern Ireland caused the Fianna Fáil leader many problems in the late 1960s and early 1970s. The same problem faced Lynch at the end of that decade and also contributed to the end of his leadership. In September 1979, Lynch, as Taoiseach, was still attempting to press upon the British government, now led by Margaret Thatcher, the need to ensure that talks between the two heads of government involved a political as well as a security dimension.[117] Lynch insisted that talks must get to the 'cause, not [just] the effects' of the conflict in Northern Ireland.[118] The Northern Ireland Secretary of State, Humphrey Atkins, was firm that responsibility of Northern Ireland's affairs rested with the British government and the people of Northern Ireland: 'There is no responsibility anywhere else – in Dublin or anywhere else.'[119] Lynch had insisted on a political initiative,[120] but his failure to extract any political gain for his agreement to improve 'extensive [security] co-operation between the authorities of the two countries'[121] provided a section of the party with an opportunity to attack him. In an article in *The Irish Times*, Fianna Fáil senator, Patrick Cooney, claimed that Lynch's recent policy represented 'a significant shift in Fianna Fáil policy'. He pointed to the agreement with the British government on security as reflecting the party's 'shelving of a demand for a British declaration of intent to withdraw'.[122] While Cooney gave his support to the changes, an open attack came in a speech by the Fianna Fáil TD, Síle de Valera, granddaughter of Eamon de Valera, at a commemorative ceremony in honour of anti-Treaty leader, Liam Lynch. She challenged the Taoiseach to 'demonstrate his republicanism' and referred to 'so-called solutions' of seeking a devolved administration in the North as 'half-measures [which] can only serve to exacerbate and fester the problem'.[123] The Fianna Fáil parliamentary party rejected the challenge to Lynch's Northern Ireland policy[124] but Haughey ensured that the matter did not rest. When speaking at the Patrick Pearse commemoration dinner he delivered what was viewed as a 'coded attack' on Lynch.[125] Haughey claimed that the idea of partition was 'totally inconceivable' to Pearse.[126] This came in the midst of confusion relating to Lynch's leadership when he confirmed, while on a trip to Washington, that agreement had been reached with the British government as to security measures in the border area.[127] Neil Blaney, no longer a member of Fianna Fáil, declared his support for Haughey as leader[128] and Lynch finally announced his resignation, 'precipitated by uncertainty about recent events',[129] on 5 December 1979.

CONCLUSION

Lynch's record on Northern Ireland appears to present a confusing and conflicting picture but amidst this there were definite consistencies. Firstly, he was very clear that he viewed reunification as the only long-term solution to the Northern Ireland conflict and consistently called on the British government to become persuaders of unity. Secondly, he consistently rejected the use of force in the pursuit of this goal, both on moral and on practical grounds. Thirdly, he was pragmatic in his acceptance that an interim arrangement, providing participation of northern nationalists in the governance of Northern Ireland, was necessary. Finally, while Lynch promoted reconciliation with northern Protestants, his understanding of the unionist case was minimal. This reflects the fact that the outbreak of the Troubles in Northern Ireland did not produce any real meaningful political debate about unionism but instead saw the prevalence of traditional, uninformed attitudes to the northern majority.

Lynch failed to exert his policy of friendship and conciliation in a strong enough manner, so as to ensure his complete control of Northern policy, and this contributed to the Arms Crisis in 1970. In the years after that crisis, Lynch continued to make anti-partitionist statements. In the past, resolutions passed at successive Fianna Fáil Árd Fheiseanna reiterated the party's commitment to unity. The party did not, however, pass resolutions which committed it to action, for example at the United Nations.[130] Now in the early 1970s, for the first time in the history of the party it put in place, at Anglo-Irish level, a policy of unification. This was aimed at both assuring the republican wing of the party as well as undermining the IRA and its support base. It is not fair, however, to lay the failure of the policy of conciliation completely with Lynch. The unwillingness on the part of the wider party to engage with his attempts to challenge their traditional views on partition and persistent IRA violence are important factors here. The collapse of a conciliatory policy is also attributable to British intransigence and its reluctance to involve the Irish government in any political initiative in the North, which thus disabled Lynch's attempts to disprove the need for a violent IRA campaign. In addition, the fact that the British government appeared intransigent also allowed notions to prevail that the conflict was the fault of the British government, which thus postponed the day when Irish nationalism as an ideology would address its internal contradictions, and when the Irish public would debate alternative solutions to the conflict and redress its interpretation of unionism.

NOTES

1. Jack Lynch: Born in Cork in 1917; barrister at law prior to entering politics; elected as Fianna Fáil TD in 1948; appointed as Parliamentary Secretary to the Government and to the Minister for Lands by de Valera in 1951; Minister for Education, 1957–9; Minister for Industry and Commerce, 1959–65; Minister for Finance, 1965–6; Taoiseach, 1966–73, 1977–9.
2. Townshend, C. *Ireland: The Twentieth Century* (London: Arnold, 1998), p. 216; Lee, J.J. *Ireland 1912–1985: Politics and society* (Cambridge: Cambridge University Press, 1989), pp. 458–69.
3. See Hayes, B.C. and McAllister, I. 'British and Irish public opinion towards the Northern Ireland problem', *Irish Political Studies*, 11 (1996), p. 65.
4. See Fanning, R. 'Anglo-Irish Relations: Partition and the British dimension in historical perspective', *Irish Studies in International Affairs*, 2, 1 (1985), pp. 1–20.
5. Keogh, D. *Twentieth Century Ireland: Nation and state* (Dublin: Gill and Macmillan, 1994), p. 307.
6. Ruane, J. and Todd, J. *The Dynamics of Conflict in Northern Ireland: Power, conflict and emancipation* (Cambridge: Cambridge University Press, 1996), p. 251.
7. One exception to this is Ronan Fanning's 'Playing It Cool: The response of the British and Irish Governments to the crisis in Northern Ireland, 1968–9', *Irish Studies in International Affairs*, 12 (2001).
8. English, R. *Armed Struggle: A history of the IRA* (London: Macmillan, 2003), p. 362. The author quotes a record of a British cabinet meeting on 18 Sept. 1969 in which the British Ambassador to Ireland, Andrew Gilchrist, set out the view that 'it would be in our interest, as well as that of southern Ireland, to explore means by which the Dublin Government could be associated with the creation of new arrangements for Ulster'.
9. National Archives of Ireland (hereafter National Archives), Department of the Taoiseach, File No. 2000/6/657, Note of discussion at the Foreign Office at 12:00 noon on Friday 1 Aug. 1969.
10. National Archives, Department of the Taoiseach, File No. 2000/6/657, Letter from the Irish Ambassador, J.G. Molloy to Hugh J. McCann, Secretary, Department of External Affairs, Nov. 1968.
11. National Archives, Department of the Taoiseach, File No. 2000/6/658, Report of discussion at the Foreign and Commonwealth Office, London, 15 Aug. 1969.
12. Crossman, R. *The Diaries of a Cabinet Minister: Volume three, Secretary of State for Social Services 1968–70* (London: Hamish Hamilton and Jonathan Cape, 1977), p. 619n.

13. National Archives, Department of the Taoiseach, File No. 2000/6/657, Note of discussion between the Tánaiste, Frank Aiken, and Edward Heath at a reception in Lancaster House held by the Secretary of State for Foreign and Commonwealth Affairs on 5 May 1969 sent to Lynch on 20 May 1969.

14. As printed in Lynch, J. *Speeches and Statements on Irish Unity, Northern Ireland, Anglo-Irish Relations, August 1969–October 1971* (Dublin: Government Information Bureau, 1971), p. 78.

15. National Archives, Department of the Taoiseach, File No. 2000/6/657, Letter from the Irish Ambassador, J.G. Molloy to Hugh J. McCann, Secretary, Department of External Affairs, the Taoiseach to Mr. Wilson, Nov. 1968.

16. National Archives, Department of the Taoiseach, File No. 2000/6/657.

17. National Archives, Department of the Taoiseach, File No. 2000/6/657, Notes made by Jack Lynch.

18. National Archives, Department of the Taoiseach, File No. 2001/6/515: Cosgrave's letter of request and Lynch's rejection are in this file.

19. They formed the Social Democratic and Labour Party (SDLP). For a study of the SDLP see Murray, G. *John Hume and the SDLP: Impact and survival in Northern Ireland* (Dublin: Irish Academic Press, 1998).

20. John Hume: Elected to Stormont as Nationalist MP in 1969; founding member of the SDLP in 1970; appointed leader of the party in 1979; elected as MP in 1983; involved in controversial talks with the Sinn Féin leader in 1988 and again in 1992; joint winner of the Nobel Peace Prize in 1999 for his role in the Northern Ireland peace process.

21. Austin Currie: Born in Co. Tyrone in 1939; Stormont MP for East Tyrone, 1964–72; active participant in the Northern Ireland Civil Rights movement, 1968–9; founding member of SDLP in 1970; member of the Northern Ireland Assembly, 1973–5; Chief Whip of SDLP, 1974; elected to Dáil in 1989 as Fine Gael TD; Fine Gael Presidential candidate, 1990; Minister of State at the Departments of Education, Justice and Health, 1994–7; lost his Dáil seat in 2002.

22. National Archives, Department of the Taoiseach, File No. 2001/6/520.

23. Neil Blaney: First elected as a Fianna Fáil TD in a by-election in the constituency of Donegal North-East in 1948; appointed Minister for Posts and Telegraphs, 1957; Minister for Local Government, 1958–66; appointed as Minister for Agriculture in 1967; dismissed from government as a result of accusations of his involvement in the illegal importation of arms for the IRA, the Arms Crisis, in 1970; expelled from Fianna Fáil in 1971; continued as Independent Fianna Fáil TD until his retirement in 1994; Member of European Parliament, 1979–84, 1989–94.

24. Charles Haughey: Elected to the Dáil as Fianna Fáil TD in 1957; appointed as Minister for Justice, 1961–4; Minister for Agriculture, 1964–6; Minister for Finance, 1966–70; dismissed from government, May 1970 for suspected involvement in the importation of illegal arms for use by the IRA, the Arms Crisis; acquitted of the charge of conspiracy to import arms, October 1970; restored to government when appointed Minister for Health and Social Welfare by Jack Lynch in 1977; leader of Fianna Fáil, 1979–1992; Taoiseach, 1979–81, 1982, 1987–92.

25. Arnold, B. *Jack Lynch: Hero in crisis* (Dublin: Merlin Publishing, 2001), pp. 116–19.

26. O'Brien, J. *The Arms Trial* (Dublin: Gill and Macmillan, 2000), see Chapter 4. See also Dwyer, T.R. *Nice Fellow: A biography of Jack Lynch* (Cork and Dublin: Mercier Press, 2001), pp. 200–1.

27. Bew, P., Hazelkorn, E. and Patterson, H. *The Dynamics of Irish Politics* (London: Lawrence and Wishart, 1989), p. 99.

28. In its most basic form this principle recognizes that Northern Ireland's constitutional status cannot be altered without the consent of a majority of the people there.

29. Arnold, *Jack Lynch,* p. 101.

30. Lynch, *Statements and Speeches,* p. 10.

31. Address by Jack Lynch at Fianna Fáil Ard Fheis 28 Jan. 1969, Fianna Fáil Archives, University College, Dublin, P176/775.

32. Árd Fheis Material 28–29 Jan. 1969, Fianna Fáil Archives, University College, Dublin, P176/775.

33. Lynch addressing the Dáil 27 Feb. 1969, National Archives, Department of the Taoiseach, File No. 2000/6/657.

34. National Archives, Department of the Taoiseach, File No. 2000/6/657, Copy of statement by Captain O'Neill in response to Blaney's suggestion of a Federal Council sent to Lynch by his secretary.
35. National Archives, Department of the Taoiseach, File No. 2000/6/657, Speech by Lynch at Clonmel and Tipperary town, Tuesday 8 Oct. 1968.
36. National Archives, Department of Taoiseach, File No. 2000/6/657, Address by Lynch to the Anglo-Irish Parliamentary Group, 30 Oct. 1968.
37. National Archives, Department of the Taoiseach, File No. 2000/6/657, Letter from Irish Ambassador, J.G Molloy to H.J. McCann, Secretary Department of External Affairs, Nov. 1968.
38. National Archives, Department of the Taoiseach, File No. 2000/6/657, Press conference given by the Taoiseach at the Irish Embassy, London, Oct. 30 1968, also see *Irish Press* 1 Nov. 1968.
39. Ibid.
40. National Archives, Department of Taoiseach, File No. 2000/6/657, Address by Lynch to the Anglo-Irish Parliamentary Group, 30 Oct. 1968.
41. National Archives, Department of the Taoiseach, File No. 2000/6/657, Presidential address by Lynch to Fianna Fáil Ard Fheis, Mansion House, Dublin 28 Jan. 1969.
42. Arnold, B. *What Kind of Country: Modern Irish politics 1968–1983* (London: Jonathan Cape, 1984), p. 27.
43. National Archives, Department of the Taoiseach, File No. 2000/6/657, Letter from Irish Ambassador, J.G. Molloy to H.J. McCann, Secretary, Department of External Affairs, Nov. 1968.
44. National Archives, Department of the Taoiseach, File No. 2000/6/658, Report of discussion at the Foreign and Commonwealth Office, London, 15 Aug. 1969. In his speech on 13 Aug. 1969, Lynch announced his intention to set up military hospitals at a number of points along the border so that those injured during riots in Derry, for example, would not have to utilize the Altnagelvin Hospital, which is located in the mainly Protestant Waterside area of Derry.
45. National Archives, Department of the Taoiseach, File No. 2000/6/657, Meeting on 15 Aug. 1969. Notes made by Jack Lynch dated 16 Aug. 1969.
46. National Archives, Department of the Taoiseach, File No. 2000/6/657, Notes made by Jack Lynch 16 Aug. 1969: Austin Currie's description, in a meeting with Lynch on 15 Aug. 1969, of the situation in the North at that time.
47. National Archives, Department of the Taoiseach, File No. 2000/6/658, Cabinet Minutes 16 Aug. 1969. It is worth noting that Pádraig Faulkner, another member of the Cabinet sub-committee on Northern Ireland, has stressed in his recent memoirs that the sub-committee had no authority to purchase arms. See Faulkner, P. *As I Saw It: Reviewing over 30 years of Fianna Fáil and Irish politics* (Dublin: Wolfhound Press, 2005), p. 94.
48. National Archives, Department of the Taoiseach, File No. 2000/6/657, Cabinet Minutes, 15 Aug. 1969.
49. National Archives, Department of the Taoiseach, File No. 2000/6/657, Memorandum for the information of the Government, 16 Aug. 1969.
50. National Archives, Department of the Taoiseach, File No. 2000/6/658, Government Information Bureau, 16 Aug. 1969.
51. Hugh McCann confidential circular as quoted in Fanning, 'Playing It Cool', p. 67.
52. As quoted in Arnold, *Jack Lynch*, p. 96.
53. Lynch, *Speeches and Statements,* p. 3.
54. National Archives, Department of the Taoiseach, File No. 2000/6/657, Dr N. ÓNúalláin, Secretary Department of the Taoiseach, in a letter attached to two possible drafts of the Taoiseach's speech, 13 Aug. 1969.
55. Arnold, *What Kind of Country,* p. 20.
56. National Archives, Department of the Taoiseach, File No. 2000/6/657, Taoiseach speaking at the Annual Dinner of Cavan Comhairle Cheantair, Fianna Fáil at Kingscourt, 1 May 1969.
57. Lynch, *Speeches and Statements,* p. 22.
58. National Archives, Department of the Taoiseach, File No. 2002/8/487, Address by Lynch 22 Oct. 1970 to the commemorative session of the General Assembly on the occasion of the 25th Anniversary of the United Nations.
59. Ibid.
60. Staunton, E. *The Nationalists of Northern Ireland 1918–1973* (Dublin: The Columba Press, 2001), pp. 269–70.

61. National Archives, Department of the Taoiseach, File No. 2001/8/6, 'The Constitutional Position of Northern Ireland', 24 Nov. 1969.
62. Ibid.
63. *Irish Press* 2 March 1971.
64. *Irish Independent* 9, 10 April 1971.
65. National Archives, Department of the Taoiseach, File No. 2002/8/251, Lynch speaking at the annual dinner of the Cork Soroptimists Club, Imperial Hotel Cork, 2 Oct. 1971.
66. *Irish Press* 20 Nov. 1971.
67. Ibid. Lynch addressing the Donogh O'Malley Fianna Fáil Cumann on 'The Political, social and economic future of Ireland'.
68. Ibid.
69. National Archives, Department of the Taoiseach, File No. 2002/8/251, Extract from '7 days' interview with Lynch, 30 Nov. 1971.
70. *Irish Independent* 9, 10 April 1971.
71. *The Irish Times* 2 Sept. 1971.
72. *The Irish Times* 3 Sept. 1971.
73. National Archives, Department of the Taoiseach, File No. 2003/17/30, Meeting between The Taoiseach Mr Lynch and Mr Heath at Chequers, 6 Sept. 1971.
74. National Archives, Department of Foreign Affairs, File No. 2003/13/6, Report of discussions on 6 and 7 Sept. 1971 at Chequers between the Taoiseach and the British Prime Minister.
75. Ibid.
76. Ibid.
77. National Archives, Department of the Taoiseach, File No. 2001/8/10, Transcript of Press conference by Lynch after meeting with Prime Minister Mr Edward Heath MP at Chequers on 6 and 7 Sept. 1971.
78. National Archives, Department of the Taoiseach, File No. 2002/8/487, Transcript of Press conference by Lynch after meeting with Prime Minister Mr Edward Heath MP at Chequers on 6 and 7 Sept. 1971.
79. *Irish Press* 27 Sept. 1971.
80. *The Irish Times* 3 Sept. 1971.
81. National Archives, Department of the Taoiseach, File No. 2002/8/487, Note from Seán Rowan 4 Aug. 1971.
82. National Archives, Department of Foreign Affairs, File No. 2003/13/7, Report of discussions on 27 and 28 Sept. 1971 at Chequers between the Taoiseach, the British Prime Minister and Mr Brian Faulkner.
83. National Archives, Department of the Taoiseach, File No. 2002/8/251, Statement issued after Chequers meeting, 28 Sept. 1971.
84. National Archives, Department of the Taoiseach, File No. 2002/8/487, Note of discussion between An Taoiseach and Mr Heath 6 Dec. 1971, written by Donal O'Sullivan, Irish Ambassador to London.
85. National Archives, Department of the Taoiseach, File No. 2002/8/489, Address by An Taoiseach, Mr Lynch at a luncheon at Parliamentary Press Gallery Group, House of Commons, Westminster, London, 6 Dec. 1971.
86. National Archives, Department of the Taoiseach, File No. 2003/16/461, Note on call to Taoiseach by British Ambassador, 6 Jan. 1972.
87. National Archives, Department of the Taoiseach, File No. 2003/16/461, Notes on meeting between Eamonn Gallagher and Cecil King in London, 24 Jan. 1972.
88. National Archives, Department of Foreign Affairs, File No. 2003/13/16, Meetings between the Minister for Foreign Affairs and Sir Alec Douglas Home, Secretary of State for Foreign and Commonwealth Affairs and William Whitelaw, 27 April 1972.
89. *The Irish Times* 23 Oct. 1971.
90. *The Irish Times* 18 Sept. 1971.
91. Kevin Boland, quoted in *The Irish Times* 20 Sept. 1971.
92. *The Irish Times* 27 Sept. 1971.
93. *Connacht Tribune* 22 Dec. 1971.
94. *Irish Press* 16 Dec. 1971.
95. National Archives, Department of the Taoiseach, File No. 2002/8/252, Dáil question addressed to the Taoiseach by Deputy Barry Desmond for answer on 16 Dec. 1971.
96. Northern Ireland Minister for Finance, Mr Kirk, *The Irish Times* 18 Dec. 1971.

97. *Irish Press* 21 Dec. 1971.
98. *Irish Press* 16 Dec. 1971.
99. *Connacht Tribune* 22 Dec. 1971.
100. See National Archives, Department of the Taoiseach, File Nos. 2002/8/251–2.
101. National Archives, Department of the Taoiseach, File No. 2002/8/487, Letter to Ambassador from C.V. Whelan 26 Jan. 1972.
102. Ibid.
103. National Archives, Department of the Taoiseach, File No. 2002/8/489, Address by Lynch at a luncheon at Parliamentary Press Gallery Group, House of Commons, Westminster, London, 6 Dec. 1971.
104. The British government was unwilling to commit to future meetings. National Archives, Department of the Taoiseach, File No. 2002/8/487.
105. *The Irish Times* 23 Sept. 1971.
106. Bew, Patterson and Teague, *Between War and Peace:* the authors suggest that this only changed from 1973 onwards through joint membership of the EEC, pp. 43–4.
107. Crossman, *The Diaries of a Cabinet Minister,* p. 622, see also pp. 381–2, 891. However, this is not how British policy was viewed by unionists, see Mulholland, Marc, *Northern Ireland at the Crossroads: Ulster Unionism in the O'Neill years, 1960–9* (London: Macmillan Press, 2000). Also see Rose, Peter, *How the Troubles came to Northern Ireland* (Hampshire, Palgrave, 2001), pp. 122–3.
108. Fanning, 'Playing it Cool', p. 84.
109. Peck, J. *Dublin from Downing Street* (Dublin: Gill and Macmillan, 1978), p. 45.
110. National Archives, Department of the Taoiseach, File No. 2001/8/6, 'The Constitutional Position of Northern Ireland', 24 Nov. 1969.
111. Fianna Fáil was in opposition from 1973–7, when Fine Gael and the Labour Party formed a coalition. Jack Lynch remained as leader and returned to the Dáil in 1977 as Taoiseach.
112. *Dáil Éireann Debates* Vol. 269, Col. 425–6, 28 Nov. 1973.
113. *Dáil Éireann Debates* Vol. 269, Col. 426, 28 Nov. 1973.
114. *Dáil Éireann Debates* Vol. 273, Col. 1583, 26 June 1974.
115. *Dáil Éireann Debates* Vol. 273, Col. 1587, 26 June 1974.
116. *Dáil Éireann Debates* Vol. 273, Col. 1588, 26 June 1974.
117. *The Irish Times* 1 Sept. 1979.
118. *Irish Press* 3 Sept. 1979.
119. *The Irish Times* 3 Sept. 1979.
120. *Irish Press* 6 Sept. 1979.
121. *The Irish Times* 6 Sept. 1979.
122. *The Irish Times* 8 Sept. 1979.
123. *The Irish Times* 10 Sept. 1979.
124. See *The Irish Times* 29 Sept 1979.
125. Dwyer, *Nice Fellow: A biography of Jack Lynch*, p. 375.
126. *The Irish Times* 12 Nov. 1979.
127. *Irish Press* 10 Nov. 1979.
128. *Irish Press* 21 Nov. 1979.
129. *Irish Press* 6 Dec. 1979.
130. See material relating to the 1957 Fianna Fáil Árd Fheis, Fianna Fáil Archives, University College, Dublin, P176/764.

CHAPTER TWO

Charles J. Haughey and Sinn Féin 1979–92: Towards a consensus on partition?[1]

INTRODUCTION

Charles J. Haughey was one of the most complex and controversial leaders in modern Ireland and examinations of his contribution to Irish politics have provided conflicting portrayals, particularly of his approach to Northern Ireland. This is no doubt due to, as T. Ryle Dwyer has identified, the contradictory nature of Haughey's approach, dependent on whether he was Taoiseach or leader of the opposition.[2] Former Deputy Leader of Fianna Fáil, Mary O'Rourke, believes Haughey was 'cautious' on Northern Ireland. According to O'Rourke, Haughey's main aim until 1987 was to get into government and his actions in that period are to be understood in that light.[3] Indeed, there is much to suggest that the period after 1987 is most crucial when judging Haughey in relation to Northern Ireland, as his approach to Northern Ireland after 1987 was much more proactive and innovative than it had been in the past. His position as Taoiseach or opposition leader is a crucial point in understanding his motives and political approach, but there is another central factor in understanding Haughey in the 1980s that will feature strongly throughout this chapter: his relationship with republicanism and the presence of Sinn Féin.

Dermot Ahern, who was chosen by Charles Haughey to participate in a delegation which met with Sinn Féin in 1988, set out his view that no position adopted by Fianna Fáil should be influenced by any perceived electoral threat posed by Sinn Féin: 'There was always the danger and there is always the danger that the more Sinn Féin come on the constitutional route, they may take part of our constituency, but that's politics and that shouldn't enter into what our view was.'[4] We know, however, that the political parties in the Republic, amongst them the governing Fine Gael party of the 1980s, thought that it was necessary to respond to events in Northern Ireland. Some of these events had become election issues, such as the politicization of Sinn Féin in the course of the hunger strikes, and this motivated the New Ireland Forum and the Anglo-Irish process which culminated in the Anglo-Irish Agreement.[5] Again in 1986, Sinn Féin can be seen as a motivating factor in Haughey's rejection of the Anglo-Irish Agreement. The Fine Gael Minister for Foreign Affairs, Peter Barry, accused Haughey of allowing his judgement to be influenced by Sinn Féin: 'For the first time, we have a leader of the Fianna Fáil party who is afraid of Sinn Féin and their IRA masters, afraid that unless he joins Sinn Féin in opposition to the Agreement, he might lose votes to the party of the "armalite".'[6]

For many reasons, including the existence of such accusations, Haughey's involvement in the Arms Crisis and the important role which republicanism played in his acquisition of power and subsequent policy, an assessment of the extent to which Sinn Féin impacted on his language and approach to Northern Ireland is needed. Therefore, this chapter concentrates on the importance of the interplay between Fianna Fáil and Sinn Féin in order to understand Haughey's northern policy and Fianna Fáil's role in the peace process. It will expose the need to look beyond such landmarks in nationalist Ireland as the New Ireland Forum in order to understand the origins of consensus within Irish nationalism which has been central to the peace process. Specifically, the chapter will discuss conflicting accounts of Charles Haughey's northern policy and of his role in the peace process in order to draw some conclusions on the topic.

Secondly, this chapter will also outline the extent to which Fianna Fáil's ideological position throughout the 1980s was conditioned by the emergence of Sinn Féin as an electoral force in Northern Ireland and potentially in the Republic of Ireland and provide an analysis of the importance for Fianna Fáil of the 1988 Fianna Fáil–Sinn Féin talks. Thirdly, an argument will be advanced as to the significance of these talks for the principles of consent and self-determination and for the peace process itself. The ideological contribution made by Fianna Fáil to the peace process is highlighted through an examination of the reformulations of the principles of consent and self-determination which were informed by the party's talks with Sinn Féin. The effort to build a consensus between Fianna Fáil and Sinn Féin provided the basis for the peace process. Thus, the chapter's final task will be to demonstrate the importance of the relationship between Fianna Fáil and Sinn Féin to understanding the origins and dynamics of the Northern Ireland peace process.

CHARLES HAUGHEY AND NORTHERN IRELAND POLICY

There have been many previous academic and journalistic studies of Charles Haughey. These have emphasized certain themes such as the fact that Haughey's policy stances and rhetoric were determined by his position, in and out of power, which was alluded to above. Dwyer also refers to the different positions adopted by Haughey and Garret FitzGerald, the leader of Fine Gael in the 1980s. FitzGerald, as the champion of revisionist thought at that time, advocated pursuing certain measures, which were aimed at placating unionists.[7] Dwyer maintained that Haughey's response was wholly inadequate: 'He did not try to refute the Taoiseach's suggestions with reasoned arguments of his own; instead he resorted to an emotive appeal that impugned the patriotism of FitzGerald and those who agreed with him.'[8]

While Dwyer does not provide a clear exposition as to why Haughey adopted such language, Justin O'Brien has argued that this can be explained in Machiavellian terms.[9] O'Brien explained that Haughey's political career was defined in reference to nationalism. He claimed that Haughey used this in his quest for, and maintenance of, power and that he also utilized the national question to provide Fianna Fáil with a distinctive position in Irish politics.[10] This was particularly relevant given that little else divided the two main parties.[11] O'Brien demonstrated the manner in which Haughey utilized his newly formed association with republicanism in the aftermath of the Arms Crisis in 1970 as a mechanism for challenging the party leadership and, once power was achieved, maintain it: 'Haughey demonstrated just how much he wanted that power and what he was prepared to sacrifice in order to maintain it.'[12] His ability to remain as leader despite the considerable numbers of dissatisfied members within the party is explained by the way in which he came to 'personify the wider Fianna Fáil organisation', and by the fact that 'Fianna Fáil always differentiated itself from its rivals by its commitment to the national question'. This allowed Haughey to 'tap into a visceral feeling within the party that ending partition was an achievable goal'.[13] O'Brien attributes Haughey's loss of power to a change in policy, away from a distinctive position, when he formed a coalition with the Progressive Democrats in 1989: 'The loss of the ideological prop fatally undermined Haughey's claim that only he could ensure Fianna Fáil retained internal cohesiveness as the repository of the revolution's ideals.'[14] O'Brien's emphasis on Haughey's relationship with republicanism in explaining his motives makes a valuable contribution to understanding his politics.

O'Brien, Dwyer and Stephen Collins recognize the achievements made by Haughey in taking the first steps towards building favourable Anglo-Irish relations and in placing the question of Northern Ireland within their confines. Collins heralds the establishment of Anglo-Irish summits, with his 'tea-pot' summit in 1980, as the launch of 'a major political initiative'.[15] O'Brien also attributes great significance to this; indeed he has labelled it the starting point from which the Good Friday Agreement developed. This is due to the summit's emphasis on the 'totality of relations between these two islands'.[16] However, while this is acknowledged, generally Haughey is given little credit for his contribution to the peace process. Indeed, O'Brien believes that Haughey sacrificed the opportunity for a breakthrough while in coalition with the Progressive Democrats in the late 1980s because of his preoccupation with maintaining power. Despite O'Brien's identification of the significance of republicanism to Haughey's politics, in the end he reduces his explanation of Haughey's motivations to his coalition with the Progressive Democrats. He claims that Haughey did not give adequate support to talks with Sinn Féin from 1988 onwards because of his fear of losing power if the Progressive Democrats were to discover the talks series. He stated that: '[T]he failure to deliver on issues Haughey had repeatedly deemed of profound importance was perhaps the greatest paradox of his political career. Defined for a generation by reference to his republicanism, in the end he was unprepared to risk power to achieve a breakthrough.'[17] Moreover, O'Brien asserts that: 'During his years as Taoiseach from 1987 there was simply no evidence of his preparedness to risk power to achieve a strategic breakthrough on the Northern question, the very issue that defined his political life.'[18]

O'Brien argued that Haughey's decision to 'remain aloof' from the talks between Sinn Féin and Fianna Fáil indicated a lack of 'moral courage'.[19] He also attributed the inconclusiveness of these talks to the absence of 'the backing of higher authority'.[20] It is understandable that Haughey would have been cautious regarding these talks; he had no way of knowing whether he could trust the republican leaders not to publicize the talks. In the political environment after the Enniskillen bombing the likely repercussions for Haughey and Fianna Fáil would not have been favourable and would have probably led to a crisis of government. Fianna Fáil minister, John O'Donoghue, has described the 1988 Fianna Fáil–Sinn Féin talks as a 'watershed' and as evidence of courage on the part of Haughey, given the fact that Sinn Féin members were seen as pariahs in this era.[21] By sanctioning both Dermot

Ahern and Martin Mansergh,[22] his special advisor on Northern Ireland, to engage in these talks, which could have been easily linked back to him, Haughey clearly illustrated the 'moral courage' which O'Brien believes to be absent. While the associated 'risks'[23] were a consideration in the termination of the talks, what was more important was the fact that the time for Sinn Féin to enter constitutional politics had not yet arrived. In that sense the process was not yet 'ripe'.[24] To blame Haughey solely for the unsuccessful outcome of the talks fails to take into account other relevant factors. Any attempt at finding a solution would have needed the support of the British government and there was a realization that this was unlikely while Thatcher was in government. While in theory the Anglo-Irish Agreement meant that the two governments would work as a partnership, that 'partnership had severe limitations'.[25] While the direct talks ended, a channel of contact with the republican movement was maintained through Father Alex Reid[26] and Mansergh[27] without the knowledge of Fianna Fáil's coalition partner, the Progressive Democrats.[28] To conclude, as O'Brien has, that these talks with Sinn Féin were insignificant to the peace process and lacked backing from Haughey is shortsighted and dismissive of the importance of these contacts in later years. Whether or not Haughey stood back from the talks, and despite their short duration, they are nonetheless important in understanding Haughey's subsequent northern policy and the peace process, which has not previously been acknowledged.

Ed Moloney in his book *A Secret History of the IRA* certainly takes a different view of the talks and of Haughey's role in the peace process to that of O'Brien.[29] Moloney describes Haughey's contribution as follows:

> His contribution was twofold. The first was that many of the political ideas on Northern Ireland developed during his time as Fianna Fáil leader were incorporated almost wholesale into the strategy worked out by (Gerry) Adams[30] and Reid. In many important ways the strategy was Haughey's, not theirs. The second contribution was that by the time he left office in 1992, the theology of the peace process had been fully worked out, and the completion of the enterprise was then only a matter of internal management and negotiation. Whatever about Haughey's role as midwife to the Provos, there is no doubt that he was in there at the beginning of their end.[31]

According to Moloney, the important contribution of political ideas made by Haughey related to his dedication to the idea of an all-Ireland constitutional conference and to his call for the British government to declare their interest in a united Ireland.[32] Moloney lends great weight to Haughey's willingness to open contacts with Sinn Féin as the basis for the IRA ceasefire. It is important to be clear as to Haughey's exact contribution to the process. While Moloney's concentration on Haughey as the starting point for the peace process is useful, his conclusion that the idea and strategy central to the peace process was Haughey's is inaccurate. The significant part played by Haughey in the peace process was not the idea but the decision to facilitate, as far as was possible at the time, Sinn Féin's desire to move republicans away from violence and towards constitutional politics through the establishment of contacts which formed the basis of a strong pan-nationalist alliance in the course of the Reynolds administration. It was the decision to react to shifts within northern republicanism that came to define Fianna Fáil's role within the peace process and its position on Northern Ireland throughout the 1990s.

In 1987 Haughey received a document from the republican movement through Father Reid, outlining Sinn Féin's desire to establish a wide nationalist movement, or what has become known as a pan-nationalist front.[33] Gerry Adams, the President of Sinn Féin, and Reid had been discussing the need to initiate a process which would enable co-operation within Irish nationalism. Father Reid wrote a letter to the SDLP leader, John Hume, in May 1986, outlining a proposal that

> the nationalist parties, North and South, would agree, through dialogue between themselves, to formulate and then to co-operate in a common nationalist policy of aims and methods for resolving the conflict and establishing a just and lasting peace. This would mean that while retaining their own separate identities the nationalist parties would make an ad hoc agreement to combine their political forces and to act in unison in a common campaign for reconciliation and peace.[34]

In a subsequent meeting with Hume, Adams reiterated the need for co-operation between the nationalist parties, in an effort to move the British government on Northern Ireland.[35] The talks with Fianna Fáil were a vital part of Sinn Féin strategy at this time. A Sinn Féin document outlining the path *Towards a Lasting Peace* published in 1992 referred to the crucial role which the Irish government ought to play in persuading unionists of the benefits of unity.[36] Another Sinn Féin document which was uncovered in 1995 outlines the thinking within Sinn Féin in the early 1990s. The *TUAS* document, as it became known, listed the movement's 'main strategic objectives' as including the creation of 'an Irish nationalist consensus with international support on the basis of the dynamic contained in the Irish peace initiative'. The motivation behind this was simple: 'The struggle needs strengthening most obviously from other nationalist constituencies led by the SDLP [and the] Dublin government'.[37] Adams described a further Sinn Féin policy paper, *Scenario for Peace*,[38] as an acknowledgement that any peace strategy would only succeed if it had the support 'of a wide representation of Irish, British and international opinion'.[39] While an in-depth analysis of why the republican movement came to reassess the usefulness of its concentration on the armed struggle in favour of a new broader approach is beyond the scope and intentions of this volume,[40] it is important however to have a sense of the number of differing factors which were relevant. Michael Cox has, for example, pointed to international developments which impacted upon the direction taken by the republican movement in the late 1980s. Cox refers to the changing international landscape at the end of the Cold War, which both enabled the erosion of the 'special relationship' between the USA and Britain and also necessitated a reappraisal on the part of republicans as to British motives in staying in Northern Ireland. He also argues that the European Union impacted upon attitudes in the Republic as well as upon Anglo-Irish relations in a way which enabled a process of dialogue to develop between the two states.[41]

The success of Sinn Féin's attempt to gain a wider basis for its struggle was aided by the complementary nature of SDLP strategies in the 1980s. The SDLP had by this stage been concerned to 'persuade the republican movement that the circumstances existed enabling Sinn Féin to participate in negotiations'.[42] The SDLP had also come to the conclusion that the search for a solution necessitated the support of the Dublin government and 'goodwill throughout Ireland'.[43] According to Seán Farren, the SDLP chairman from 1981–6, the failure of a number of devolution initiatives in 1974 and 1982 meant the SDLP now argued that 'a solution to political division … would not be found on the narrow ground of Northern Ireland alone'.[44] The Anglo-Irish Agreement of 1985 was the first step in the SDLP's strategy as outlined in 1979.[45] In the period after the Anglo-Irish Agreement, Hume 'was looking for a strategy to develop the political process to the next stage where violence would be taken out of the political equation' and he hoped the Anglo-Irish Agreement could act as a leverage in persuading the republican movement that the British government was neutral in terms of Northern Ireland.[46] John Hume has recalled how the Anglo-Irish Agreement of 1985 resulted in a public debate between the SDLP and Sinn Féin as to the nature of the British government's motives in relation to Northern Ireland.[47] It is in this context that the SDLP, particularly John Hume, was prepared to engage in dialogue with Sinn Féin. Seán Farren has said that the failure of these talks did not discourage the SDLP from this strategy.[48] Despite the fact that relations between the SDLP and Fianna Fáil were damaged by differing interpretations of the Anglo-Irish Agreement, it is unlikely that either the Irish government or later the American government would have been persuaded to support this process, had John Hume not advocated that they do so. It is therefore not just in his impact on Sinn Féin's thinking that Hume's contribution lies; it is also his influence on Dublin and American attitudes.[49] By the late 1980s Sinn Féin, the SDLP and Fianna Fáil were searching for an alternative and broader approach to advance their aims. The strategies of the three parties coincided, since Sinn Féin recognized the need for the support of wider nationalist opinion and both the SDLP and Fianna Fáil had come to accept that Sinn Féin must be involved in any future negotiations with the British government and the unionists. The 1988 talks process involving these three parties formed an early manifestation of these ideas and strategies. The search for a new and inclusive approach was assisted by the fact that the 1988 mission statement of the Redemptorist Peace Ministry endorsed Father Reid's involvement in direct talks with representatives of Sinn Féin and the IRA. The statement outlined the ministry's 'duty to intervene directly to do all it can to bring its violent dimension and their [sic] tragic consequences to an end'.[50] Father Reid was to form an invaluable link between the three different parties at crucial points in the process.

The peace process can be viewed as originating from the formation of this intra-nationalist co-operation. Haughey's willingness to develop talks and a lasting contact, if not to the extent to which the republican movement aspired, proved the basis of the peace process. During the talks with Sinn Féin, the Fianna Fáil representatives made it clear that more progress could be made if Irish nationalists were politically united but that this was prohibited by the IRA's use of violence. Subsequently, they attempted to persuade Sinn Féin of the benefits of accepting democratic principles.[51] The crucial nature of these talks on this level is therefore evident: Haughey was offering Sinn Féin the coveted pan-nationalist front but only on the basis that the IRA would call a ceasefire.[52] Moloney's study is the first to examine the role of Haughey in the peace process; he is the first to claim that Haughey was crucial to the early stages of the peace process. While Moloney's sources remain confidential, his new account seems more acceptable than O'Brien's dismissal of the talks, given that Haughey selected those Fianna Fáil representatives who attended the talks and sanctioned the maintenance of the contacts. Also, taken together with the speeches outlined in the next section and Dermot Ahern's admission that 'a lot of the messages that Haughey would have given publicly would have been flowing from his knowledge of the meetings',[53] we know that the talks slotted into and influenced Haughey's agenda in relation to Northern Ireland.

All accounts of Haughey's record on Northern Ireland have failed to deal systematically with the changing influences on his position. O'Brien shrewdly portrays the importance of Haughey's relationship with nationalism to understanding his use of republican rhetoric, but, rather than being viewed in purely Machiavellian terms, his use of republican rhetoric can be related to diverse challenges posed at one level by FitzGerald and at another by the republican movement and Sinn Féin. It is because of his affiliation with nationalism and its necessity as a distinguishing marker that these challenges were relevant. Overlooking these factors is misleading. In fact they are crucial to understanding why Haughey reversed his earlier acceptance of the principle of consent. The response from Haughey to FitzGerald's call for a constitutional crusade can also be seen in this light. Haughey's position was threatened by this new challenging approach offered by FitzGerald in the wake of failed Fianna Fáil rhetoric, given that this represented a challenge to the very core of what distinguished Fianna Fáil and Haughey from Fine Gael: a commitment to the national question on republican terms. While Haughey was in power he displayed openness to these progressive moves but was forced to object to them while in opposition.

THE IMPORTANCE OF SINN FÉIN TO FIANNA FÁIL'S
NORTHERN IRELAND POLICY

There are a number of points to be made in explaining why the presence of Sinn Féin was of particular relevance to Haughey and Fianna Fáil throughout the 1980s. Firstly, Fianna Fáil had been relegated to the opposition benches in 1981 partly due to the relative success of a number of the H-Block candidates who stood in the election that Haughey had mistakenly called during the hunger strikes. Their success in two constituencies was enough to deprive Fianna Fáil of the required majority to form a government. Placing Northern Ireland at the centre of the election despite the failure of Haughey's administration to make an impact on Thatcher's stance during the crisis enabled the IRA hunger strikers to gain on polling day.[54] From this point until 1987 when Haughey returned to power, the substance of the threat from Sinn Féin remained an unknown quantity. It was not clear whether Sinn Féin could capitalize on the success of the hunger strikers' election victories when it took the decision to take its seats in the Dáil in November 1986.[55] Sinn Féin's performance remained at an average of 2 per cent[56] but there remained the potential for the party to deprive Fianna Fáil of government, as had occurred in the case of the H-Block candidates in 1981. There was a danger that if Fianna Fáil did not appear to be in control of the Northern Ireland issue Sinn Féin could capitalize on this. This is seen most clearly in Haughey's position on the Anglo-Irish Agreement in 1985 (see below).

Secondly, the rivalry between the two parties went to the very core of the republican ethos of Fianna Fáil. Sinn Féin represented a challenge to the republican credentials of Fianna Fáil. In 1971, Sinn Féin set out its view of the southern state and its institutions and pledged itself 'to replace them with an All-Ireland Parliament, the successors to the First Dáil and Second Dáil'.[57] The ideological struggle between the two parties essentially related to the legitimacy of the southern state and the ownership of the ideals of 1916, which both parties claimed.[58]

Thirdly, Sinn Féin's growth in the North as well as continued IRA violence meant that Fianna Fáil's northern policy could not simply bypass the republican movement. An approach which involved the SDLP and not Sinn Féin was inadequate in these circumstances; it was this realization which informed Haughey's approach when he returned to power in 1987. While the decline in the Sinn Féin vote reduced the electoral threat to Fianna Fáil at this time, both the SDLP and Fianna Fáil believed that the search for a solution must involve Sinn Féin and, consequently, Hume and Haughey, independently, decided to maintain contacts with Sinn Féin. It is on these terms that Sinn Féin influenced Fianna Fáil's rhetoric and approach to Northern Ireland in this period.

Republicans had long since been critical of Fianna Fáil. Lynch, who was continually referred to as 'Union Jack', was cited as giving 'moral and material aid and comfort to the enemies of our people, the British forces of Occupation in Ireland'.[59] He was also criticized for his willingness to employ repressive methods against the IRA.[60] These attacks on the political parties in the Republic continued throughout. The republican movement accused both main parties of 'constituting different brands of Free-Statism, both with the same pro-British and partitionist message. In reality, the attitude to the North of Fianna Fáil, which makes capital out of its republican roots differs very little from that of Fine Gael, whose roots go back to the original Free Staters'.[61] Fianna Fáil was also faulted for 'bogus' republicanism and for engaging in 'collaboration with enemy forces in the North'.[62] Although Haughey was to oversee the first act of reaching out to Sinn Féin in the late 1980s he had earlier been subject to the same accusations and insults reserved for Fine Gael and Labour. In his 1986 publication, *The Politics of Irish Freedom,* Adams was strident in his criticism of Fianna Fáil's failure to 'tackle the partition issue in a meaningful way which could have led to independence'.[63] So, while there were hints from Haughey in the early 1980s (the summit with Thatcher in 1980 and the New Ireland Forum in 1983) that he might embrace constitutional change, the inability to ignore such challenges from Sinn Féin and the republican movement meant Fianna Fáil remained committed to the use of traditional republican language. This, Martin Mansergh explains, 'meant that Fianna Fáil in the early to mid 1980s, reverted under Charles Haughey to its republican roots, in a way not seen since Eamon de Valera'.[64] This was particularly true of the party's time in opposition. Mansergh argues that this was a result of the party's 'determination to hold the republican ground and not cede it to anyone else',[65] in particular to Sinn Féin.

This constraint was expressed in Haughey's response to a submission from Robert McCartney[66] entitled *The Unionist Case*.[67] Haughey argued that:

> It is a great illusion to suppose that if the Irish government were to recognise the validity of partition and to abandon the concept of a united Ireland that this would necessarily bring a diminution of violence. On the contrary, the only likely consequence would be a threat to the stability of the twenty-six counties as well as the six counties. An Irish government which would abandon the fundamental democratic aspiration of the Irish people on both sides of the border would invite repudiation, possible in a form which would only aggravate the existing conflict in Northern Ireland.[68]

This is a clear illustration that Haughey believed that the Irish government's approach to Northern Ireland must aim to limit the strength of Sinn Féin and the IRA. The varying challenge posed by Sinn Féin explains Fianna Fáil's changing attitude towards Northern Ireland and, in particular, the alteration between revisionism and republicanism. At his first Árd Fheis as leader and Taoiseach in 1980, Haughey denounced IRA violence:

> All but a tiny minority understand that violence can never bring a solution and that it serves only to perpetuate division and hatred. Let us make it absolutely clear that no Irish Government will tolerate any attempt by any group to put themselves above the law or to arrogate to themselves any of the functions of the Government. There is only one army in this State, one police force and one judiciary, appointed under the Constitution, to uphold the laws. The Government, acting for the people, will ensure that these laws are effective and are enforced. Democracy will be defended and the rule of law upheld. That is an essential element of national policy.[69]

Arguing that Northern Ireland had been created and sustained artificially and had failed as a political entity, he stressed the need for the Irish and British governments to 'work together to find a formula and lift the situation onto a new plane that will bring permanent peace and stability to the people of these islands'. He envisaged that this new Anglo-Irish approach would begin with 'a declaration by the British Government of their interest in encouraging the unity of Ireland, by agreement and in peace [and this] would open the way towards an entirely new situation in which peace, real lasting peace, would become an attainable reality'.[70] By advocating unity and seeking a declaration from the British government on unity, Haughey followed Lynch's approach, and he too hoped to remove the reasons for IRA violence.

From an early point Haughey was dedicated to a two-pronged approach. Firstly, he sought to launch a diplomatic crusade with the objective of applying international pressure on Britain.[71] Secondly, and most importantly, there was his emphasis on Anglo-Irish relations as the key to a settlement. This was evident in his attempt at a 'major political initiative'[72] through the 1980 meeting with Margaret Thatcher. Haughey was in agreement with the SDLP's analysis of the Northern Ireland problem and believed that Anglo-Irish relations offered an appropriate framework to proceed towards a solution.[73] In the period prior to the Anglo-Irish Agreement, Haughey's position was similar to that of the SDLP, for example both parties rejected the rolling devolution initiative of the Secretary of State for Northern Ireland, Jim Prior, in 1982.[74]

Haughey signed up to a form of the principle of consent in the joint communiqué issued by him and Margaret Thatcher in 1980 by agreeing that 'any change in the constitutional status of Northern Ireland would only come about with the consent of a majority of the people of Northern Ireland'.[75] However, he also maintained that this was not prejudicial to 'our view [that] while no part of the Irish nation has the right to opt out of our nation, we recognise that unity cannot be imposed by force, and can only come about by negotiation and agreement'.[76] In the aftermath of the hunger strikes, when Fianna Fáil was in opposition, the party's position was less conciliatory on the issue of consent. With the inauguration of the constitutional crusade by Garret FitzGerald and Fine Gael in September 1981 Fianna Fáil retreated to the sanctity of familiar republican language.

Haughey challenged the recommendation by FitzGerald's government that the 1937 Constitution should be altered with the aim of assuaging unionists. Haughey's objection to the notion of change was not absolute but rather was premised on timing.[77] Subsequently, Haughey vehemently opposed FitzGerald's efforts towards an open and widespread adherence to the principle of consent that gave a majority in Northern Ireland a veto over unity. In his joint communiqué with Thatcher, issued after their summit together in November 1981, FitzGerald committed his government to a strong formulation of the principle of consent, much to Fianna Fáil's consternation.[78] At this stage, Haughey adhered to a formulation of consent which provided unionists not with the right to consent to the future of Northern Ireland but with the right to be involved with deciding, not the fact of a united Ireland but rather the shape it would take (see below).

FitzGerald declared his intention to seek 'the kind of pluralist society that might have evolved had Ireland not been divided sixty years ago'[79] through a re-examination of the relevant provisions of the 1937 Constitution. Yet the interpretation of the Irish question that he endorsed through the New Ireland Forum, which he initiated and sponsored in 1983, was fairly conservative in its preference for a unitary state.[80] However, this was a concession to ensure Fianna Fáil and Haughey would support the report. Despite concluding in favour of unity, J.H. Whyte believed that the New Ireland Forum report con-

tained progressive elements.[81] The reformulation of nationalist thinking in the New Ireland Forum report, detected by Whyte, was disguised by Haughey's choice of language afterwards and by the narrow
interpretation of the report, which he employed in order to 'undermine the reality, which was that the actual written text represented an
agreed, four-party position' and thereby 'restored to him the rem-
nants of his earlier Northern Ireland policy'.[82]

There were two major concerns for Haughey in his response to the
New Ireland Forum report. First was his desire not to be outmanoeu-
vred by Garret FitzGerald on the issue of Northern Ireland. Arnold
has argued that damaging FitzGerald and his government was the
only objective that Haughey cared about at this stage.[83] This was certainly a great consideration in electoral terms, and we have seen Mary
O'Rourke's assertion that Haughey's main concern was to regain
office. Secondly, his preoccupation with becoming Taoiseach once
again led him to acknowledge the potential for an ideological and
electoral threat from the republican movement. The New Ireland
Forum was the response of nationalist Ireland to the electoral growth
of Sinn Féin, and the fact that Haughey did not want to be outflanked
by Sinn Féin adds to our understanding of the contrast between what
the New Ireland Forum report entailed and Haughey's choice of language. Mansergh explained that the 'rigorous constitutional republicanism' pursued by Haughey at this time was aimed at 'limiting challenges to your [Fianna Fáil's] republican flank'.[84]

The alternation between government and opposition, together
with the continued potential for Sinn Féin to challenge Fianna Fáil on
an ideological and electoral level, was most significant in Haughey's
reaction to the Anglo-Irish Agreement. Haughey warned prior to the
Anglo-Irish Agreement in 1985 that it was 'a time for great vigi-
lance'.[85] He sent his deputy, Brian Lenihan, to the United States in an
unsuccessful effort to reduce American support for any Anglo-Irish
Agreement.[86] In particular, Haughey objected to the formal acceptance by the Irish government of the principle of consent, affirming
that it represented a concession to the effect that 'the legitimacy of
partition, which is contrary to unification, has been recognised by an
Irish government in an international agreement'.[87] FitzGerald brought
Haughey's attention to the fact that he himself had accepted such a
position in the joint communiqué issued with Thatcher in 1981. At
this point Haughey reiterated previous statements which emphasized
a distinction that he employed on the issue of consent: 'When we
speak of the need to secure the agreement of the unionist population

that agreement applies to the new arrangements for, but not to the concept of, a united Ireland.'[88]

When Haughey was in government he appeared open to the idea of consent. However, when in opposition, partly as a result of the success of a number of H-Block candidates, he retreated to a traditional republican concentration on unity. Similarly, as had been the case in his reaction to the New Ireland Forum report, Haughey's position as leader of the opposition, the potential for Sinn Féin to gain votes, as the H-Block candidates has done so in the early 1980s, influenced his decision to reject the Anglo-Irish Agreement. Again Fianna Fáil reneged on the principle of consent by drawing the above distinction. While Haughey's rejection of the Anglo-Irish Agreement was based on his ideological objection to recognizing the right of the British government to have jurisdiction over Northern Ireland, it was also politically motivated.

It must be acknowledged that this categorical adherence to constitutional republicanism as espoused by Haughey in the first half of the 1980s was not held dear by all Fianna Fáil party members. Dwyer maintains that certain members, like George Colley, did not admire Haughey's doctrinaire rhetoric, preferring to note that Fianna Fáil had envisaged similar changes in the 1960s to those championed by Fine Gael, and also the fact that this movement 'had been endorsed by Haughey's idol, Seán Lemass'.[89] Mary O'Rourke stated that she and many others on the shadow front bench in 1985 believed that the party should 'roll on with it [Anglo-Irish Agreement]'.[90] Frank Fahey declared that he and many other younger members of the party at that time had no problem with the principle of consent.[91] A Fianna Fáil engagement with the revisionist nationalism as espoused by FitzGerald might have been possible in the 1980s, had Haughey endorsed such a shift in ideological position. Instead, his position on the opposition benches required a response to Sinn Féin which meant Fianna Fáil displayed, in declared rhetoric at least, an adherence to a traditional republican position on partition and Northern Ireland. In addition, Haughey's support within the party came from the republican wing and, as such, a shift in intellectual perspective on Northern Ireland was problematic since this was the subject which motivated his support base. Haughey's tactical use of language on Northern Ireland meant he lacked consistency on the issue. However, once Haughey returned to power in 1987 he had a clear view of how to proceed in the search for a settlement in Northern Ireland and developed a clear agenda in the aftermath of the Anglo-Irish Agreement.

One key element of Haughey's search for a solution to the Northern Ireland Troubles after the Anglo-Irish Agreement was based on his recognition that a process which concentrated solely on the principle of consent would be unacceptable to the republican movement. Such a process, as inherent in the Anglo-Irish Agreement, designed to exclude Sinn Féin and, with a short-term approach, overlooked the need to make reciprocal gestures to republican demands. Therefore Haughey sought to build a process which was inclusive of all relevant parties and which addressed both republican and unionist demands. Support for a process based on this kind of inclusiveness must be accredited to Haughey as his lasting legacy.

Haughey's time in opposition witnessed both a lack of innovation in terms of Northern Ireland and a return to a traditional anti-partitionist stance. He could not engage with the ideas and principle of consent as espoused by FitzGerald while in opposition, despite intimating a convergence to those principles while in government, because of his desire to ensure his party did not lose seats to Sinn Féin. The relationship between Sinn Féin and Haughey's position on Northern Ireland was altered after 1987, when Fianna Fáil returned to power and Sinn Féin looked less of a potential electoral rival. However, by this stage, Haughey had come to be convinced that Sinn Féin must be brought into a wider inclusive process that would 'transcend the Anglo-Irish Agreement'.

FIANNA FÁIL AND SINN FÉIN IN THE POST-ANGLO-IRISH AGREEMENT PERIOD

The period following the Anglo-Irish Agreement is one of great significance in understanding the developments in Fianna Fáil's position in relation to Northern Ireland. Haughey had argued that the Anglo-Irish Agreement constituted a 'major setback' for Irish unity: 'The agreement is in complete conflict with the Irish National aspiration of Unity and the provisions of the Constitution.'[92] He originally threatened to mount a legal constitutional challenge to the Anglo-Irish Agreement but later mellowed on the issue. Mansergh explained that Haughey accepted the agreement because he was compelled to, despite the fact that 'he was not emotionally sold on the agreement'. Subsequently he accepted the principle of consent 'despite doubts about the legitimacy of Northern Ireland'.[93] While reiterating his grave concerns about the 'constitutional implications' of the agreement, Haughey pledged to 'offer support and approval for anything that would benefit people in the six counties'.[94]

After Fianna Fáil's success in the 1987 general election, Brian Lenihan explained that the working of the Anglo-Irish Agreement would be done without 'prejudice to our long-term objective of a united Ireland'.[95] This amounted to a blatant U-turn from Fianna Fáil's already stated interpretation of the agreement that it violated Articles Two and Three of the Constitution. The change in rhetoric was stimulated by the level of support among the general public for the agreement,[96] the intensity of unionist dissatisfaction[97] that suggested nationalists had gained from the agreement and by the level of support within the US administration for the accord. On his first visit to the US as Taoiseach in 1987, Haughey was forced to face this realization. He said on his return: 'There was a sort of tacit assumption about the Anglo-Irish Agreement. It's there in place now and we will continue to operate it.'[98] Therefore, despite his earlier vocal objections to the agreement, Haughey now 'reversed engines'[99] and 'despite his hostility to the Anglo-Irish Agreement, whose terms he had excoriated in 1985, once in office he proceeded to use it for all it was worth'.[100]

In the context of this study, the dynamics of the relationship between the two competing republican parties, Fianna Fáil and Sinn Féin, at that juncture is important. Once Haughey and Fianna Fáil returned to power after February 1987 the electoral threat from Sinn Féin was substantially diminished, since Sinn Féin had made no impact in the election in the Republic and had appeared to have peaked in the North. This diminishing of the Sinn Féin threat in the Republic at this stage was a crucial precursor to the subsequent developments in Haughey's position, allowing Haughey to distance his party from its traditional position and rhetoric.[101] The decision by Fianna Fáil to engage in dialogue with the republican movement was based upon the realization that Sinn Féin's ability to maintain, while not necessarily extending, its support in Northern Ireland necessitated a process inclusive of Sinn Féin.

Haughey's aim was to transcend rather than implement the Anglo-Irish Agreement and thus he attempted to build bridges with unionists and it was reported that Haughey had offered to convene a committee to analyze the need for changes in the Constitution.[102] He sought to extend his contacts with the unionist parties when he stated his willingness to meet with 'responsible' unionist politicians if they so wished.[103] At the 1988 Fianna Fáil Árd Fheis, in the wake of the Enniskillen bombing,[104] Haughey reiterated his commitment to broaden the framework within which the northern process was situated. He outlined the contention that a political solution must involve the establishment of 'new political structures, which accommodate the diverse traditions of this island, guarantee the rights of all and substitute a community of interest and a community purpose for confrontation and division'. He continued:

> [T]he future constitutional arrangements for this island should be decided by all the people of Ireland acting through their representatives to shape new institutions in which we could all take pride because of the wisdom and fairness of their provisions and the generosity of spirit they display. Under them the rights and beliefs of every individual would be guaranteed and all would feel secure.[105]

Calling for 'a new monument ... to common-sense and the willingness of both traditions in Ireland to come together' he reiterated the government's readiness to embrace unionism by outlining the contribution he would make at this stage: 'For our part we will avail of any opportunity for open and honest dialogue ... [any] opportunity to hear at first hand from the representatives of the unionist tradition how they would see these things come about'.[106]

This language would seem finally to indicate a realization on the part of the Fianna Fáil party that agreement with unionists and not just the British government was necessary. Haughey's suggestion that the talks would be unconditional hinted that he might be open to an alternative solution. However, despite such seemingly friendly words and gestures towards unionists, Haughey's quest to improve relations never had the potential to succeed as he prefaced such invitations to talks with statements of his belief that unity represented the best outcome. For example, he began his Árd Fheis speech above, calling for a new monument dedicated to bringing the traditions together, by saying that: 'The unity of Ireland, achieved by constitutional political means, is not only the best way but the only way of finally bringing to an end the divisions and conflicts which have and are inflicting such a heavy cost, morally, socially and economically on our people, North and South.'[107] Haughey's speech in 1988, which was a mixture of a traditional Fianna Fáil commitment to unity together with a conciliatory gesture towards unionists, was probably the best he could deliver given the number of resolutions proposed by a range of

Cumann across the country calling on 'the Fianna Fáil Party to reaffirm its Republican and Nationalist Traditions and the traditions that Fianna Fáil have stood for since the foundation of the Party'.[108]

Despite his references to unity and failure to build bridges with unionists, he was convinced, in the aftermath of the Anglo-Irish Agreement, of the need to promote a wider, more extensive agenda. He argued, despite his commitment to utilize the agreement to his advantage, for a process transcending the agreement. This represented Haughey's central focus on Northern Ireland from this point on. Thus, from the point of his return to power in 1987, the basis of his rejection of the Anglo-Irish Agreement was no longer premised on its violation of the Irish Constitution, but rather the need to extend it to a more inclusive framework. He was unsupportive of devolution[109] and dedicated to the notion of a round table conference to decide the basis of an agreed Ireland with Sinn Féin involved in the event of an IRA ceasefire.[110]

THE 1988 SINN FÉIN/FIANNA FÁIL TALKS INITIATIVE: IMPLICATIONS FOR THE PEACE PROCESS

Unionist leaders were not the only representatives that Haughey was endeavouring to develop relations with. The period after the Anglo-Irish Agreement initially saw hostility between Fianna Fáil and the SDLP, when they adopted diverging positions on the agreement. However, by the time Fianna Fáil returned to office in 1987 Haughey was seeking reconciliation. From this point on Fianna Fáil appeared to be operating its northern policy with close reference to the SDLP. Within months of returning to government in 1987 Haughey arranged a meeting with an SDLP delegation and this heralded a joint stance by both parties. The joint communiqué that was issued following this meeting pledged both parties' support for the implementation of the Anglo-Irish Agreement.[111] Early in 1988 the *Irish News* reported that Haughey had been aware of, and had 'approved' of, a meeting held a week previously between Hume and Adams.[112] Just prior to this report, Haughey predicted 'a fair amount of movement' on the North in the next year.[113] He ruled out any specific 'signs of movement in regard to devolution' but contended 'there is general movement in the whole arena of northern politics'.[114] Given that he was party to the talks process taking place between the SDLP and Sinn

Féin, he was most probably referring to this dialogue. Similarly, he asserted, in reference to the Enniskillen bombing, that 'there has been in some ways a very beneficial outcome of that terrible incident'.[115] He detected that it was bringing about rethinking within the republican movement about the utility of violence.[116] These were indications of Haughey's appreciation of the changes in the republican movement, hints too that this was to have a profound effect on Fianna Fáil's republican agenda. From this juncture Haughey continued to support the analysis of Hume. In the Dáil on 27 January 1988 he stressed his belief that the SDLP–Sinn Féin meetings were beneficial[117] and that he had 'the greatest respect for the integrity and judgement of the leader of the SDLP'.[118]

This was the beginning of a new attempt to build a nationalist consensus, similar to that achieved by the New Ireland Forum. However, on this occasion the project was more ambitious, envisaging the involvement and co-operation of Sinn Féin. This emanated from a request from Father Reid and Cardinal Tomas Ó Fiaich in 1987. They asked if Haughey would meet with a Sinn Féin delegation.[119] Despite Haughey's reservations he instructed Martin Mansergh to remain in touch with Father Reid. So, while Haughey was not talking personally with Adams, he was aware of developments within the republican movement. Dermot Ahern outlined his view of the motivation behind Haughey's decision to establish contacts with Sinn Féin: 'He said he had been asked by Fr Alex Reid through Cardinal O'Fiaich to participate in these talks to mirror what John Hume was doing at that time, the Hume–Adams talks, the original Hume–Adams talks. That we were to more or less mirror what they were doing in the North to give a southern nationalist, constitutional nationalist perspective.'[120] Two meetings took place between the Irish delegation and Sinn Féin in March and June of 1988. Martin Mansergh and two Fianna Fáil colleagues, Dermot Ahern and Richie Healy (a senior Fianna Fáil figure) met the Sinn Féin president, Gerry Adams, and two other leading Sinn Féin members, Mitchel McLaughlin[121] and Pat Doherty.[122] Dermot Ahern provided an insight into what these discussions entailed and what form of arguments the Irish government was utilizing on the key issues at that stage:

> Most of the discussion was along the lines of getting Sinn Féin to go the constitutional route exclusively and trying to get the consent of a unionist majority and some sort of communication that you cannot have a united Ireland with a reluctant unionist

[population] … We were basically telling them that the broad mass of the people in the South were against the violence, were against forcing unionists into a minority situation against their will. I think it was that sort of basis.[123]

However, these were brought to a close when Haughey decided that agreement was unlikely. It became apparent that Sinn Féin was more concerned, in the post-Enniskillen bombing atmosphere, with ending the political isolation from which they suffered rather than with bringing about a cessation of violence.[124]

The search for a consensus within nationalism through the 1988 Sinn Féin–Fianna Fáil talks altered the relationship between the two parties and these talks are therefore vital to understanding Haughey's evolving policy on Northern Ireland. Firstly, the talks give an insight into the direction in which he wanted to steer his party on this issue and what opinion within the party he wished to have dominate. Secondly, a look at the nature of the discussion explains what was taking place within the republican movement at that time and we can subsequently determine how Haughey sought to react to the knowledge emanating from these talks. Dermot Ahern speculated as to why Haughey had chosen him to join this delegation. Ahern had been attempting to provoke a reassessment of the party's position on Northern Ireland and wondered if Haughey was influenced by his open challenges to the customary viewpoint on Northern Ireland:

> I often wonder was that the reason Haughey picked me, I'd made a few speeches in the Dáil and publicly, more or less giving the view … it was the issue of consent, the whole issue of fifty percent plus one. I made the point that, we in Fianna Fáil and Sinn Féin, we have the same ideals of a united Ireland, I said publicly and was prepared to say publicly, I probably would have articulated that having a united Ireland would in effect only be changing the minority, from a nationalist minority in the North, to a unionist minority on the island, on the basis of fifty percent plus one. You're far better getting sort of mutual consent and understanding long before that.[125]

Dermot Ahern has said that, while ideas within the party were changing in a way that was influenced by John Hume, the concept of unity by consent was not widely accepted among the rank and file of the party.[126] By choosing Dermot Ahern and ensuring that the principle of

consent was emphasized by the Fianna Fáil delegation when it met
with the republican movement in 1988, Haughey both encouraged
and engaged with the section of the party that was both involved with
and advocating a reassessment of ideas on Northern Ireland.

What is vital here is the influence these talks had on Haughey's
subsequent thinking and decisions regarding Northern Ireland. While
Dermot Ahern holds the view that 'the thinking amongst Fianna Fáil
was changing generally and that change was moulded by Hume particularly',[127] he acknowledged the fact that the process to a 'certain
extent would have been fed into by speeches by Haughey. A lot of the
messages that Haughey would have given publicly would have been
flowing from his knowledge of the meetings' with Sinn Féin.[128] We
have already discovered that Sinn Féin was conveying, in the talks
with Fianna Fáil, the desire to end the IRA's violent campaign and
this, in turn, motivated Haughey's policy of transcending the Anglo-
Irish Agreement. During the 1988 discussions the principle of consent
was addressed. According to Dermot Ahern, Sinn Féin appeared to be
taking his points relating to consent on board; in general there was an
'engagement' and 'an understanding'.[129] This movement on the part of
Sinn Féin provided Haughey with the intellectual space in the following years to re-engage his party with the process of rhetorical revision that he had begun in 1980 at his 'tea-pot' summit with Margaret
Thatcher. What is reinforced here is the argument that the Irish government's position on key issues of Northern Ireland policy has been
influenced and developed in cognizance of alternative nationalist
opinion on the same issues.

The development of a new point of view by Fianna Fáil over the
next decade was the product of the party's willingness to involve itself
in the debate sparked by the Hume–Adams dialogue inaugurated in
1988. As Ivory points out: 'political discourses in the Republic of
Ireland … was heavily informed by the Hume–Adams deliberations'.
He also states that, in relation to the principle of consent, 'the development of policy on this issue within the Irish political parties must
take these exchanges as their starting point'.[130] This is certainly true;
the Hume–Adams dialogue guided the reformulation of ideas in the
Republic. But what was central here was not the 'alternative interpretation'[131] provided by the Hume–Adams dialogue in itself, but Fianna
Fáil's involvement through dialogue with these parties. The Sinn
Féin–SDLP and the Sinn Féin–Fianna Fáil talks must be viewed as one
process. The SDLP's involvement was crucial to Northern Ireland
politics; the involvement of Fianna Fáil was vital to popular support

in the Republic of Ireland and to the building of a wider nationalist consensus which formed the basis of the peace process.

What is interesting here are the differing roles of the SDLP, John Hume and Fianna Fáil. Moloney[132] provides an alternative interpretation of Hume's contribution to that previously presented by Mallie and McKittrick.[133] Contrary to the view expressed by Mallie and McKittrick that Hume contributed massively to the peace process on an intellectual level, Moloney argues that Hume was brought into the peace process, which was the brainchild of Father Reid, Adams and to a certain extent Haughey, in order to lend it the credibility it needed. His immediate role was as 'a sort of go-between for the Irish government. This would solve the problem of [Haughey] having to meet Adams directly while preserving the initiative'.[134] Moloney goes on to explain why Hume was not told of Fianna Fáil's talks with Sinn Féin:

> The dialogue between him [Haughey], Reid, and Adams was to be kept hidden from the SDLP for fear that it would be leaked and Haughey ruined. Hume was deliberately not told about the contacts and for long afterwards believed that his subsequent meetings with Adams marked the start of the peace process ... The SDLP's leader's association with the Reid–Adams enterprise gave it a level of acceptability it otherwise would have lacked, especially in the Republic, where Hume's standing was exceptionally high. Haughey began the Irish part of the peace process, but Hume gave it respectability.[135]

When asked about this account of Hume's input into the peace process, Mansergh conceded that Hume and 'the SDLP could do publicly what Fianna Fáil couldn't'.[136] While he said that Hume was not essential to accessing the republican movement due to the continued 'triangular relationship' of contacts involving Adams, Mansergh and Hume, he maintains that it was necessary to ensure 'co-operation'[137] with both Hume and Adams. Therefore, while arguing that the reformulation of the ideas of consent and self-determination was developed through the Fianna Fáil–Sinn Féin talks, Moloney's suggestion that Hume was used by Haughey, Reid and Adams solely to add credibility to their process appears too cynical. As leader of the largest nationalist party in the North at that time, his input would have been vital. Each party to the process had differing roles and Hume was probably aware that part of his role was to harness public support for these changing attitudes originating from within Sinn Féin and Fianna Fáil.[138]

THE PRINCIPLES OF CONSENT AND SELF-DETERMINATION

Gareth Ivory has maintained that Fianna Fáil succeeded in re-estab-
lishing the position of constitutional republicanism through the compromises and reformulations that it accepted in the course of the
peace process and that this has culminated in a new 'revitalised'[139]
republican agenda. The basis of his argument is as follows:

> Fianna Fáil now recognises fully the political expression of the
> unionist political identity in Northern Ireland, including that
> aspect which places unionists outside the Irish nation. In return
> for such recognition, Fianna Fáil has secured from the British
> government recognition of the right to Irish national self-deter-
> mination throughout the entire island, although the exercise of
> this right is qualified. But as the northern unionist political iden-
> tity is recognised, the integrity of the island has been enhanced
> economically, socially, and culturally.[140]

While it will be illustrated that Ivory's claim that the acceptance by
the British government of the right of national self-determination represented a major ideological achievement for Fianna Fáil is correct,
his view that, in return, the right of the unionist community to opt
out of the Irish nation was granted by Fianna Fáil is rejected. This is
central to understanding the way in which Fianna Fáil ensured that,
in the course of the peace process, the party gave recognition to the
reality of Northern Ireland while still maintaining the integrity of the
nation, a principle that has been at the core of its ideology. The result,
therefore, has been that Fianna Fáil has reconciled its ideology with
the reality of partition without significantly revising its ideology.

According to Mallie and McKittrick,[141] the connection between
consent and self-determination was one which John Hume began to
think about during the talks sponsored by the Northern Ireland
Secretary of State, Peter Brooke, as a means of reconciling unionist
demands with those of republicans. While it is true that Hume contributed to the final wording of the formula, the view that the process
of reaching this formula originated solely from Hume is restrictive
and overlooks Fianna Fáil's involvement in the effort to find a satisfactory mechanism of reconciling the two concepts. Thus, in delin-
eating the origins of this combination a new importance is attributed
to the Sinn Féin–Fianna Fáil talks in 1988. Despite the appearance
that the talks ended fruitlessly, it was at this point that self-determi-

nation was introduced into the equation.[142] For this reason, these talks provided the parameters within which future nationalist and republican debates would be contained. In reference to the debates, which were stimulated by the 1988 talks, Mansergh explained that the contentious issue was not consent, but rather that of self-determination and 'squaring these two things'.[143] The importance of this is fourfold: Firstly, this represents the beginning of the peace process which, in Haughey's view, would transcend the Anglo-Irish Agreement. According to Mansergh, the problem for Fianna Fáil and the republican movement with the process in place under the auspices of the Anglo-Irish Agreement was that it pointed in the wrong direction through its concentration on consent.[144] For this reason, Mansergh dismisses the Anglo-Irish Agreement as the starting point of the current peace process. Given the absence of any reciprocal reference to republican language, the agreement was too exclusive.[145] Mansergh argues that Haughey's aim after the Anglo-Irish Agreement was to bring the process in a new direction, which would be inclusive of republican as well as unionist ideas. This new direction became informed by the 1988 talks with Sinn Féin. The talks provided the reasoning behind the introduction of self-determination, which was crucial because it was an important 'republican concept'.[146] While self-determination is not an exclusively republican ideal since unionists have also sought recognition for the right of the people of Northern Ireland to self-determination,[147] the debate in the late 1980s as to how to reconcile self-determination and consent was aimed at finding a formula that republicans could accept. The implication here is that Fianna Fáil and perhaps even Sinn Féin were not rejecting the Anglo-Irish Agreement because of the presence of consent but because of the absence of self-determination.

Secondly, this interpretation raises questions as to the strength of the principle of consent. Not only had Fianna Fáil and Sinn Féin managed to manipulate the direction of the peace process, they had also altered the meaning of the principle of consent. By attaching self-determination, the principle was now subject to a republican manipulation. The inauguration of this 'republican concept' can be viewed as a dilution of the principle of consent since a condition has been placed upon it. It is necessary at this point to assess the definition of the principle and the conflicting interpretations of its nuances. In its written form, consent encompasses an assurance given to unionists that no change will be made to the constitutional status of Northern Ireland without the agreement of a majority of people in Northern Ireland.[148]

Paragraph 4 of the Downing Street Declaration deals with the British government's position regarding Irish self-determination: 'The British government agree that it is for the people of the island of Ireland alone, by agreement between the two parts respectively, to exercise their right of self-determination on the basis of consent, freely and concurrently given, North and South to bring about a united Ireland, if that is their wish.'[149] The 1993 Downing Street Declaration and the 1998 Good Friday Agreement have defined the relationship between self-determination and the principle of consent in a manner which enables a majority in Northern Ireland to veto reunification even if a majority in the Republic were to favour unity. While a single exercise of self-determination, North and South, is coordinated, the Good Friday Agreement has ensured that it will be effected only on the basis that a majority in both jurisdictions give their consent. A majority in the North must give its consent before any constitutional change can take place. The integrity of the nation has been maintained but in this case consent takes precedence and the form of self-determination, as outlined in the Good Friday Agreement, appears to be a radically altered concept to that which was traditionally understood by republicans.

However, there are a number of points from which republicans can draw comfort. Not only has the understanding of self-determination been altered, so too has that of the principle of consent. While republicans, including Fianna Fáil, have accepted the principle of consent, the right of a majority of the people in Northern Ireland to self-determination has been re-determined and no longer operates independently of the island as a whole; it is instead exercised within the context of the island of Ireland. The strength of the pan-nationalist alliance and the fact that the principle of consent has been placed within the context of national self-determination have made it easier for Sinn Féin to accept the principle. Even if consent is deemed to be paramount, taking a literal interpretation would suggest that the unionist community has no right to self-determination except when it enjoys majority status within Northern Ireland. With the absence of an explicit reference of the right of unionists to veto any constitutional change if they do not comprise a majority of the people in Northern Ireland, it cannot be construed as a clear unionist veto or recognition of their right to opt out of a united Ireland if that were to be the wish of a majority of the people in Northern Ireland in the future. The acceptance of consent amounts to little more than a recognition on pragmatic terms of the existence of Northern Ireland.

While Fianna Fáil concedes the existence of Northern Ireland, the integrity of the nation has been maintained as the self-determination of Northern Ireland can only be exercised within the confines of the republican definition of the nation, the island as a whole. Thus the position of republicanism has been strengthened and the principle of consent weakened through its appendage to self-determination.

It is not clear how the relationship between consent and self-determination would be applied in the event that a majority in the North were to vote in favour of unity without agreement from unionists. A deliberate ambiguity has been employed in order to 'square the two' principles, and this is critical to the future of the peace process. In 1990 Michael Gallagher addressed the question of whether Ulster unionists have a right to self-determination. He concluded that 'the very idea of an absolute right to self-determination for either nationalists or unionists is a chimera'.[150] The fact that both unionists and nationalists have been able to present cases in favour of their respective rights to self-determination has meant that the reconciliation of these two opposing claims to self-determination has necessitated a level of ambiguity. Jerry Burke views this lack of clarity as an inherent strength of the Agreement. He argued that the Good Friday Agreement involved a satisfactory compromise between both unionist and nationalist conflicting interpretations of self-determination[151] and he claimed that, because that agreement 'simultaneously accommodates different, legitimate unionist and nationalist interpretations of self-determination', it had the advantage of enabling the leaders of both communities to concentrate on what they viewed as the positive points of the agreement.[152] However, this has not manifested itself within the unionist community. For anti-agreement unionists the value of the principle of consent is in question because national self-determination has assumed a new revitalised position within the peace process. John Wilson Foster sums up the problems which this has created for unionists. Referring to the 1993 Downing Street Declaration, he maintains that the British government has begun to use 'a different dialect. "Self-determination by the people of Ireland"; "democratically national and political aspirations"; "both traditions in Ireland"; these key phrases in the Declaration are from the lexicon of nationalism, not unionism'.[153] This underlines the third significance attached to the introduction of the concept of self-determination in 1988. Even if the concept took on a radically altered shape and is conditioned by the principle of consent, the subtle change in emphasis through the introduction of self-determination metamorphosed the entire nature of the process, from one of compromise on the part of nationalism to one designed to transfer the republican movement into constitutional politics.

Fourthly, this new understanding of the reasoning behind the introduction of self-determination together with its origins has ramifications for unionists. Contrary to the view that the combination of consent and self-determination involved a concession on the part of republicans, it in fact represented a change of emphasis in a process which was previously primarily concerned with consent but which now equally addressed the republican ideal of self-determination. The new process is in stark contrast to its predecessor. From this point onwards the peace process has been conducted with a bias in favour of meeting republican concerns and this is key to understanding anti-agreement unionists' misgivings about the entire process.

Gareth Ivory has traced the development of the principle of consent as a barometer against which to measure Fianna Fáil's position on Northern Ireland. It is argued here instead that it is the relationship between Fianna Fáil and Sinn Féin which acts as such a barometer. Of course these are not mutually exclusive. The integration of consent and self-determination was informed by debates stimulated by the 1988 talks. This was essential to the development of the ideological standpoints relating to Northern Ireland held by successive Irish governments, in particular those led by Fianna Fáil. In other words this attempt to remove dissent and division from within the wider nationalist spectrum enabled the Irish government, under Fianna Fáil, to shift its position in a manner not undertaken by any previous Fianna Fáil government.

CONCLUSION

Gareth Ivory has argued that, by the time Haughey left office in 1922, he had engaged in a process through which he had accepted a principle, long since advocated and promoted by Garret FitzGerald, which recognized the right of a majority in Northern Ireland to determine their future; the principle of consent. Ivory maintains that, since 1990: 'Fianna Fáil has reasserted the importance of constitutional republicanism, a position that eluded the party throughout much of the 1970s and 1980s, as a revisionist nationalism challenged party orthodoxy. During that period, despite considerable backbench resistance the Fianna Fáil leadership has opted for moderate revisionist nationalism.'[154] It has been shown that the opposite is the more appropriate conclusion; that Fianna Fáil resisted any change to its traditional constitutional republicanism until the late 1980s. It is apparent that Fianna Fáil felt a greater challenge from Sinn Féin than from revisionist nationalism. Fianna Fáil's amenability to a process, which involved replacing intra-nationalist competition with consensus through contacts with both the SDLP and Sinn Féin, enabled a reappraisal of ideas in a manner unprecedented for Fianna Fáil and indeed for the other Irish political parties. Thus, the significance of the decision by Fianna Fáil to open contacts with Sinn Féin in 1988 for future Irish governments' policy formation regarding partition and Northern Ireland cannot be over-emphasized.

Fianna Fáil, under Haughey, was able to familiarize itself with the ideological shifts taking place within the republican movement through contact with that movement. This in turn enabled Haughey and his successors to retreat from the 'greening of the party' necessitated in the early 1980s by the Sinn Féin threat, given that the republican movement was now reassessing its own doctrinaire position. This process was not only slow for Sinn Féin but also for Fianna Fáil. While the catalyst for change appeared in the late 1980s and while there were new signs of flexibility on the part of Fianna Fáil after 1988, it was the early 1990s before Fianna Fáil engaged in substantive and public debate on issues relating to Northern Ireland and the party's republican rhetoric. These debates and indications of the party's intention to embrace a revised and conciliatory approach aimed not only at the republican movement but also at unionist concerns culminated in the constitutional change of the Good Friday Agreement in 1998. The problem was that for the past decade Fianna Fáil had clung to its republican credentials and was now not immediately prepared to relinquish this ground, remaining reluctant to move on the issues of Articles Two and Three of the Constitution. Martin Mansergh, among others, points to the March 1990 Supreme Court judgment, in the case taken by Michael and Chris McGimpsey[155] of the UUP, as the catalyst for change within Fianna Fáil on the issue of consent.[156] The real significance of the judgment was not to act as an impetus towards an acceptance of the principle, since we have seen that Haughey and a section of the party were already open to the notion of consent and had presented an argument in favour of consent in its first meetings with Sinn Féin in 1988. The importance of the McGimpsey judgment was that the principle of consent, inculcated into Irish nationalist discourse through the Anglo-Irish Agreement, was declared to be constitutional. While in government Haughey suggested a reassessment of the 1937 Constitution, presumably because he wanted to work with the Anglo-Irish Agreement as a basis for any future settlement   but believed the Constitution represented an impediment to the principle of consent intrinsic to the Anglo-Irish Agreement. The McGimpsey judgment facilitated a process of widespread reform on the national question within the Fianna Fáil party without necessitating convincing the party and the electorate at that early stage in the peace process of the appropriateness of amending the Constitution. Haughey and those within Fianna Fáil who were already in favour of changing the party's traditional position now acquired a new intellectual justification and integrity for their project. It was from this point on that the first debates took place within the party and there were signs of changing ideas, even though Haughey was open to this transformation of doctrine at an earlier stage.

In the first half of 1989 Haughey appeared to have little to say on Northern Ireland and there appeared to be very little progress, given that the Hume–Adams dialogue had officially come to a conclusion, as had Fianna Fáil's talks with Sinn Féin. Simultaneously, overtures made by Hume and Haughey to unionists in the hope that talks might result were failing to convince the unionist parties to become involved.[157] However, 1989 witnessed a major turning point in relation to Haughey's position regarding devolution. Haughey had earlier made his objection to devolution clear.[158] Little more than a week after entering coalition with the Progressive Democrats in 1989, Haughey indicated that he was now amenable to the idea of supporting some form of devolution for the North.[159] It was obvious that this shift had been forced upon Haughey by the exigencies of coalition, as the leader of the Progressive Democrats, Des O'Malley,[160] had made it clear prior to the general election that he thought that a solution for the North must entail a devolved system.[161] This is a recurring theme in the story of Haughey's approach to Northern Ireland. He never seemed to be able to pursue his policy without having to take into account a number of influencing pressures, whether it was from within his own party, FitzGerald's constitutional crusade, Sinn Féin, or the realities of coalition. This is why Haughey's true position is so difficult to ascertain, because it cannot be understood in isolation of these diverse challenges and the manner in which he responded to them. In that sense, Haughey's political career appears reactionary, while his clandestine dialogue with Sinn Féin from 1988 onwards was his sole attempt at being proactive.

NOTES

1. A shorter version of this chapter has previously been published as O'Donnell, C. 'Fianna Fáil and Sinn Féin: The 1988 Talks Reappraised', *Irish Political Studies*, 18, 2 (Winter 2003), pp. 60–81.
2. Dwyer, T.R. *Short Fellow: A biography of C. J. Haughey* (Dublin: Marino, 2001), p. 201.
3. Interview with Mary O'Rourke,15 Nov. 2005.
4. Interview with Dermot Ahern 1 Nov. 2002.
5. FitzGerald, G. *All in a Life: An autobiography* (Dublin: Gill and Macmillan, 1992), pp. 496–7. Sinn Féin had not contested elections in either Northern Ireland or the Republic prior to the hunger strikes in 1981. The success of a number of H-Block candidates indicated to elements within Sinn Féin the benefits of entering the political arena. Sinn Féin gradually built on this initiative and became a permanent fixture in Northern Irish politics. The party took the decision in 1986 to drop the policy of abstentionism in the Republic. See, for example, Feeney, B. *Sinn Féin: A hundred turbulent years* (Dublin: O'Brien Press, 2002).
6. *The Irish Times* 18 Oct. 1986.
7. FitzGerald proposed amending certain constitutional provisions which were perceived by unionists as hostile, for example Articles Two and Three, or as unacceptable, such as the ban on divorce.
8. Dwyer, *Short Fellow*, p. 203.
9. O'Brien, J. *The Modern Prince: Charles J. Haughey and the quest for power* (Dublin: Merlin Publishing, 2002).
10. O'Brien, *The Modern Prince*, p. 4.
11. See Chubb, B. *The Government and Politics of Ireland* (Stanford: Stanford University Press, 1982).
12. O'Brien, *The Modern Prince*, p. 6.
13. O'Brien, *The Modern Prince*, p. 7.
14. O'Brien, *The Modern Prince*, p. 9.
15. Collins, S. *The Power Game: Ireland under Fianna Fáil* (Dublin: O'Brien Press, 2001), p. 143. The summit is remembered as the 'tea-pot' summit because of the Georgian tea-pot which Haughey presented to Thatcher on that occasion.
16. O'Brien, *The Modern Prince*, p. 82.
17. O'Brien, *The Modern Prince*, p. 127.
18. O'Brien, *The Modern Prince*, p. 128.
19. O'Brien, *The Modern Prince*, p. 146.
20. Ibid.
21. Interview with John O'Donoghue, 7 Feb. 2006.
22. Martin Mansergh: Born in England in 1946; son of Irish historian, Nicholas Mansergh; entered the Department of Foreign Affairs as a civil servant in 1974, promoted to First Secretary, 1977; former Head of Research for Fianna Fáil and Special Advisor, in particular on issues relating to Northern Ireland, to Fianna Fáil leaders, Charles Haughey, Albert Reynolds and Bertie Ahern; involved in talks with Sinn Féin and Church intermediaries prior to the first and second IRA ceasefires; involved in the drafting of the Downing Street Declaration in 1993 and in the negotiations leading to the Good Friday Agreement in 1998; elected as Fianna Fáil Senator on the Agricultural Panel in July 2002.
23. Interview with Martin Mansergh 12 Dec. 2002.
24. Ibid. Zartman has suggested that peace processes are produced at times when they are ripe, at points in the conflict where 'mutually hurting stalemates' occur. See Zartman, I. W. 'The Timing of Peace Initiatives: Hurting stalemates and ripe moments', in J. Darby and R. MacGinty (eds), *Contemporary Peacemaking: Conflict, violence and peace processes* (Hampshire: Palgrave Macmillan, 2003). It is not suggested here that Mansergh is referring to this academic debate.
25. Interview with Martin Mansergh, 12 Dec. 2002. See McGarry J. and O'Leary, B. *The Politics of Antagonism: Understanding Northern Ireland* (London: The Athlone Press, 1996), pp. 243–9 for the nature of disagreements between the two governments relating to the objectives of the Anglo-Irish Agreement and matters relating to public policy and security.
26. Alex Reid: A Tipperary–born Redemptorist priest based in West Belfast's Clonard Monastery; had been involved as an intermediary in republican feuds during the 1970s;

trusted by republicans, particularly by Adams.

27. Mallie, E. and McKittrick, D. *The Fight for Peace: The secret story behind the Irish peace process* (London: Heinemann, 1996), p. 72.
28. Interview with Martin Mansergh, 12 Dec. 2002.
29. Moloney, E. *A Secret History of the IRA* (London: Penguin Press, 2002), Chapter 9.
30. Gerry Adams MP MLA; born in Belfast 6 Oct. 1948; has continuously denied membership of the IRA but this is not widely believed; first elected at MP for West Belfast in 1983; became Vice-President of Sinn Féin in 1978 and President in 1983.
31. Moloney, *A Secret History of the IRA,* p. 263. Moloney, in his remark 'midwife to the Provos', is referring here to the suggestion that the actions of those involved in the Arms Crisis were deliberately aimed at making contact with a certain section within the IRA, with the intention of causing a split within the movement and thereby being responsible for the establishment of the PIRA. See O'Brien, J. *The Arms Trial* (Dublin: Gill and Macmillan, 2000).
32. Moloney, *A Secret History of the IRA,* p. 268.
33. Moloney, *A Secret History of the IRA,* p. 269.
34. As quoted in Adams, G. *Hope and History: Making peace in Ireland* (Kerry: Brandon, 2003), p. 42.
35. Adams, *Hope and History,* p. 43.
36. Sinn Féin, *Towards a Lasting Peace in Ireland* (Dublin: Sinn Féin, 1994), also available at http://sinnfein.ie/pdf/TowardsLastingPeace.pdf; accessed 15 March 2006.
37. Mallie and McKittrick, *The Fight for Peace,* p. 381. There has been controversy as to whether TUAS referred to the Totally Unarmed Strategy or whether in fact it denoted Tactical Use of Armed Struggle, though the consensus now seems to favour the latter.
38. This document is available at http://www.sinnfein.ie/pdf/AScenarioforPeace.pdf; accessed 15 March 2006.
39. Adams, *Hope and History,* p. 51.
40. For such a comprehensive assessment of the development of republican thought in the twentieth century see English, R. *Armed Struggle: A history of the IRA* (Oxford: Macmillan, 2003), alternatively see Patterson, H. *The Politics of Illusion: A political history of the IRA* (London: Serif, 1997); Feeney, *Sinn Fein: A hundred turbulent years* or Moloney, *A secret history of the IRA.*
41. Cox, M. 'Bringing in the "International": The IRA ceasefire and the end of the Cold War', *International Affairs,* 93.4 (1997); Cox, M. 'Thinking "Globally" about Peace in Northern Ireland', *Politics,* 18.1 (1998); Cox, M. 'Northern Ireland after the Cold War', in M. Cox, A. Guelke and F. Stephen (eds), *A Farewell to Arms? From 'long war' to long peace in Northern Ireland* (Manchester: Manchester University Press, 2000). On the importance of the European Union see Meehan, E. 'Europe and the Europeanisation of the Irish Question', in Cox, Guelke and Stephen (eds), *A Farewell to Arms?*
42. Farren, S. 'The SDLP and the Roots of the Good Friday Agreement', in Cox, Guelke and Stephen (eds), *A Farewell to Arms?,* p. 52.
43. Hume, J. *Personal Views: Politics, peace and reconciliation in Ireland* (Dublin: Town House, 1996), pp. 89–90.
44. Farren, 'The SDLP and the Roots of the Good Friday Agreement', p. 49.
45. Murray, G. *John Hume and the SDLP: Impact and survival in Northern Ireland* (Dublin: Irish Academic Press 1998), p. 101.
46. Murray, *John Hume and the SDLP:* p. 172.
47. Hume, *Personal Views,* p. 93.
48. Farren, 'The SDLP and the Roots of the Good Friday Agreement', p. 52.
49. For an analysis of the extent to which Hume influenced opinion in America in his attempts to counteract republican support there, see Wilson, A.J. *Irish America and the Ulster conflict, 1968–1995* (Belfast: Blackstaff Press, 1995).
50. As quoted in Rafter, K. 'Priests and Peace: The role of the Redemptorists Order in the Northern Ireland peace process', *Etudes Irlandaises,* Printemps, 28.1 (2003), p. 170.
51. Interview with Martin Mansergh, 12 Dec. 2002. Also note the debate in academia as to whether Irish republicanism is devoid of democratic principles per se. See, for example, Augusteijn, J. 'Political Violence and Democracy: An analysis of the tensions within Irish republican strategy, 1914–2002', *Irish Political Studies,* 18, 1 (Summer 2003), pp. 1–26, and Bourke, R. *Peace in Ireland: The war of ideas* (London: Pimlico, 2003).
52. A broad nationalist alliance involving Fianna Fáil was so appealing to republicans given the

level of political isolation which the movement had been faced with. The aim of such an alliance was to ensure a tougher stance against the British government. See Patterson, *The Politics of Illusion*, p. 236.

53. Interview with Dermot Ahern, 1 Nov. 2002.
54. Patterson, H. *Ireland since 1939* (Oxford: Oxford University Press, 2002), p. 277.
55. For the debates within Sinn Féin regarding abstentionism at the time of the 1985 and 1986 Árd Fheiseanna, see English, *Armed Struggle*, pp. 249–52.
56. See Laver, M., Mair, P. and Sinnott, R. (eds), *How Ireland Voted: The Irish general election 1987* (Dublin: Poolbeg and PSAI Press, 1987), pp. 67, 81.
57. Sinn Féin pamphlet, *Sinn Féin Yesterday and Today* (1971), p. 2.
58. Adams has been clear on this point: see Adams, G. *The Politics of Irish Freedom* (Kerry: Brandon, 1986), Chapter 3.
59. *An Phoblacht/Republican News* Sept. 1971.
60. *An Phoblacht/Republican News* 8 Sept. 1979.
61. *An Phoblacht/Republican News* 21 March 1981.
62. *An Phoblacht/Republican News* 10 Jan. 1981.
63. Adams, *The Politics of Irish Freedom*, pp. 41–2.
64. Mansergh, M. 'The Background to the Irish Peace Process', in Cox, Guelke and Stephen (eds), *A Farewell to Arms?*, p. 16.
65. Ibid.
66. Robert McCartney: Joined the UUP in 1981; elected to the Northern Ireland Assembly, 1982–6 for North Down; expelled from the UUP in 1987; elected to Westminster as UK Unionist in 1995 but lost his seat in 2001; elected to the Northern Ireland Assembly 1998.
67. *The Unionist Case* was written by Robert McCartney and brought to Dublin by a number of prominent business and professional unionists to put the unionist case there.
68. As quoted in Mansergh, M. (ed), *The Spirit of the Nation: Speeches by Charles J. Haughey 1957–1986* (Cork and Dublin: Mercier Press, 1986), p. 574.
69. Address by Charles Haughey at the Fianna Fáil Árd Fheis 16 Feb. 1980, Fianna Fáil Archives P176/785.
70. Ibid.
71. Dwyer, *Short Fellow*, p. 181. Martin Mansergh outlined that Haughey favoured Irish-America as a starting point for this crusade; Interview with Martin Mansergh, 12 Dec. 2002.
72. Collins, *The Power Game*, p. 143.
73. Murray, *The SDLP and John Hume*, p. 102.
74. Murray, *The SDLP and John Hume*, p. 121. It is important to note that it was not just Haughey who was unhappy with this initiative. The British Prime Minister, Margaret Thatcher, also felt that the chances that it would produce a settlement were remote.
75. Dwyer, *Short Fellow*, p. 182.
76. Ivory, 'Constitutional Republicanism, and the Issue of Consent 1980–1996', p. 95.
77. See Dwyer, *Short Fellow*, p. 204.
78. Dwyer, *Short Fellow*, pp. 205–6.
79. Boyce, D.G. '"Can Anyone Here Imagine": Southern Irish political parties and the Northern Ireland problem', in Barton, B. and Roche, P.J. *The Northern Ireland Question: Myth and reality* (Aldershot: Ashgate, 1991), p. 182.
80. O'Halloran, C. *Partition and the Limits of Irish Nationalism: An ideology under stress* (Dublin: Gill and Macmillan, 1987), pp. 194–210. The Forum Report stated: 'The Parties in the Forum are convinced that such unity (a united Ireland in the form of a sovereign, independent Irish state) in agreement would offer the best and most durable basis for peace and stability'. *The New Ireland Forum Report*, 2 May 1984 (Dublin: Stationery Office, 1984), chapters 5.4–5.5.
81. Whyte, J.H. *Interpreting Northern Ireland* (Oxford: Clarendon Paperbacks, 1990), p. 140.
82. Arnold, B. *Haughey: His life and unlucky deeds* (London: HarperCollins Publishers, 1994), pp. 220–1.
83. Arnold, *Haughey*, pp. 186–7.
84. Interview with Martin Mansergh, 12 Dec. 2002.
85. Dwyer, *Short Fellow*, p. 299.
86. Wilson, *Irish America and the Ulster Conflict*, p. 246.
87. Dwyer, *Short Fellow*, p. 302.
88. *Dáil Éireann Debates*, Vol. 361, Cols. 2579–2600, 19 Nov. 1985, also quoted in Ivory, 'Constitutional Republicanism, and the Issue of Consent 1980–1996', p. 104.

89. Dwyer, *Short Fellow,* p. 205.
90. Interview with Mary O'Rourke ,15 Nov. 2005.
91. Interview with Frank Fahey, 13 Dec. 2005.
92. *The Irish Times* 16 Nov. 1985. Note that the Supreme Court ruled in the course of the 1990 McGimpsey judgment that in fact the Anglo-Irish Agreement was not contrary to the 1937 Constitution.
93. Interview with Martin Mansergh 12 Dec. 2002.
94. *Irish Independent* 21 Nov. 1985.
95. *Irish Press* 17 March 1987.
96. Support for the agreement ranged from 59% in Nov. 1985 to 69% in Feb. 1986, Cox, W.H. 'Public opinion and the Anglo-Irish Agreement', *Government and Opposition,* 22 (1987), p. 345.
97. See Cochrane, F. *Unionist Politics and the Politics of Unionism since the Anglo-Irish Agreement* (Cork: Cork University Press), 1997.
98. *Irish Press* 18 March 1987.
99. Collins, *The Power Game,* p. 180.
100. Collins, *The Power Game,* p. 182.
101. Adams has speculated that Haughey was able to engage with Sinn Féin at this time because his party did not pose an electoral threat to Fianna Fáil at the time: Adams, *Hope and History,* p 81. Sinn Féin's vote in the 1987 election was 1.9%, which meant that the party had failed to increase its vote even though it had abandoned abstentionism from the Dáil one year earlier, see Laver, M., Mair, P. and Sinnott, R. (eds), *How Ireland Voted: The Irish general election 1987* (Dublin: Poolbeg Press and PSAI Press, 1987), p. 67.
102. *The Irish Times* 25 March 1987.
103. *Irish Independent* 11 Feb. 1988.
104. The Enniskillen bombing of 8 Nov. 1987: The IRA bombed a Remembrance Day ceremony, killing eleven protestant civilians. See McDaniel, D. *Enniskillen: The Remembrance Sunday bombing* (Dublin: Wolfhound, 1997).
105. *Sunday Press* 21 Feb. 1988.
106. Ibid.
107. Presidential address by Charles Haughey at the Fianna Fáil Árd Fheis 20 Feb. 1988, Fianna Fáil Archives, P176/790.
108. Material relating to Fianna Fáil Árd Fheis 19–21 Feb. 1988, Fianna Fáil Archives P176/781.
109. *Irish Independent* 22 April 1988.
110. Patterson, *The Politics of Illusion,* p. 203.
111. *Belfast Telegraph* 11 Sept. 1987.
112. *Irish News* 18 Jan. 1988.
113. *Irish Press* 11 Jan. 1988.
114. *Newsletter* 11 Jan. 1988.
115. Ibid.
116. Dermot Ahern remembers Adams' reply to a challenge regarding the IRA's violent campaign: 'Isn't that the very reason why we're talking to try to prevent those from happening?' Interview with Dermot Ahern, 1 Nov. 2002.
117. *Irish Press* 28 Jan. 1988.
118. Ibid.
119. Mallie and McKittrick, *The Fight for Peace,* pp. 70–1.
120. Interview with Dermot Ahern, 1 Nov. 2002.
121. Mitchell McLaughlin: elected to the Derry City Council for Sinn Féin in 1985; party talks negotiator, 1996–8, elected to the Northern Ireland Assembly 1998; party spokesperson on EU affairs and regional development.
122. Pat Doherty: Born in Glasgow of Donegal parents; returned to Donegal in 1968; Sinn Féin vice-president since 1988; headed the Sinn Féin delegation to the Forum for Peace and Reconciliation in 1994; stood for Dáil election in the Donegal North-East constituency in 1989 and in the Connacht/Ulster constituency in the EU elections in 1989 and 1994; elected to the Northern Ireland Assembly in 1998; elected as Westminster MP in 2001 for West Tyrone.
123. Interview with Dermot Ahern, 1 Nov. 2002. For details of attitudes in the Republic of

Ireland regarding Northern Ireland, see, for example, Cox, W.H. 'Who Wants a United Ireland?', *Government and Opposition*, 20, 1 (Winter 1985).
124. Interview with Martin Mansergh, 12 Dec. 2002.
125. Interview with Dermot Ahern, 1 Nov. 2002.
126. Ibid
127. Ibid.
128. Ibid.
129. Ibid.
130. Ivory, G. 'Revisions in Nationalist Discourse among Irish Political Parties', *Irish Political Studies*, 14 (1999), p. 94.
131. Ivory, 'Revisions in Nationalist Discourse among Irish political parties', p. 94.
132. Moloney, *A Secret History of the IRA*, p. 277.
133. Mallie and McKittrick, *The Fight for Peace*, see Chapters 4, 7 and 8.
134. Moloney, *A Secret History of the IRA*, p. 277.
135. Moloney, *A Secret History of the IRA*, pp. 277–8. Dermot Ahern confirmed Hume was not informed of the 1988 Fianna Fáil–Sinn Féin talks; Interview with Dermot Ahern, 1 Nov. 2002.
136. Interview with Martin Mansergh, 12 Dec. 2002.
137. Ibid.
138. Hume was not immediately successful in winning support for the process involving Sinn Féin. He was subjected to fierce criticism when his meetings with Adams were exposed in 1993. See Mallie and McKittrick, *The Fight for Peace*, pp. 214–17.
139. Ivory, 'Fianna Fáil, Constitutional Republicanism, and the Issue of Consent', p. 116.
140. Ibid.
141. Mallie and McKittrick, *The Fight for Peace*, pp. 117, 121.
142. Mansergh has outlined how the talks between Sinn Féin and the SDLP and Sinn Féin and Fianna Fáil in 1988 'centred on the concept of self-determination': Mansergh, M. 'Mountain-Climbing Irish Style: The hidden challenges of the peace process', in M. Elliott (ed), *The Long Road to Peace in Northern Ireland: Peace lectures from the Institute of Irish studies at Liverpool University*, p. 110.
143. Interview with Martin Mansergh, 12 Dec. 2002.
144. Ibid.
145. Ibid.
146. Ibid. Republicans such as Gerry Adams had, from the early period of the Troubles, labelled the republican campaign as one 'for national self-determination' and *An Phoblacht/Republican News* expressed the need for 'the most basic right of all – the right of self-determination', Bourke, *Peace in Ireland: The war of ideas*, p. 25 n. 11.
147. The records of submissions made by the unionist parties to the Strand Two meetings in July 1992 call on the Irish government to recognize such a right. See, for example, Ian Paisley's (UDUP) opening statement and the opening statement of the UUP at the Second Plenary meeting of Strand Two at Lancaster House, London, 7 July 1992.
148. The talks chairman, Senator George Mitchell, is quoted as suggesting that the concentration by unionists on the demand for the principle of consent may prove to be a 'strategic error' in the long term. As quoted in Bourke, *Peace in Ireland*, p. 308.
149. Mallie and McKittrick, *The Fight for Peace*, p. 381.
150. Gallagher, M. 'Do Ulster Unionists Have a Right to Self-Determination?', *Irish Political Studies*, 5 (1990), p. 28.
151. Burke, J. 'On Walzer's Hermeneutics of Justice, Gadamer's Criterion of Openness and Northern Ireland's Belfast Agreement' *Irish Political Studies*, 14 (1999), p. 17.
152. Burke, 'On Walzer's Hermeneutics of Justice', p. 20.
153. Foster, J.W. 'The Downing Street Declaration (1993)', in J.W. Foster (ed), *The Idea of the Union: Statements and critiques of the Union of Great Britain and Northern Ireland* (Canada: Belcouver Press, 1995), p. 100.
154. Ivory, G. 'Constitutional Republicanism, and the Issue of Consent 1980–1996', *Eire-Ireland* (Summer/Fall 1997), p. 93.
155. These two members of the UUP utilized their right under the Irish Constitution to claim Irish citizenship and mounted a legal challenge to the Anglo-Irish Agreement in the Irish courts on the basis that it was contrary to Articles Two and Three of the Constitution. The Supreme Court delivered a very important judgment stating that the agreement merely

gave *de facto* recognition to Northern Ireland and therefore was not contrary to the relevant articles. The judgment went on to say that the Irish government was compelled by a 'constitutional imperative' to seek unity.

156. Mansergh, 'The Background to the Irish Peace Process', p. 16.
157. *The Irish Times* 2 Feb. 1989.
158. *The Irish Times* 8 Jan. 1988.
159. *The Irish Times* 20 July 1989.
160. Desmond O'Malley: Elected as Fianna Fáil TD in 1967; succeeded Michael Moran as Minister for Justice in 1970, when Lynch sacked Moran on health grounds in the midst of the Arms Crisis; split from Fianna Fáil in 1985 to form the Progressive Democrats owning to his personal antipathy towards Charles Haughey and, in particular, his decision to oppose the Anglo-Irish Agreement; entered coalition with Fianna Fáil in 1989.
161. See Jim Cusack's report in *The Irish Times* 10 July 1989 for coverage of the issues which divided Fianna Fáil and the Progressive Democrats in the 1989 election.

CHAPTER THREE

Albert Reynolds and the Northern Ireland Peace Process 1992–4

INTRODUCTION

When Charles Haughey resigned as Taoiseach in February 1992 Garret FitzGerald offered a critical evaluation of Haughey's career. He was particularly disapproving of his record on Anglo-Irish relations and Northern Ireland. However, he did admit that 'the evaluation of Charles Haughey's political career will require a long perspective; we are too close to events to make much sense at this stage of the light of the shadow. Some of the more positive elements may loom larger in the future than they do at this moment.'[1] Certainly this has proved true in relation to Haughey's role in the foundation of the present peace process, as we have seen.[2] Conversely, the role of Albert Reynolds in the peace process has never been scrutinized.[3] This is explained by the contrasting approaches between of the two leaders. Initially, in government with the Progressive Democrats, Reynolds, like Haughey, allowed his contacts with the republican movement to be known only to very few within the party and the government.[4] However, the change in coalition partner resulted in better relations between the coalition parties and Reynolds was able to conduct the process with much more widespread knowledge and support[5] while in government with the Labour Party led by Dick Spring.[6] This has caused many to see the Reynolds–Labour administration as the starting point of the peace process. This chapter will assess the role and contribution made by Albert Reynolds to the peace process and to the shifts in Fianna Fáil policy on Northern Ireland. In keeping with the approach utilized in the study of Charles Haughey in the previous chapter, the significance of Sinn Féin to these shifts is highlighted.

THE POLITICAL ENVIRONMENT

Reynolds' quest for a breakthrough on the North was furthered by the occurrence of a series of complementary circumstances. Firstly, the political and social changes in the Republic in the 1990s sponsored a number of political debates and created an environment for reassessment and change. This was influenced by a number of factors. For example, Alvin Jackson points to the impact of European Union membership as 'involv[ing] a movement away from the old culturally xenophobic and economically protectionist verities of the Sinn Féin tradition'.[7] This, he claims, has led to 'the maturing of Ireland's relationship with Britain'.[8] In addition, Brian Girvin points to the Anglo-Irish Agreement as the catalyst for debate, particularly with regards to Articles Two and Three of the Constitution.[9] As we have seen in the previous chapter, sections within Fianna Fáil had already been debating the future of Articles Two and Three of the Constitution.[10] This process of debate and change was aided and made public by the McGimpsey case in 1990. The judgment in this case resulted in a unionist backlash with the Ulster Unionist Party (UUP) leader, James Molyneaux,[11] declaring that any possibility of an agreement had been lost. This, he said, proved that 'the assurances attached to the Anglo-Irish Agreement were deceitful and fraudulent'.[12] Despite the negative effect on unionist attitudes the case heralded a positive process of debate in the Republic in relation to Northern Ireland and, in particular, to the offending articles of the Constitution.

Many viewed the judgment as increasing the urgency for change in relation to Articles Two and Three. *The Irish Times* claimed that it was now time to question whether the articles were representative of public opinion[13] and argued that Fianna Fáil, in particular, needed to address this question.[14] The *Sunday Independent* was critical of the state's constitutional position on Northern Ireland and branded the articles as a 'constitutional licence to kill'.[15] The issue also caused problems within the government itself, bringing to the fore diverging attitudes on the North held by the two coalition parties, Fianna Fáil and the Progressive Democrats. The Progressive Democrats reiterated their support for constitutional reform in a Senate motion and put pressure on their coalition partner by repeatedly calling on Fianna Fáil to support changes to Articles Two and Three. The party chairman, Michael McDowell,[16] called on Fianna Fáil to make a gesture of reconciliation since the articles provided 'no useful purpose' other than to serve as a '"comfort blanket" for traditional nationalists'.[17]

Progressive Democrats leader, Des O'Malley, proclaimed his support for change[18] and the party's spokesperson on Northern Ireland, Helen Keogh, argued that the articles gave justification to violence and caused unionists to 'regard the territorial claim in the Constitution as a desire to annex or dominate them and force them into a united Ireland'.[19] This dissension from the Progressive Democrats was significant in that it came in response to the Taoiseach's pronouncement that he envisaged no immediate changes to Articles Two and Three of the Constitution. Haughey did not suggest that constitutional change could never be considered but that it could only occur as part of an overall agreement in the context of future unity.[20] In his speech to the 1990 Fianna Fáil Árd Fheis, Haughey defended the articles against the unionist claim that they encouraged violence by lending moral legitimacy to the IRA by asserting the need for the articles to be read in conjunction with Article Twenty Nine of the Constitution, which committed the government to peaceful means.[21] This, he thought, should assuage unionist fears.

In addition to continued discussion about constitutional change, the question as to when and under what circumstances Sinn Féin could become involved in the talks process was also being addressed, not just in Ireland but also in Britain. As early as November 1989 the Secretary of State for Northern Ireland, Peter Brooke, was promoting debate within Sinn Féin through his pledge of an imaginative response to an IRA ceasefire.[22] A year later he made a similar plea to terrorists to remove the 'impediment on the road to peace and greater understanding and to new political institutions which adequately reflect everyone's interests'.[23] In March 1990 Charles Haughey intimated that there could be a place for Sinn Féin in the building of the future arrangements in Ireland if the IRA announced a total cessation of violence.[24] Significantly, John Taylor, an Ulster Unionist MP, remarked that 'all parties which renounce violence certainly become involved in the normal democratic procedures'.[25] There were also growing levels of support in Britain (especially among Irish people living in Britain) for talks including Sinn Féin and loyalist groupings.[26] Consequently, the political atmosphere was suitable for Reynolds to support a process that placed such dialogue at its centre, and this was a second favourable circumstance for an alternative approach to finding a solution to the Northern Ireland Troubles under Reynolds' leadership.

Thirdly, the failure of the Brooke talks[27] because of the SDLP's lack of faith both in that talks process and in the British government's ability to act independently of the unionist parties[28] meant that the new process found support from both the SDLP and the Irish government. Michael Cunningham has illustrated how the failure of the 1992 talks provided momentum for an alternative approach: 'the construction of an inclusive policy to bring in the paramilitaries rather than to try to marginalize the "men of violence" through the bolstering of the "middle ground" via consociationalism'.[29]

Fourthly, just as Haughey had responded to activities within the republican movement when he decided to open a channel of contact with Sinn Féin in 1988, Albert Reynolds' decision to do the same was influenced by the level of debate within Sinn Féin regarding the future role of the militant tradition. This debate had become more pronounced since the beginning of the 1990s. Not only were republicans engaging in 'discussions about the ongoing struggle, about policy matters, about the unionists and most importantly, about the process by which peace can be established in this island (Ireland)',[30] they were also calling for both the SDLP and the Irish government to move away from what they termed 'active collaboration',[31] in the search for a new direction.[32] Adams has outlined that, when the idea of a joint-governmental declaration was being worked out, Sinn Féin realized that 'a common Irish nationalist position independent of or in tandem with a joint position of the two governments' was necessary and that an end to the armed struggle could only be brought about through cooperation with the SDLP and the Irish government.[33] Reports from the 1992 Sinn Féin Ard Fheis described a sense of agony in the search for a new direction amidst the party's widespread isolation and inability to extend its political campaign due to continued IRA violence.[34] In his speech at Bodenstown in June 1992, Árd Comhairle member Jim Gibney provided an additional insight into 'evolutionary changes which have taken place in republican thinking over the last 10 years', which had meant the party had acknowledged the need for 'a sustained period of peace' before a British withdrawal was possible.[35] In short, Reynolds' commitment to a peace process would have been of little significance had Sinn Féin and the IRA not have been interested in pursuing an alternative to the armed struggle which had the establishment of a strong pan-nationalist alliance involving the Irish government at its core. In fact, Reynolds' interest in the peace process was very much stimulated by encouraging signals from Sinn Féin and the IRA.

Fifthly, the precedent of dialogue with paramilitary organizations had already been set. Meetings were taking place at Clonard Monastery in west Belfast between Gerry Adams, Father Reid, and other church members since September 1990.[36] *The Irish Times* reported in June 1992 that church leaders had been conducting talks with both loyalist and republican paramilitary groups since the beginning of that year. Meetings had taken place in Derry between Martin McGuinness[37] and Bishop Edward Daly,[38] while a Presbyterian minister, Dr Jack Weir, had met both UDA and Sinn Féin leaders.[39] This undercurrent of activities created the momentum for dialogue through direct contact with republicans, which Reynolds established in October 1992.[40]

Finally, the peace strategy was aided by changes in attitudes among the British administration. Cunningham has outlined a number of ways in which the British government was reassessing its approach to the Troubles in Northern Ireland. In general, they were rethinking the way in which terrorist groups in Northern Ireland had been dealt with. There was a realization that shunning the paramilitary groups was counterproductive and that there was a desire within all groups to abandon the violent campaign.[41] Cunningham also points to the fact that the 1990s had witnessed the 'internationalisation' of the Northern Ireland Troubles. Britain's place within the European Union also enabled a movement away from the traditionally narrow concept of national sovereignty. This facilitated the acceptance of the need to involve the government of the Irish Republic in the search for a solution to the conflict in Northern Ireland.[42] Shifts in international opinion and a willingness by both the United States of America and the European Union administrations to give support to the peace process also advanced the new approach inherent in the peace process.[43] The British government's willingness to find a way to end the stalemate was crucial to the peace process. The determination by Reynolds to support a process involving the search for an IRA ceasefire and subsequent talks with Sinn Féin at a time when Sinn Féin felt most isolated may be explained by the nature of the debates outlined above and the readiness of both governments to look for an alternative approach to that which had been sponsored by Peter Brooke and his successor as Northern Ireland Secretary of State, Patrick Mayhew.

As with Haughey, any study of Reynolds' approach to Northern Ireland must be placed within the context of the political environment, both in Northern Ireland and in the Republic, which both leaders responded to. Appreciating that context illustrates the debates and circumstances which informed Reynolds' approach and ability to give prominence to the Northern Ireland problem and also that his success at this level was aided by existing circumstances.

THE REYNOLDS ADMINISTRATION

Martin Mansergh has referred to the 'prevailing orthodoxy' which dictated against dialogue with paramilitaries 'as a means of demonstrating moral distance and indeed repugnance'.[44] But, as has been illustrated, conditions amendable to a new approach involving Sinn Féin were in place when Reynolds came to power. That had not been the case in 1988, when Haughey first initiated talks with the republican movement. Also, there was a significant debate already underway, as we have seen, in relation to essential constitutional and attitudinal change needed in the Republic in order to facilitate a settlement. Reynolds said that his administration:

> effected a major change in that, prior to that, successive governments tended to call on republicans and others to lay down their arms and then and only then they would talk to them. Seeing that that had failed for thirty years I felt a change of policy was desirable and necessary. So I set out to change the government policy, to try to get a ceasefire before any guns were laid down, to try to arrange, to negotiate a ceasefire by setting up a communications link with the leaders of Sinn Féin through Dr Martin Mansergh who was my personal advisor on the North of Ireland.[45]

Certainly his government institutionalized the Irish government's role in the peace process as one which involved promoting Sinn Féin's place within it, but this idea predated the Reynolds administration. Reynolds' contribution was to pursue this notion so vigorously and successfully that no future government could depart from it. Reynolds was willing and able to take political risks that Haughey, because of his political past, was never in a position to do. Haughey had been more concerned with power than Reynolds. With regards to the issue of electoral repercussions that might result from this approach, Reynolds recalled that:

> It wasn't an issue at the time because every party looks after their own patch and their own people and political movement is a question for political parties to move forward … but I was prepared to take the risk and give it a go because it was saving lives that were at stake. I was prepared to try and fail rather than not try at all.[46]

While Reynolds' lack of political baggage may have enabled him to build trust between the Irish government and unionists,[47] it will be clear that he felt that his responsibility was to 'look after' republicans and that John Major would have a reciprocal role to play in relation to unionists.[48] This is not to say that Reynolds did not recognize the value of including unionist opinion, but it is apparent that his first priority was to his own republican constituency and to the republican movement. The Ulster Unionist Party leader, James Molyneaux, was soon to criticize Reynolds' government for its selective communication with parties in the North and because the government was dependent 'solely on advice channelled by Mr Hume'.[49] This was unfortunate given that Molyneaux had hinted at the need for unionists to open contacts with Irish ministers, which may have paved the way for a historic development. Initially the prospect of a meeting between Reynolds and unionists had looked promising; soon after coming to power Reynolds spoke of his sympathy for unionists and the concerns that they had. He denounced 'republican paramilitaries [who attempt] to coerce the unionist people' as having no 'historical sanction'.[50] However, rather than offer a gesture in relation to Articles Two and Three, Reynolds' approach was to seek to remove the reasons for republican violence by assisting nationalists in 'combating all manifestations of discrimination, injustice or intolerance. We will uphold their right to pursue their rights and aspirations through peaceful, democratic means.'[51]

Constitutional Change Linked to the 1920 Government of Ireland Act and North–South Bodies

Debates taking place at the Fianna Fáil Árd Fheis in March of 1992 illustrated the party's reluctance to abandon Articles Two and Three of the Constitution and also indicated a sympathy towards Sinn Féin's inclusion in future talks.[52] Reynolds introduced a new dimension to discussions about Articles Two and Three. He now said that, while the Irish government was willing to negotiate possible changes to the articles, this would be part of wider constitutional discussions relating to the Government of Ireland Act 1920,[53] seen by republicans as having institutionalized partition in Ireland.[54] Reynolds outlined how Sinn Féin's response to this had encouraged him to believe that he had embarked on the correct approach on this issue:

> I had been talking about problems created by the partition of the north of Ireland and that particularly section 74 [sic] of the

Government of Ireland Act 1920 – that was really the legislation
introduced by Britain that created the partition of Ireland – that
would have to be on the table for discussion. And Martin
McGuinness at one stage took up that challenge, said that he was
quite happy, and prepared to be at any table where section 74
[sic] of the Government of Ireland Act was on the table.[55]

In addition to introducing the Government of Ireland Act, Reynolds
also insisted that concurrent referenda would have to take place in the
North and the South. Moreover, he made it clear that changes to
Articles Two and Three would have to be matched with 'innovative
and attractive'[56] North–South structures. Reynolds also argued that
the British government should adopt a role in which it would
'encourage [Irish unity] as a long term solution'.[57] Recognizing the
bargaining value of Articles Two and Three, Reynolds placed a high
price on constitutional change.[58]

Constitutional Change as Part of an Overall Settlement

In addition to demanding revision of the relevant provision of the
1920 Government of Ireland Act and strong North–South bodies, the
Irish government was consistent in its claim that Articles Two and
Three could not be presented to the electorate in isolation but 'solely
and merely in a package situation ... we are looking at it totally in the
context of a package and not in any other way'.[59] According to
Reynolds, to have a referendum on the articles that could be defeated if not part of a settlement would 'do more harm than good ...
would resurrect old bitterness and old divisions'.[60] A submission by
the Minister for Foreign Affairs, David Andrews, to the Strand Two
Brooke–Mayhew talks in 1992 reiterated that the government was
unwilling to alter its stance that change could only come when
accompanied by commitments from both unionists and the British
government on North–South institutions.[61] Despite an offer of 'a fair
and honourable accommodation'[62] from Andrews on the matter, stalemate resulted. This was followed by the decision from the Democratic
Unionist Party (DUP) to boycott the Strand Two talks that were scheduled to take place in Dublin, claiming the articles were not 'going to
be realistically addressed'.[63] Despite the level of criticism which the
government was subjected to and the continued clashes between the
government and opposition members,[64] the government did not
depart from the position that insisted upon constitutional amendment

only as the basis of an overall settlement. It is no real surprise that the government's rigid stance on the above issues impacted on the ability of the Brooke–Mayhew talks initiatives to succeed. On 27 April 1992, as a concession to unionists and in order to allow talks to proceed, a three-month suspension of the inter-governmental conference was agreed.[65] But there was little progress in the talks on Strand One with unionists rejecting the SDLP's European-inspired proposal for government.[66] Unionists were also distrustful of the SDLP's close relationship with the Irish government.[67] The Irish government's intransigence in relation to Articles Two and Three added to these problems and threatened the progress of the talks on Strand Two. The DUP called for written assurances from the Irish government that Articles Two and Three would be addressed.[68] This request was denied, as was Ian Paisley's[69] later demand that the issue be placed top of the agenda.[70] With the lack of agreement on Strand One, Reynolds was anxious not to concede anything without gaining something in return. He also expressed his view that the concentration on Articles Two and Three as the basis of a solution was misguided.[71] Reynolds contributed to the debate regarding constitutional change by introducing a number of new conditions, which were followed by Ahern in the 1998 negotiations: that change would be discussed as part of an overall settlement and that North–South bodies, the 1920 Government of Ireland Act and constitutional change would be interdependent.

Building the Pan-Nationalist Alliance

The establishment of a pan-nationalist alliance became the fundamental driving force behind Reynolds' approach to Northern Ireland. Before his departure, Haughey informed Reynolds of the initiative involving the republican movement.[72] Reynolds committed his government to placing 'no limits'[73] on endeavours to achieve peace in Northern Ireland. He concentrated on providing the conditions necessary for an IRA ceasefire rather than on the establishment of good Anglo-Irish relations or building bridges with unionists. With the knowledge of a very small number of people, Reynolds sanctioned direct talks between his advisor on Northern Ireland, Martin Mansergh, and Sinn Féin representatives, which had been taking place since October 1992.[74] Meetings also took place between Michael Lillis, a diplomat in the Department of Foreign Affairs, and Sinn Féin delegates in March of 1992.[75] In April 1993 it was revealed that talks had taken place between the SDLP leader, John Hume, and the Sinn Féin president, Gerry Adams. It was not disclosed at this stage whether or to what extent the Irish government was involved in this exercise but a new debate emerged. Amid speculation as to the nature of the talks, Hume and Adams published a statement outlining their attempts to establish 'an overall political strategy'. The statement reaffirmed the right of the Irish people 'as a whole to national self-determination' and rejected the feasibility of an internal solution.[76]

The Hume–Adams initiative was subject to much criticism[77] and both Hume and Adams were forced to defend their initiative. Adams explained that the talks, which he said were prompted by clergy, were part of an effort to create a peace process that would engender a new approach to break the current logjam. Significantly, Adams stressed the role the Irish government must play in this so as to ensure success.[78] Hume aimed to alleviate unionist concerns about the process by providing assurances that he was not pursuing any hidden agenda other than dialogue and an agreement which gave 'minimal' recognition to the nationalist identity.[79] The possibility of further talks between the parties in the North was, however, undermined by the Hume–Adams talks and Ian Paisley refused to meet Hume while he was engaged in discussions with Adams.[80] Reynolds nonetheless continued to concentrate on what by now had generated the idea of the joint-governmental declaration. Meetings between Irish officials and republicans were still taking place, in attempts to negotiate the basis of a declaration to be passed to the British government.[81] The Hume–Adams dialogue continued and the two leaders periodically issued statements in relation to their progress. The statement which provoked much more controversy than the original announcement of the talks came in September 1993. In it Hume and Adams proclaimed that they had made progress and that an unreleased statement of principles had been forwarded to Dublin in order to stimulate debate between the two governments.[82]

The Irish government gave a cautious response, clearly irritated at the decision by Hume and Adams to put the future of the initiative in their hands.[83] For the first time Hume's judgement was called into question in a number of circles in Dublin. It was reported that Dick Spring, Tánaiste and Minister for Foreign Affairs, was angered by the apparent 'pan-nationalist *fait accompli*' that the government had been presented with.[84] Reynolds was compelled to assert his commitment to the principle of consent in an attempt to assuage unionist fears that an arrangement had been secretly reached with republicans.[85] Despite this, government members were publicly quite supportive.[86] Dick Spring said 'any statement that gives the appearance of wanting to establish peace in Ireland is something that has to be dealt with'.[87] Following a meeting with Hume, Spring and Reynolds stated that it was a time for 'reflection, assessment and discussion' of Hume's position in order to ensure that 'it can make a very important contribution towards a consensus for peace'.[88] *The Irish Times* claimed that it had learnt that central to the Hume–Adams document was a statement by the British government on national self-determination that was aimed at prompting an IRA cease-fire.[89] It was also reported that the document envisaged a pivotal role for the Irish government, firstly, in convincing the British government to convene all-party talks and, secondly, in the process of enforcing any agreement which might be reached.[90] In effect this would amount to an exercise of the Irish people's right to national self-determination with the consent of the unionist community incorporated through dialogue. Reynolds expressed optimism in relation to the Hume plan as the 'basis for peace'[91] when he presented the document to his cabinet.[92] However, any expectation that the Irish government might be able to publicly support the Hume–Adams initiative was lost in the wake of the Shankill bombing on 23 October 1993.[93] In the circumstances, the Irish government was compelled to distance itself from the language of Hume–Adams[94] if there was to be any hope of convincing the British government to proceed with the notion of a joint-governmental statement. At this stage negotiations between Reynolds' government and republicans ceased and the emphasis shifted to engaging both the British government and unionists in the process. Reynolds announced his resolution to press ahead with efforts for peace, but stressed that that would entail negotiations with the British government.[95]

ANGLO-IRISH RELATIONS

Reynolds' ability to convince the Major administration to embrace the idea of a joint declaration, which had been a central demand of the pan-nationalist alliance, was his major success. Reynolds was confident from the beginning that he could convince Major to support any feasible approach he might pursue: 'I also knew that if I had reasonable proposals to put to John Major that our friendship over a period and our trust was certainly a big plus in going forward as well.'[96] But it was not until November of 1993 that Reynolds' attention turned from republicans towards the area of Anglo-Irish relations.

The prevailing consensus within the literature assumes that joint sponsorship of the peace process by the two governments was underway under the guise of the Anglo-Irish Agreement. Thus a link is made between that accord, the peace process and the Good Friday Agreement despite the obvious divergence in emphasis between the two agreements. Based on this assumption, Richard Bourke claims that the Anglo-Irish Agreement fostered 'a common understanding about the affairs of Northern Ireland' between the two governments.[97] It is true that the Anglo-Irish Agreement of 1985 was a significant development in terms of future Irish government policy towards Northern Ireland, since it gave the Irish government a degree of responsibility not previously afforded to it.[98] The Anglo-Irish Agreement also provided the two governments with the opportunity to meet under the workings of the Anglo-Irish Inter-Governmental Conference.[99]

Roger MacGinty and John Darby, in their analysis of the 'background of the peace process', have pointed to the post-Anglo-Irish Agreement period as generating an 'intergovernmental relationship … to the degree that it could support a peace process and the strains that would entail … The signing of the 1985 Agreement secured the long-term policy goal of developing a permanent working relationship with the British government on Northern Ireland'.[100] But we have seen in the previous chapter that Haughey was much more influenced by domestic forces, namely developments within northern republicanism. Similarly, Reynolds has been shown to focus on the same movement. This is not to say that neither recognized the imperative of involving the British government, but this was not their primary task. MacGinty and Darby have also argued that, 'since the signature of the 1985 Anglo-Irish Agreement, the British and Irish governments have shared the aim of engineering a comprehensive political settlement for Northern Ireland that could be endorsed by a majority of its citizens and undermine the legitimacy for political violence'.[101] But future administrations in both London and Dublin had very different notions as to how a settlement might be achieved and what it would entail. Despite the Progressive Democrats' enthusiasm for the inter-party talks,[102] Fianna Fáil endorsed the Hume–Adams initiative. The British government, on the other hand, was much more supportive of the talks process pursued by both Peter Brooke and Patrick Mayhew.

Paul Arthur has explicitly made the link between the Anglo-Irish Agreement and the Good Friday Agreement.[103] He has argued that 'it is inconceivable that there would have been the 1993 Declaration or the 1995 Framework Documents had there not been the Anglo-Irish Agreement, which established the context for the three-stranded approach'.[104] Equally, Sir David Goodall, a British official involved in the negotiating process leading up to the Anglo-Irish Agreement, has argued that 'it [the Good Friday Agreement] is also in important respects an extension and development of the Hillsborough Agreement rather than (as unionists maintain) its supplanter'. In his view there are many 'common threads in the two agreements'.[105] However, the continuity between the two agreements, most notably the principle of consent, belies the divergence in language, actors and process. Certainly the Anglo-Irish Agreement established a basis for closer inter-governmental co-operation, but the problem with an approach to understanding the Irish government's role in the peace process which starts with the Anglo-Irish Agreement is the tendency to reduce that role to one within the confines of Anglo-Irish relations. This overlooks the Irish government's contribution and, in particular, that of Fianna Fáil to the building of an ideological consensus within nationalism, which took primacy in the earlier stages of the peace process. Crucially the Downing Street Declaration in 1993 could not have taken place without that consensus building exercise.

Brendan O'Duffy makes a much more important point: 'the Anglo-Irish Agreement represented a shift *towards* parity of status of the two opposing sovereigns as patrons of the rights to self-determination of the two ethno-national communities in Northern Ireland.'[106] While there has been debate over the actual symmetry created by the Anglo-Irish Agreement,[107] this was no doubt the way that Fianna Fáil viewed the political implications of the accord; the Irish government would act with the British government as a sponsor of their respective communities. If there is a link between the agreement in 1985 and the peace process which culminated in the Good Friday Agreement in 1998, it is the institutionalization of this notion. However, this has been altered by the joint management of the peace process by both governments in the aftermath of the 1998 agreement. Speaking in 2003 on the role of the Irish government in the implementation of the Good Friday Agreement, the then Minister for Foreign Affairs, Brian Cowen, described the two governments as 'joint guarantors of the Agreement'.[108]

Viewing the Anglo-Irish Agreement and Anglo-Irish relations as the primary determinant of future Irish government policy on Northern Ireland is minimalist. The difficulties in Anglo-Irish relations in the months running up to the Downing Street Declaration highlight the fact that there was no common view as to how to proceed and that a joint governmental approach hung in the balance until the final days of negotiations in December 1993. This joint statement of December 1993 was of utmost importance in defining relations between the two countries in the context of the peace process of the 1990s. However, while the Downing Street Declaration was testimony to the realization that both governments must adopt a joint approach, this did not materialize until much later in the course of the Ahern–Blair administrations.[109] It is not until the position of Sinn Féin at the negotiating table had been secured in 1997 that lasting favourable Anglo-Irish relations developed.

Despite the friendship between John Major and Albert Reynolds, differences began to emerge between their administrations on a suitable approach to Northern Ireland. Bew and Gillespie have acknowledged that there was no evidence even three months prior to the signing of the Downing Street Declaration that the British government was moving away from its concentration on inter-party talks.[110] A look at relations between Dublin and London prior to the Downing Street Declaration confirms this. In May 1993, Ulster Unionist Party leader, James Molyneaux, suggested that the two governments were facing a major disagreement over Dublin's demand for joint sovereignty. While spokespersons for both governments denied this, the Minister for Foreign Affairs, Dick Spring, conceded there were certain differences and that there needed to be a more balanced approach to a solution.[111] The SDLP's continued demands on the 'Irish dimension' and the inability of the Irish government to move on Articles Two and Three were further damaging relations between the governments.[112] Extra pressure was put on the relationship by a row over President Mary Robinson's visit to Belfast. The British government lobbied Irish officials in the hope that Reynolds, as Taoiseach, would exercise his constitutional right to deny the President permission to leave the state. This created, in particular, strain between Patrick Mayhew and Dick Spring who, in meetings with British officials, was forced to defend the government's decision not to stop the President's visit.[113] The matter was exacerbated by the President's decision to shake the hand of the Sinn Féin president, Gerry Adams, when visiting west Belfast. Criticism came not just from the British government[114] and unionists[115] but also from the opposition benches.[116] Anglo-Irish relations were put under further strain and Spring was subjected to a 'cool reception' when the inter-governmental conference met.[117]

A further obstacle to the establishment of a joint approach between the two governments was Major's precarious position in the House of Commons and the belief that a deal had been struck between the Ulster Unionist Party and John Major. The Irish government was worried that concessions had been made to Molyneaux and his party in return for their vote in favour of the Maastricht Treaty and that this would lead to the British government abandoning the three-stranded approach to the talks process.[118] Dick Spring expressed concern that the 'understanding' between the Ulster Unionist Party and Major would 'jeopardise the prospect for talks'.[119] The nature of the deal was still an issue in September, when the next Anglo-Irish conference was held.[120] It was not until Dick Spring presented his six principles (see below) to the Dáil in October of 1993, in the aftermath of the Shankill bombing and Greysteel shootings, that relations improved. Spring's statement received a positive response from Patrick Mayhew, who saw it as proof of 'thinking which is a source for great hope', and John Major also expressed 'great interest'.[121] It provided the basis for progress when the two leaders met for the Brussels European summit on 29 October.[122] According to Major: 'We agreed that the Hume–Adams process was so tainted as to be unusable; the only way forward was for the two governments to take matters into their own hands.'[123] However, Reynolds was becoming impatient with Major and resented his repeated claims that he had abandoned the Hume–Adams approach.[124] There appeared to be a difference of opinion as to what had been agreed in Brussels. But, while relations were temporarily tempered by Spring's announcement of his six principles, they were once again damaged by the revelation that the British government had been in contact with Sinn Féin and the IRA.[125] This exposure came just as London had presented an alternative document to Dublin which was in stark contrast to that which had originally been negotiated, through its concentration on inter-party talks rather than on securing a ceasefire.[126] The Irish government continued to try to coax the British government into supporting its peace plan, which sought to 'reach a formula for peace and [then] a whole political solution can be sought thereafter in the talks'.[127] Reynolds, at the Fianna Fáil Árd Fheis, claimed there could be peace within a year if the British government showed a willingness to take political risks.[128] Far from there being an agreed way forward, it is obvious that, right up until the Downing Street Declaration was signed, the British government was still considering abandoning the idea, and all accounts of the negotiations demonstrate the level of disagreement between the two sides.[129] Reynolds' success related to the fact that he persisted with his approach and succeeded in convincing Major to take the risk of supporting this new approach, which had its origins in pan-nationalism.[130] The role of Dick Spring in this is important (see below).

A closer examination of Anglo-Irish relations in this period therefore illustrates that Arthur, O'Duffy and O'Leary quoted earlier have inaccurately assumed that good Anglo-Irish relations sponsored the early stages of the peace process. Reynolds certainly recognized that, because of its part in the conflict, the British government had to be involved in any solution for Northern Ireland and thus the Anglo-Irish arena provided the natural avenue for any political initiative. The institutions that had been put in place under the Anglo-Irish Agreement complemented rather than spawned the peace process. Rather, it was spawned from within nationalism and the British government was only involved at a point which the participants of the pan-nationalist alliance deemed necessary. Similarly, Reynolds recognized the need to have a process inclusive of loyalist and unionist interests and he was clear about this.[131] At this early stage of the peace process, however, he believed that it was the British government who had the responsibility of including such interests in the same way that he represented the interests of northern nationalism and republicanism.

THE CONTRIBUTION OF DICK SPRING

Albert Reynolds insisted that his approach to the Northern Ireland peace process was a balanced one and was premised on his belief that 'it couldn't have been done, and wouldn't have been successful if everyone wasn't involved; the SDLP, Sinn Féin, the IRA, unionists and the unionist paramilitaries [sic]. My view was that we needed everyone involved and we needed everyone around the table.'[132] However, we have established that Reynolds believed that his role was to 'look after' republicans and therefore he gave personal priority to the creation of a wider nationalist position in the quest for a ceasefire. Indeed he offered a number of incentives to the republican movement. He summarised them as follows:

> [T]o bring about a ceasefire and as a recognition of the ceasefire that I was prepared to try to get a visa for Gerry Adams, and later for Joe Cahill, to go the United States and that we would take away section 35 [sic] of the Broadcasting Act which would allow Sinn Féin and the republican movement onto the airways

again. That we were prepared to look at parole of prisoners and I would try to get the British government to do the same. And that if we were able to demonstrate that we could get changes from the British government and that we could win the argument at international level on the public stage, that there was real hope for going forward. So it was demonstrated over a period that we did do it and so over a period we convinced them to look at the possibility of a permanent ceasefire and that we could show that there was progress on the alternative route of peace.[133]

The willingness of Fianna Fáil under Reynolds to play a role defined by a commitment to Sinn Féin's inclusion and pan-nationalism had consequences for Anglo-Irish affairs and for the development of positive relations with unionists. Fortunately, the Taoiseach's approach was balanced by that of his coalition partner and Minister for Foreign Affairs, Dick Spring, who was much more active in addressing unionist concerns. However, apart from his statement of six principles, Spring never completely achieved the trust of the unionist community. There was tension within the Irish government's approach to Northern Ireland at this time. As early as April 1993 the Taoiseach was forced to deny reports of a rift between the coalition parties and state that 'there is close and continuous consultation between the Tánaiste and myself on all policy matters'.[134] Again, in May 1993, differences of opinion and problems within the partnership were commented upon[135] and in June this became evident in relation to Northern Ireland. In a Dáil debate opposition members alluded to Labour's diverging stance from that of Fianna Fáil. The deputy leader of Fine Gael, Nora Owen, outlined the impression that 'the difference between these two men about Articles Two and Three, and at what stage they should be involved in discussions, are very obvious'.[136] Spring's advisor, Fergus Finlay, relays the struggle both he and Spring underwent in adopting a new approach towards the republican movement.[137] Spring, like Reynolds, was willing from the beginning to give priority to the Northern Ireland conflict but was convinced of the need to involve the British government in any new initiative.[138] Spring advocated a cross-party approach to Northern Ireland and had called on politicians to abandon the 'history book mentality and the Civil War politics'.[139] He also supported British efforts to get inter-party talks up and running in the autumn of 1993.[140]

As Minister for Foreign Affairs, Spring outlined an even-handed and conciliatory position in relation to the talks process. He challenged the two governments to find agreement on the way forward and stated that dialogue which sought to allow either side to control or intimidate could not occur. He offered a genuine approach to compromise if unionists agreed to enter negotiations, which he said must commence with no preconditions in place.[141] However, his efforts were not initially successful. Molyneaux claimed that Spring's suggestion that a failed talks process should result in a return to a commitment to the Anglo-Irish Agreement amounted to an attempt to achieve 'unity by enforced consent'.[142] Likewise, DUP leader, Ian Paisley, declared the Tánaiste's speech to be 'absolute nonsense'.[143] Spring's endorsement of a referendum on the outcome of talks also did not help to establish a common approach between the two governments.[144] Neither was the idea of joint referenda supported by unionist opinion. The April 1993 edition of the *New Ulster Defender* denounced the proposal on the grounds that 'it would be asymmetrical and undemocratic for the people of the Republic to have a say on a settlement for the people of Northern Ireland' and also denied that it was 'a safeguard for unionists', as had been suggested by Hume.[145] Spring defended his suggestions in relation to a joint British–Irish approach. He was dismayed that unionists were unable to accept his guarantee on Articles Two and Three 'in good faith'.[146] He clarified that his government attached primary significance to inter-party dialogue but also stated that both governments must not let failure in this area affect the governments' commitment to progress. The establishment of a position of commonality between the two governments was a consistent facet in Spring's approach to the Northern Ireland talks and, therefore, the Labour leader made a vital contribution to the building of good Anglo-Irish relations and to promoting the notion of a joint governmental stance.

Spring's approach was two-pronged; the multi-party talks were to be encouraged,[147] but the way forward was the responsibility of the two governments: 'We in the wider British and Irish communities owe it to the people of Northern Ireland to acknowledge that the quarrel is not merely a baffling local phenomenon. It flows directly from the troubled history of our two islands.'[148] He envisaged new options being considered by both governments in order to reach agreement and appeared to have convinced the Northern Ireland Secretary of State, Patrick Mayhew, of this approach. Mayhew, in the aftermath of an inter-governmental conference, expressed the view that the British government must be involved in constitutional negotiations with the Irish government while also conducting bilateral talks with the Northern Ireland parties.[149] Spring's contribution was to seek a balance between the different interests involved. From becoming Minister for Foreign Affairs, he had made a number of innovative speeches on the correlation between the talks process and Anglo-Irish relations. But the input which sparked the most debate and opened the way towards a better understanding between the Irish government and the unionist parties came in the aftermath of a week of intense violence in October 1993. During a Dáil debate on Northern Ireland, Spring took the opportunity to present six principles aimed at providing a means to move forward which he hoped would allow 'reason and hope' to prevail.[150] Spring's fourth and fifth principles were the most thought-provoking and introduced a new dynamic into the government's position. He stated:

> Let us once and for all accept that if we talk about the freedom of unionists to give their consent to constitutional change, we must also recognise the freedom of unionists to withhold their consent from such change, unless and until they are persuaded by democratic political means only ... if we believe in consent as an integral part of any democratic approach to peace, we must be prepared at the right time and in the right circumstances to express our commitment to that consent in fundamental law.[151]

Spring's principles were received positively by the Fine Gael leader, John Bruton,[152] and Liz McManus of Democratic Left referred to the positive response from all parties in the Dáil.[153] The positive response from Fine Gael and the Progressive Democrats, parties generally more sympathetic to unionist opinion, reflected the fact that Spring was attempting to counterbalance the approach of the Taoiseach. This was mirrored by republicans, who interpreted the principles as 'reinforc[ing] support for the British government backed unionist veto on the future of the six counties' and reiterated that peace could only be attained in 'the exercise of self-determination without impediment of any kind, by the Irish people as a whole'.[154] This forced Spring to clarify his statement and he assured republicans that 'no Irish government will ever turn its back on the nationalist community in Northern Ireland'.[155] Reynolds was particularly keen to correct the 'drafting error'[156] included in the statement. Spring's reference to the right of unionists, and not just a majority of the people in Northern Ireland, to veto constitutional change represented an inherently different concept and one which Fianna Fáil, republicans and Hume could not accept. Speaking in the Dáil, Reynolds was clear that the principle of consent could not be worded in favour of an explicit veto for unionists and explained: 'What we are talking about here is the consent of a majority to constitutional change, as precisely defined in Article 1 of the Anglo-Irish Agreement. The government have in no way departed from that position.'[157] Dick Spring confirmed that 'the principles which I outlined were intended to be complementary to the efforts which John Hume has been making to find a basis for peace'.[158] This underlined the point that the Irish government's approach to the peace process prioritized Sinn Féin's inclusion and ending IRA violence. This eclipsed Spring's attempts to build trust with unionists, which would have been a truly historical achievement. The fact that this opportunity was lost highlights the inherent shortcomings of the peace process.

Nevertheless, the speech resulted in an offer from the British government to renew discussions on constitutional issues. John Major pinpointed this speech 'as open[ing] the road to a genuine negotiation and a much more balanced process, not one driven by Adams'.[159] Spring's principles were heavily informed by the points agreed by Hume and Adams[160] and which were presented to the government, but they were now presented as an Irish government initiative: 'These principles are the Irish government's position on a necessary process if we are going to establish peace on this island.'[161] Fine Gael's Austin Currie described how the Hume–Adams agreement had been 'subsumed into the democratic principles announced by Mr Spring. The Irish government can now approach the British government with a package that bears the fingerprints only of the Irish government'.[162] This was a moment of ingenuity on the part of Spring and the Irish government. The significance of Spring's principles in rescuing the Hume–Adams approach and in convincing the British government of the viability of this approach cannot be exaggerated. On the signing of the Downing Street Declaration, Spring was able to state that 'they (the six principles) are all contained, implicitly and explicitly, in the Declaration we are now considering' and to ask unionists to trust in the 'good faith' of the Irish government.[163]

THE 1993 DOWNING STREET DECLARATION

The Downing Street Declaration of 15 December 1993 emerged from an initiative which was specifically 'an Irish one'[164] and had an objective distinct from any previous initiative. The public statement of intent on the part of the two governments was aimed at removing any justification for the republican campaign and was thus meant to act as an incentive for a ceasefire.[165] In doing so the two governments hoped not to isolate unionists. Reynolds made it clear that the declaration was not a blueprint for an agreement: 'My guiding principle has been that we should not seek to prejudice or predetermine the shape of a final political settlement.'[166] Clearly the declaration was concerned with the achievement of a peaceful environment, which could then be followed by negotiations which could take any form decided by the parties involved, but which would involve Sinn Féin. Reynolds made this explicit when questioned after his meeting with Major in Brussels, when he stressed the need for a statement that would pro- voke a 'response from the two sets of paramilitaries'.[167] Martin Mansergh has also confirmed that Reynolds was more attentive to the need of 'securing an IRA ceasefire than a talks process'.[168] Reynolds again stressed this after the declaration was published, which he said 'provides ... the first step towards a lasting peace ... it's a statement of principles, not a basis for negotiation. The next stage of negotia- tions only come after peace has first been established.'[169] The declara- tion proposed the establishment of a Peace Forum which would involve all democratically mandated political parties. In the Dáil debate on the Downing Street Declaration, the Taoiseach stated that the aim of the Forum would be to ensure that 'all differences between the Irish people relating to the exercise of self-determination will be resolved exclusively by peaceful, political means'.[170] Reynolds acknowledged that the importance of the Forum for Peace and Reconciliation was that it 'provided the forum for people to come together and it provided an entry for Sinn Féin to meet the other par- ties, many of which would not even look at the same side of the road they walked'.[171] Evidently Reynolds saw this as the central part of the declaration; it created the environment as well as the mechanism to draw Sinn Féin into the democratic process.

Paul Arthur has highlighted the number of points contained with- in the Hume–Adams document that have been reproduced in some form within the declaration of 15 December 1993; the suggestion of some type of peace forum, the pledge by the British government once more as to its neutrality in relation to the future constitutional posi- tion of Northern Ireland and the statement in relation to self-deter- mination.[172] These points serve to reinforce the fact that Fianna Fáil's approach to addressing ideological issues in the Downing Street Declaration and the peace process in general was directed both by the desire to facilitate the republican movement's conversion to constitu- tional politics and by the need to ensure that the party's ideology maintained a commitment both to national self-determination and to the integrity of the nation. The Downing Street Declaration thus provides an opportunity to understand the two priorities of the peace process at this point. The first of these is the recognition of the concept of self-determination. This was key to bringing about the second objective, that of securing an IRA ceasefire.

Ideological Implications of the 1993 Downing Street Declaration

The Downing Street Declaration gave expression to the British government's acceptance of the Irish government's role in the affairs of Northern Ireland. It also entailed a clear statement on the right of the Irish to national self-determination.[173] This was the *raison d'être* of the Downing Street Declaration and was aimed at eliciting a response from the republican movement. Securing such a satisfactory statement on self-determination from the British government was a crucial advance for Irish nationalists. In particular, it was of huge importance for Fianna Fáil. Fianna Fáil TD, Noel Treacy, argued that the statement by the British government on self-determination gave the Irish people the right to work out their future for themselves. The Downing Street Declaration also included the first formal recognition of the principle of consent by a Fianna Fáil government but this has also been interpreted as beneficial to northern nationalists. Noel Treacy has pointed out that any future administration in Northern Ireland must now secure the consent of northern nationalists.[174] More importantly, the acknowledgement by the British government of the right of the Irish people to self-determination, while premised on the consent of the majority of the people in the North, ensures that the Republic is also granted a say.[175] Sinn Féin TD, Aengus Ó Snodaigh, elected to the Dáil in 2002 for Dublin South Central, conceded that accepting consent in reference to Northern Ireland and not, as the republican movement had demanded, on the basis of the whole island was 'a major concession' and an acceptance that they would now have to 'persuade people [unionists]'. However, he pointed to the statement on the part of the British government in the Downing Street Declaration and later in the Good Friday Agreement as being of great significance:

> It was the first time, in writing, in an international agreement that a British government had accepted that the Irish had a right to a united Ireland and that they were willing to, with the consent of the majority, that they were willing to allow that, which

is a recognition of what we've always demanded all along; the self-determination of the whole island.[176]

It is worth noting that the 1985 Anglo-Irish Agreement included a similar pledge on the part of the British government that, if a majority of people in Northern Ireland consented to a united Ireland, it would introduce legislation for this and this challenges the first part of Ó Snodaigh's statement. Nevertheless, the Downing Street Declaration is significant in that its formula for consent is set within the context of all-Ireland self-determination. Sinn Féin's Martin Ferris also interpreted the acceptance of the principle of consent in a positive light: 'As, effectively, a declaration by the British government, in particular, that they are going to accept the sovereign change in the six counties once the consent of the people of the six counties has been attained.'[177] UK Unionist Party leader, Robert McCartney, has interpreted the principle of consent as defined within the peace process of the 1990s in a manner which would support this Sinn Féin analysis. In 1997 he talked about the 'ongoing process for modifying and diluting that (consent) principle to the point where it will present no obstacle to the unification of Ireland'.[178] In his view the Downing Street Declaration 'represented a further dilution of the consent principle, both in language and tone … It is impossible to discover within the terms of the document any other solution being postulated other than that of Irish unity.'[179]

A major point of disagreement relates to the way in which self-determination has been coupled with the principle of consent and the question of which principle has been diluted in the process. Arguments have been presented that the republican concept of self-determination has had its meaning altered. But, as has been demonstrated both above and in the previous chapter, the principle of consent has been weakened and the introduction of self-determination amounts to a major advance for republicanism. However, it is not that self-determination of the island as a whole has been given precedence – since the relationship between the two concepts as set out in the Downing Street Declaration has ensured that, while a single act of self-determination will take place, it will be effected only on the basis that a majority in both jurisdictions give their consent – but rather that self-determination has been made just as central to the peace process as consent. The principle of consent appeared in its own right in the Anglo-Irish Agreement in 1985, but now has been translated to an all-Ireland basis. Also, the introduction of self-determination has

expanded the scope within which the constitutional future of
Northern Ireland will be considered, also onto an all-Ireland plane.
Reynolds has described his *quid pro quo* in relation to consent as follows: 'As far as I was concerned I saw my government and indeed any
future government would be bound by the principle of consent in
relation to going forward, but the principle of consent, provided that
as long as the principle of consent was parallel with and part of self-
determination ... fine, that's what we needed'.[180] In essence this is
what the Downing Street Declaration achieved for Fianna Fáil: the
concept of self-determination was now recognized as a central principle guiding the peace process. As a result, the process can be clearly
distinguished from that which Fianna Fáil was presented with under
the Anglo-Irish Agreement when it returned to power in 1987.

THE 1994 CEASEFIRE

The ceasefire that was announced in August 1994 was a huge achievement and Reynolds played a major part in its attainment. Immediately
after the presentation of the Downing Street Declaration, Sinn Féin
put a dampener on the celebrations in Dublin by reacting unenthusi-
astically. Reynolds was keen to point out the need for an early decision from the republican movement as to whether it could accept the
declaration.[181] Dick Spring was also clear in this rejection of Sinn
Féin's demand for talks with both governments for the provision of
clarification.[182] But, while Major was plain in his refusal to give clarification to republicans on issues relating to the declaration, Reynolds,
as always, presented the impression of being much more patient and
eager to keep the republican movement on board. He confirmed that
he would be willing to provide clarity on a number of points which
had been requested by Sinn Féin.[183]

Over the next couple of months Reynolds made a number of
attempts to convince Sinn Féin to accept the declaration. Addressing
the Irish Association, Reynolds highlighted positive points which he
felt had 'yet to be appreciated' by the republican movement. He
called on it to face the 'task ahead [which is] to practice real republicanism and reach out to the other tradition and begin in earnest the
task of reconciliation, not allowing ourselves to be discouraged by the
inevitable rebuffs along the way'.[184] The two governments were keen
to highlight for Sinn Féin the dangers of becoming isolated from the
governments' peace plans by refusing to embrace the opportunity pre-

sented by the Downing Street Declaration.[185] In another keynote speech Reynolds addressed what were perceived to be the shortcomings of the Downing Street Declaration. On the question of whether the clause relating to self-determination was a sufficient recognition of the right, he made an appeal not to allow the 'peace process to be blocked because of basic misunderstandings about how self-determination operates in international law and international politics and because something unattainable was being sought that was not consistent with international norms'.[186] He sought to convince republicans to face the realities in relation to the concept of self-determination and realize that what had been achieved represented a considerable advancement and a pragmatic position. By the end of January 1994 Patrick Mayhew hinted that there might be a change of mind on the issue of clarification. He and Dick Spring believed that to set a deadline for Sinn Féin and the IRA to accept the document would be counterproductive.[187] Reynolds was central to the change in position on clarification. Having convinced the British government on this issue, Reynolds also acted as an intermediary in subsequent communications between Sinn Féin and the British government.

Other factors were perhaps more successful in changing Sinn Féin's position; the call from the United States President, Bill Clinton, to react positively to the declaration;[188] the visit by Adams to the US; and the removal of section 31 of the Republic's Broadcasting Act. All of these provided Sinn Féin with glimpses of the extent to which they could benefit from becoming part of a very broad and powerful nationalist partnership. Hennessey has made this point; he has suggested that 'the key factor influencing the republican movement was probably the belief that there would never be a better chance to construct a pan-nationalist alliance from Belfast to Dublin to Washington which would be too powerful for the British to resist'.[189] There is no doubt that this was a key consideration for republicans and was as important as the Downing Street Declaration, given that they never accepted the principles outlined in the declaration. In other words, the ceasefire was more of a strategic policy shift than a reassessment of republican principles.

The nature of the clarification that was provided in May 1994 once again questions the importance of the Downing Street Declaration, on its own, in bringing about the ceasefire. The British government once again reiterated its constitutional stance in relation to Northern Ireland, as laid out in the Downing Street Declaration, but it pointed out that acceptance of the declaration was not a prerequisite to joining talks, only a ceasefire was required. The contents of the statement released by the British government simply confirmed much of what had been stated by the British government previously, which substantiates the view that the republican movement were simply trying to stall the process.[190] This gives extra credence to Hennessey's argument that it was Sinn Féin's desire to become involved in the process and to extend its power base that influenced the decision to call a ceasefire. If Sinn Féin did not, as Reynolds said, 'appreciate the importance of the declaration', the ceasefire was therefore very much the result of Reynolds' decision to make it a priority and of his ability to meet the demands of the IRA in a way that did not isolate the bulk of unionism. The Downing Street Declaration was crucial on an ideological basis but it was Reynolds' persistence through discussions with Sinn Féin and commitments which he made (as he outlined above) on behalf of the Irish government in the aftermath of that declaration that succeeded in bringing about the ceasefire.[191] Adams has pointed to the importance attached to the commitments made by the Irish government and by Irish America in 1994 and to the fact that he was able to report to the IRA that 'there was an identity of view between Sinn Féin, the SDLP and the Irish government on a range of issues' in persuading the IRA to call a ceasefire.[192] This was particularly crucial given that the collapse of the back channel of communications between the IRA and the British government had damaged relations and led to further distrust.[193]

Once clarification had been provided, considerable pressure was placed on the IRA to respond and 'to end the violence and to accept the generosity of the latest gesture and come into the process'.[194] The Irish government was still attempting to court republicans. Reynolds outlined the work that Irish officials were undertaking at an intergovernmental level to 'expand North–South co-operation in the various social and economic sectors'.[195] There were also discussions about the negotiations for the framework documents. Emily O'Reilly in the *Sunday Business Post* reported that the Irish government was seeking to increase cross-border co-operation through the establishment of executive bodies in a number of areas, which she described as 'pursuing a united Ireland in all but name'.[196] Later in the month, the Northern Ireland Office confirmed the Government of Ireland Act would be changed as part of an overall settlement.[197]

When the ceasefire was finally announced on 31 August 1994 there was a mixed reaction. Albert Reynolds was obviously very pleased that his efforts had brought a satisfactory conclusion. Speaking in the aftermath of the IRA announcement, he immediately declared that the government was 'willing to recognize in practical ways without delay the electoral mandate of Sinn Féin'.[198] The Irish government accepted that the ceasefire would be permanent.[199] Fianna Fáil TD for Donegal, Dr Jim McDaid, prided himself on his party's achievement, declaring that because of the party's history it had been 'well placed to bring about a ceasefire' and had done so by not 'abandoning hope' when others had.[200]

Both prior to and after the ceasefire the Irish government was keen to assure unionists that no secret deal had been agreed. Dick Spring and Albert Reynolds vowed that the Irish government would not attempt to win joint rule over Northern Ireland; Reynolds claimed that he was aware of and understood unionist objections to such an arrangement,[201] while Dick Spring stated 'unequivocally that joint authority is not on the Irish government's agenda ... we are not seeking a greater role for the Irish government in the governance of Northern Ireland'.[202] In early September, Reynolds made it clear that there 'is no deal. There are no hidden agreements'.[203] The British government had made similar gestures to unionists, promising Molyneaux 'full consultation' on talks with Dublin in the search for agreement on a future framework for talks.[204]

However, amid language aimed at persuading unionists to accept the good faith of both the Irish government and the IRA ceasefire, Reynolds was rapidly showing Sinn Féin the benefits of the ceasefire. Within a couple of days of the ceasefire announcement, Reynolds announced that he would meet with Adams for the first time.[205] This exacerbated differences of interpretation about the ceasefire statement which had emerged between the two governments. The Irish government expressed no problem in accepting the permanency of the ceasefire, while the British government and unionists took a different view in the absence of the actual word 'permanent'. In a statement on 16 September, Major welcomed the ceasefire but stressed: 'We [the British government] need to know from their words and their actions that this is a firm and unequivocal decision. They are nearly there. I hope they will have the courage to remove ambiguities and make a clear statement everyone wishes to hear.'[206] In contrast to this, Reynolds, in his meeting with Adams and Hume, said he would be continuing with his endeavours to achieve progress in the peace process despite criticism from both unionists and the British government.[207] In a statement issued on behalf of the three leaders they argued that peace necessitated 'bringing everyone in to sit around the table and to work out a new future, a new accommodation for the two traditions of this island'.[208] The Irish government and Reynolds concentrated once again on what was necessary in order to maintain the political momentum which was dictated to them by movement within the republican organization.

CONCLUSION

This chapter has illustrated a number of factors in relation to the Irish government's role in the peace process and, in particular, that of the Reynolds administration. Firstly, the analysis of the political environment which Reynolds inherited when he came to power offers a new understanding of his commitment to the peace process; it was informed by contemporaneous debates and by the fact that momentum for an alternate approach for involving Sinn Féin in talks already existed. We can conclude that the reason why the peace process took on a new momentum during Reynolds' administration was a combination of his business-like and public approach to the issue[209] and the existence of a new set of circumstances which were more amenable to the idea of a process including Sinn Féin and constitutional change on the part of the Republic.

Most importantly, and what is stressed here, is that Fianna Fáil in this period was motivated in the main by the construction of a pan-nationalist alliance. This has been overshadowed by the tendency to view the Irish government's role in the peace process within the confines of Anglo-Irish relations. The Irish government's role in this period was not, as many suggest, informed by the Anglo-Irish Agreement or by interests relating to Anglo-Irish relations. As was argued in the previous chapter, Fianna Fáil decided to work with the Anglo-Irish Agreement because of the international obligation to do so; both Charles Haughey and Albert Reynolds were consistent in the search for an alternative plan. This alternative vision was informed by movements and initiatives originating from and created within northern nationalism and republicanism. The alternative perspective presented here also challenges the perceived link between the Anglo-Irish Agreement, the peace process and the Good Friday Agreement. While the Anglo-Irish Agreement institutionalized the idea of joint sponsorship of each government's respective community, which did characterize both Haughey's and Reynolds' view of their role in the search for a settlement, it did not spawn a joint governmental approach. This was only achieved in the Ahern–Blair era. The existence of a good personal relationship between Reynolds and Major simply enabled the production of the Downing Street Declaration despite Reynolds' commitment to the interests of the pan-nationalist alliance. It did not mean that a joint governmental approach existed. The Anglo-Irish Agreement and the Good Friday Agreement generated different approaches; the former provided for joint sponsorship of individual communities, while at the heart of the Good Friday Agreement is the idea that the two governments should act as co-guarantors of the agreement. The institutions of the Anglo-Irish Agreement and the Anglo-Irish arena provided the obvious avenue for a peace process which originated from pan-nationalism to proceed. However, this did not happen until consensus had been reached within nationalism. Reynolds envisaged that any eventual settlement would be constructed within the framework of Anglo-Irish relations, but in the early years of the peace process bringing about the ceasefire through the development of a strong pan-nationalist alliance took precedence. Reynolds and the Irish government envisaged that a wider process, which involved the British government and reconciliation with unionists, would begin once an IRA ceasefire was in place.

Key to achieving that ceasefire, in ideological terms, was the statement relating to self-determination in the Downing Street Declaration in 1993. The Downing Street Declaration and the practical commitments made by Reynolds to Sinn Féin in the months before the ceasefire are the clearest illustrations of Reynolds' commitment to pan-nationalism and to making concessions to the republican movement in order to secure the IRA ceasefire. Reynolds' objective was to bring about an IRA ceasefire by challenging the arguments used by the IRA to justify its campaign. He did this by pursuing the interests of the pan-nationalist alliance and thereby demonstrating that progress could be achieved at a political level. It is important to say that, while Reynolds' approach appeared one-sided through his concentration on republicans and the pan-nationalist alliance, it was informed by two basic principles that had guided Fianna Fáil policy on Northern Ireland since the outbreak of the Troubles. The first was the natural affinity felt towards the nationalist community in Northern Ireland on the part of Fianna Fáil, as a republican party, and the Irish government in general. The second was the belief that the problem lay with IRA violence and it was within the capabilities of the Irish government, because of that affinity with northern nationalists, to do something to bring this to an end. As has already been stated, the Irish government, under Reynolds, also believed that the British government had it within its power to address loyalist violence. The quest

for a ceasefire involved making concessions to republicans and this
was sometimes detrimental to improving relations with unionists and
the British government. There is no doubt that Reynolds genuinely
wanted to secure peace for Northern Ireland, and he was willing to
sacrifice good relations with the British government and unionists at
this early point of the peace process because he believed he could
achieve more through his relations with republicans. He would work
to include both the British government and unionists as part of an
overall process but gave priority to republicans in order to secure the
IRA ceasefire. In putting into practice the principles that underlined
Fianna Fáil's approach to the Northern Ireland Troubles and bringing
about the IRA ceasefire in 1994, Reynolds succeeded where his predecessors, Lynch and Haughey, failed. This is the measure of his contribution, not just to ending the IRA campaign, but also to ensuring
that Fianna Fáil could claim the peace process and its successes as its
own.

Speaking after the IRA ceasefire announcement, Gerry Adams gave
his version of how it had come to pass: 'The last two years there has
been measurable progress. And there would not have been measurable progress if John Hume and I had not kick-started this initiative
and had the Dublin government not come in to bolster and support
us.'[210] Reynolds has described the role of his government by reference
to Hume's view of how it could contribute to the peace effort:

> I suppose the best description [of the Irish government's role in
> the peace process] I can give you is John Hume's words to me …
> the talks with Sinn Féin through Gerry Adams and himself had
> gone as far as they could go and unless the two governments
> became involved in the process there was nowhere else they
> could go so it would just fail at that stage as many other talks
> before them had failed. He put it to me that it was now up to the
> two governments to either take it and take it forward or else let
> it drop.[211]

These snippets, providing insights into Hume's and Adams' view of
Reynolds' role, are clearly similar. The idea of a peace process that
would bring about a ceasefire by facilitating Sinn Féin's route into
constitutional politics was in its early stages when Reynolds came to
government. His contribution was the cohesiveness which he gave to
the peace process through the relentless support and attention that he
gave to it while in office. His ability to bring the British government

on board was much more instrumental in ensuring co-operation between the two governments than any previous attempt and is an extremely important product of his administration. Even though a joint governmental approach was not really achieved until Ahern and Blair came to office, Reynolds nonetheless convinced Major to support the idea of the joint statement. His success is measured by the fact that he institutionalized a process, with Sinn Féin at its centre, as the approach of future Irish governments, even the one led by Fine Gael. The Fianna Fáil–Labour government under Reynolds produced a policy on Northern Ireland which commanded widespread support and produced a cross-party consensus.

NOTES

1. *The Irish Times* 1 Feb. 1992.
2. However, revelations about his tax affairs and accusations of bribery continue to overshadow Haughey's political legacy; see Keena, C. *Haughey's Millions: Charlie's money trail* (Dublin: Gill and Macmillan, 2001).
3. Mallie, E. and McKittrick, D. *The Fight for Peace: The secret story behind the Irish peace process* (London: Heinemann, 1996); Duignan, S. *One Spin on the Merry-Go-Round* (Dublin: Blackwater Press, 1996).
4. Interview with Albert Reynolds, 8 Aug. 2003.
5. Interview with Martin Mansergh, 12 Dec. 2002.
6. Dick Spring: Son of Kerry TD, Dan Spring; elected to local council as Labour Party candidate in 1979; elected as TD in 1981 and became a junior minister in the government; succeeded Michael O'Leary as leader of the Labour Party in 1982; Tánaiste and Minister for the Environment in the 1982 coalition with Fine Gael; Tánaiste and Minister for Foreign Affairs, 1992–4 in coalition with Fianna Fáil; retained these posts during the 'Rainbow Coalition' of Fine Gael, Labour and Democratic Left, 1994–7; lost his Dáil seat in 2002 to Sinn Féin's Martin Ferris in the constituency of Kerry North.
7. Jackson, A. *Ireland 1798–1998: Politics and war* (Oxford: Blackwell Publishers, 1999), p. 385.
8. Jackson, *Ireland 1798–1998*, p. 388.
9. Girvin, B. 'Northern Ireland and the Republic', in P. Mitchel and R. Wilford (eds), *Politics in Northern Ireland* (Oxford: Westview Press and PSAI Press, 1999), p. 227.
10. Joseph Lee points out that Charles Haughey had, in the aftermath of the New Ireland Forum, accepted the need for a new Constitution. This, according to Lee, was disguised by the media concentration on inter-party division subsequent to the Forum. Lee, J. 'Dynamics of Social and Political Change in the Republic', in D. Keogh and M.H. Haltzell (eds), *Northern Ireland and the Politics of Reconciliation* (Cambridge: Cambridge University Press, Woodrow Wilson Center Press, 1993), p. 131.
11. James Molyneaux: UUP MP for South Antrim, 1970–83 and for the Lagan Valley, 1983–97; leader of the UUP, 1979–95; returned to the Northern Ireland Assembly for South Antrim, 1982–6; stood down as leader in 1995.
12. *The Irish Times* 26 March 1990.
13. For a report on opinion polls on the issue in the Republic in both 1991 and 1992, see the *Irish News* 2 Oct. 1992.
14. Editorial, *The Irish Times* 2 March 1990.
15. Sunday *Independent* 18 March 1990.
16. Michael McDowell: Grandson of Eoin MacNeill, co-founder of the Gaelic League and founder of the Irish Volunteers; barrister at law since 1974; elected as Progressive Democrats TD for Dublin-South East in 1987; Attorney General, 1999–2002; President of the Progressive

Democrats since Feb. 2002; appointed Minister for Justice, Equality and Law Reform in 2002; became Tánaiste and leader of Progressive Democrats in 2006.

17. *The Irish Times* 18 Oct. 1990.
18. Sunday *Press* 20 Sept. 1992.
19. *The Irish Times* 15 March 1990.
20. *The Irish Times* 14 March 1990. This approach to constitutional change was adhered to by Fianna Fáil in future negotiations.
21. *The Irish Times* 9 April 1990. For a synopsis of the unionist argument that Irish irreden-tism, as espoused in Articles Two and Three of the 1937 Constitution, is a central cause of the Northern Ireland conflict, see McGarry, J. and O'Leary, B. *Explaining Northern Ireland: Broken images* (Oxford: Blackwell Publishers, 1995), pp. 97–105. Article 29.1 commits the State to 'the ideal of peace and friendly co-operation amongst nations'.
22. *The Irish Times* 6 Nov. 1989.
23. *The Irish Times* 10 Nov. 1990.
24. *The Irish Times* 14 March 1990.
25. *Irish News* 2 Jan. 1992.
26. As quoted in *The Irish Times* 8 Feb. 1992.
27. For a brief assessment of the failure of the Brooke dialogue, see Bew, P. and Gillespie, G. *Northern Ireland: A chronology of the Troubles 1968–1993*, pp. 277–8. For a discussion of the significance of the Brooke talks, see Arthur, P. 'The Brooke Initiative', *Irish Political Studies*, 7 (1992), pp. 111–5; see, in particular, Bloomfield, D. *Political Dialogue in Northern Ireland: The Brooke initiative, 1989–92* (London: Macmillan Press, 1998).
28. *The Irish Times* 13 Jan. 1992; see also Mary Holland's article in *The Irish Times* 16 Jan. 1992.
29. Cunningham, M. *British Government Policy in Northern Ireland 1969–2000* (Manchester: Manchester University Press, 2001), p. 88.
30. Gerry Adams, *An Phoblacht/Republican News* 29 March 1990.
31. Gerry Adams, *An Phoblacht/Republican News* 8 Feb. 1990.
32. Ibid.
33. Adams, G. *Hope and History: Making peace in Ireland* (Kerry: Brandon, 2003), pp. 106–7.
34. *The Irish Times* 24 Feb. 1992. For the difficulties associated with the ballot box and Armalite strategy, see O'Doherty, M. *The Trouble with Guns: Republican strategy and the Provisional IRA* (Belfast: The Blackstaff Press, 1998).
35. *The Irish Times* 23 June 1992. Gibney is widely believed to have made this speech at the behest of Adams. See Moloney, *A Secret History of the IRA*, pp. 399–401.
36. Mallie and McKittrick, *The Fight for Peace*, p. 135.
37. Martin McGuinness: Born in Derry in 1950; joined the IRA in 1970, becoming a leading figure and Chief of Staff in the late 1970s; elected as Sinn Féin MP in 1997 and MLA in 1998; Northern Ireland Minister for Education 1999–2002; he is the subject of a biogra-phy by Clarke, L. and Johnston, K. *Martin McGuinness: From guns to government* (Edinburgh: Mainstream Press, 2001).
38. *The Irish Times* 8 June 1992. Bishop Edward Daly had been a priest in Derry and present on Bloody Sunday 1972. The picture of him waving a white flag while moving an injured man to safety on that day is probably the most widely recognized image of Bloody Sunday, see his autobiography: Daly, Edward, *Mister, Are you a Priest?* (Dublin: Four Courts Press, 2001).
39. *The Irish Times* 27 June 1992.
40. Adams, *Hope and History*, p. 113.
41. Cunningham, *British Government Policy in Northern Ireland*, p. 160. Also see Dixon, P. *Northern Ireland: The politics of war and peace* (Hampshire: Palgrave, 2001). An account of how the conflict in Northern Ireland was internationalized and how this impacted on British policy can be found in Guelke, A. 'British Policy and International Dimensions of the Northern Ireland Conflict', *Regional Politics and Policy: An international journal*, 1, 2 (1991), pp. 140–60.
42. Cunningham, *British Government Policy in Northern Ireland*, pp. 161–2.
43. See Guelke, A. 'International and North/South Issues', in W. Crotty and D.E. Schmitt (eds), *Ireland and the Politics of Change* (London and New York: Longman, 1998), pp. 195–209.
44. Mansergh, M. 'The Background to the Irish Peace Process', in M. Cox, A. Guelke and F. Stephen (eds), *A Farewell to Arms? From 'long war' to long peace in Northern Ireland* (Manchester: Manchester University Press), p. 12.
45. Interview with Albert Reynolds, 8 Aug. 2003.

46. Ibid.
47. David Andrews, the Minister for Foreign Affairs in Reynolds' administration, had confirmed that he was inviting unionists into direct talks, *Dáil Éireann Debates* Vol. 416, Col. 880, Feb. 27 1992. See also *The Irish Times* 28 Feb. 1992.
48. Interview with Albert Reynolds, 8 Aug. 2003.
49. *Irish News* 14 Oct. 1992.
50. *Irish News* 9 March 1992.
51. Ibid.
52. Ibid.
53. *The Irish Times* 25 Feb. 1992.
54. Adams, G. *The Politics of Irish Freedom* (Kerry: Brandon, 1986), p. 19.
55. Interview with Albert Reynolds, 8 Aug. 2003; he was presumably referring to Section 75 of the Government of Ireland Act, which claimed that ultimate sovereignty over Northern Ireland rested with Westminster. Reynolds was not just influenced by Sinn Féin in bringing this on to the agenda. The SDLP had also pointed to the importance of the 1920 Government of Ireland Act; see McGarry, J. and O'Leary, B. *The Politics of Antagonism: Understanding Northern Ireland* (London: The Athlone Press, 1996), p. 319.
56. *The Irish Times* 19 Oct. 1992.
57. Ibid.
58. For an insight into how Seán Duignan, Reynolds' Press Officer, viewed the Taoiseach's dealing of Articles Two and Three, see Duignan, *One Spin on the Merry-Go-Round,* p. 100.
59. Tánaiste John Wilson at Strand Two talks, *Irish News* 1 Oct. 1992.
60. *Irish News* 20 Oct. 1992.
61. *The Irish Times* 16 Sept. 1992.
62. Sunday *Tribune* 20 Sept. 1992.
63. Saturday *Times* 19 Sept. 1992.
64. For criticism by the leader of Democratic Left, Proinsias De Rossa, see *The Irish Times* 16 Sept. 1992, and by leader of Fine Gael, John Bruton, see *Newsletter* 26 May 1992.
65. *Guardian* 28 April 1992.
66. See John Taylor, MP on the SDLP proposal in the *Irish News* 21 May 1992. See also Cadogan Group, *Northern Limits: The boundaries of the attainable in Northern Ireland politics* (Belfast: Cadogan Group, 1992) for a critique of the SDLP proposal. Their publications can be found on the internet: www.cadogan.org.
67. John Taylor MP accused the SDLP of 'sneaking' contents of Strand One discussions to the Irish Government within days of the resumption of the talks. *Newsletter* 3 May 1992.
68. *The Irish Times* 24 June 1992.
69. Ian Paisley: DUP leader and founder; MP, former MEP and MLA for North Antrim; Moderator of the Free Presbyterian Church.
70. *Irish News* 14 Sept. 1992. The DUP eventually walked out of the Strand Two talks because of this.
71. *The Irish Times* 28 April 1993.
72. Interview with Martin Mansergh, 12 Dec. 2002.
73. *The Irish Times* 7 Feb. 1992.
74. Mallie and McKittrick, *The Fight for Peace,* p. 161. The Irish government was not aware that the British government had developed a 'back-channel' of contacts with the IRA. See English, R. *Armed Struggle: A history of the IRA* (Oxford: Macmillan, 2003), pp. 267–8.
75. *The Irish Times* 30 Aug. 1993.
76. *The Irish Times* 26 April 1993.
77. See Michael McDowell's criticism in *The Irish Times* 27 April 1993 and John Bruton's argument that concentration on self-determination could not bring reconciliation in *The Irish Times* 4 May 1993.
78. *The Irish Times* 3 May 1993.
79. *The Irish Times* 10 May 1993.
80. *The Irish Times* 11 Sept. 1993.
81. This chapter is not intended to provide a narrative account of the meetings between Irish officials, Hume and the republican movement. For such an account and of the origins of the idea for the Joint Declaration see Mallie, E. and McKittrick, D. *Endgame in Ireland: The search for peace in Northern Ireland* (Belfast: Blackstaff Press, 1994), Chapter 7; Adams, *Hope and History,* pp. 105–7; Moloney, *A Secret History of the IRA,* pp. 408–12.

82. *Agreed Statement from John Hume and Gerry Adams* published by Social Democratic and Labour Party, Belfast 25 Sept. 1993.
83. See Geraldine Kennedy's report in *The Irish Times* 27 Sept. 1993.
84. *The Irish Times* 2 Oct. 1993.
85. *The Irish Times* 18 Oct. 1993.
86. For a brief synopsis of the political reaction to the statement, see the *The Irish Times* 20 Oct.1993.
87. *Newsletter* 5 Oct. 1993.
88. *Newsletter* 8 Oct. 1993.
89. As quoted in *Newsletter* 22 Oct. 1993.
90. *The Irish Times* 20 Oct. 1993.
91. *Independent* 18 Oct. 1993.
92. *Independent* 8 Oct. 1993.
93. Shankill bombing: An IRA bomb exploded prematurely in a butcher's on the Shankill Road in Belfast on the 13 Oct. 1993, killing the IRA bomber, Thomas Begley and nine other civilians. The bomb had been aimed at the headquarters of the UDA, which was located above the shop; no UDA members were present on that day. The peace process suffered hugely and looked close to collapse when Gerry Adams was photographed carrying the coffin of the bomber.
94. Reynolds has verified that his aim in declaring Hume–Adams dead was to keep it alive. See for example Mallie and McKittrick, *Endgame in Ireland,* p. 130; Duignan, *One Spin on the Merry-Go-Round,* p. 106.
95. *The Irish Times* 25, 26 Oct. 1993.
96. Interview with Albert Reynolds, 8 Aug. 2003.
97. Bourke, R. *Peace in Ireland: The war of ideas* (London: Pimlico, 2003), p. 281.
98. Connolly, M. and Loughlin, J. 'Reflections on the Anglo-Irish Agreement', *Government and Opposition,* 21 (1986), p. 150.
99. McGarry and O'Leary, *The Politics of Antagonism,* p. 234.
100. MacGinty, R. and Darby, J. *Guns and Government: The management of the Northern Ireland peace process* (Hampshire: Palgrave, 2002), pp. 21–2.
101. MacGinty and Darby, *Guns and Government,* p. 58.
102. In 'A Response to the Government of the Irish Republic' the UUP expressed disappointment at some of the Irish government's delegation, in particular Fianna Fáil's Pádraig Flynn, who had 'resorted to old and out-dated Nationalist rhetoric'. The submission went on to welcome 'helpful responses' from Desmond O'Malley of the Progressive Democrats: *Submission to the Plenary Meeting on Strand Two at Parliament Buildings,* Belfast, Friday 24 July 1992. Eamon Delaney, an ex-official at the Department of Foreign Affairs, has stated that, in the course of the 1992 talks, despite the fact that agreement was very close, the Irish government accepted that 'the Provos would have to be stitched into a settlement': Delaney, E. *Accidental Diplomat: My years in the Irish foreign service, 1987–1995* (Dublin and New York: New Island), p. 344.
103. Arthur, P. *Special Relationships: Britain, Ireland and the Northern Ireland problem* (Belfast: The Blackstaff Press, 2000), p. 144.
104. Arthur, P. 'Anglo-Irish Relations and Constitutional Policy', in Mitchell and Wilford (eds), *Politics in Northern Ireland,* p. 252.
105. Goodall, Sir D. 'Hillsborough to Belfast: Is it the last lap?', in M. Elliott (ed), *The Long Road to Peace in Northern Ireland: Peace lectures from the Institute of Irish Studies at Liverpool University* (Liverpool: Liverpool University Press, 2002), p. 123. See also Goodall, D. 'Actually It's All Working out Almost according to Plan', *Parliamentary Brief,* 5, 6 (May/June 1998).
106. O'Duffy, B. 'British and Irish conflict regulation from Sunningdale to Belfast, Part II: Playing for a draw 1985–1999', *Nations and Nationalism,* 6, 3 (2000), p. 404, italics in original.
107. See Cochrane, F. 'Any Takers? The isolation of Northern Ireland', *Political Studies,* 42, (1994), pp. 378–95; and the subsequent debate in Dixon, P. 'Internationalization and Unionist Isolation: A response to Fergal Cochrane', *Political Studies,* 43 (1995), pp. 497–505; Cochrane, F. 'The Isolation of Northern Ireland', *Political Studies* 43 (1995), pp. 506–8.
108. Brian Cowen speaking on *Hearts and Minds,* BBC1 Northern Ireland, 12 June 2003.
109. Conor Lenihan believes relations between Ireland and Britain have improved immeasurably since he came to the Dáil in 1997. Close relations and co-operation now exist in ways

that would not, in his view, have been possible in 1997. Interview with Conor Lenihan, 16 Nov. 2005.

110. Bew, P. and Gillespie, G. *Northern Ireland: A chronology of the Troubles, 1968–1999* (Dublin: Gill and Macmillan, 1999), p. 284.
111. *The Irish Times* 31 May 1993.
112. *The Irish Times* 16 June 1993.
113. Finlay, F. *Snakes and Ladders* (Dublin: New Island Books, 1998), pp. 191–2.
114. *The Irish Times* 19 June 1993.
115. See *The Irish Times* 19 June 1993; see also the *The Irish Times* 21 June 1993.
116. For John Bruton's reaction, see *The Irish Times* 22 June 1993.
117. *The Irish Times* 9 July 1993.
118. *The Irish Times* 26 July 1993.
119. *The Irish Times* 24 July 1993.
120. *The Irish Times* 9 Sept. 1993.
121. *The Irish Times* 30 Oct. 1993.
122. Ibid.
123. Major, J. *An Autobiography* (London: Harper Collins, 2000), pp. 450–1.
124. Duignan, *One Spin on the Merry-Go-Round,* p. 118.
125. For Reynolds' response to this revelation and impact on negotiations, see Duignan, *One Spin on the Merry-Go-Round,* pp. 122–3.
126. Mallie and McKittrick, *The Fight for Peace,* pp. 229–30.
127. *Guardian* 2 December 1993; see also *Dáil Éireann Debates* 436, 1072, 1 Dec. 1993.
128. *Belfast Telegraph* 8 Nov. 1993.
129. Mallie and McKittrick, *The Fight for Peace,* pp. 256–63, Duignan, *One Spin on the Merry-Go-Round,* pp. 122–6; Hennessey, T. *The Northern Ireland Peace Process: Ending the Troubles?* (Dublin: Gill and Macmillan, 2000), pp. 75–80.
130. See Finlay, *Snakes and Ladders,* pp. 202–3.
131. Interview with Albert Reynolds, 8 Aug. 2003.
132. Ibid.
133. Ibid. Presumably he is referring to section 31 of that Act, which banned both IRA and Sinn Féin spokespersons from RTÉ.
134. *The Irish Times* 28 April 1993.
135. *The Irish Times* 29 May 1993.
136. *The Irish Times* 19 June 1993.
137. Finlay, *Snakes and Ladders,* see pp. 180–82.
138. Finlay, *Snakes and Ladders,* p. 182.
139. As quoted in Ryan, T. *Dick Spring: A safe pair of hands* (Dublin: Blackwater Press, 1993), p. 195.
140. *The Irish Times* 25 May 1993.
141. *The Irish Times* 1 July 1993.
142. *The Irish Times* 9 July 1993.
143. Ibid.
144. See Joe Carroll's article in *The Irish Times* 10 July 1993.
145. *New Ulster Defender,* editorial, April 1993.
146. *The Irish Times* 16 July 1993.
147. See Frank Millar's report in *The Irish Times* 11 Sept. 1993.
148. *The Irish Times* 11 Sept. 1993.
149. *The Irish Times* 13 Sept. 1993.
150. *The Irish Times* 28 Oct. 1993.
151. Dick Spring, *Dáil Éireann Debates* Vol. 435, Col. 256, 27 Oct. 1993.
152. *Sunday Tribune* 7 Nov. 1993. John Bruton: Elected as Fine Gael TD in 1969; Parliamentary Secretary to the Minister for Education, 1973–7; Fine Gael Spokesman for Agriculture, 1977; Minister for Finance, 1981, 1986; Minister for Industry, Trade, Commerce and Tourism, 1982; elected leader of Fine Gael, 1990; became Taoiseach in December 1994 in the Rainbow Coalition involving Fine Gael, Labour and Democratic Left; deposed from leadership, 2001.
153. *Sunday Tribune* 7 Nov. 1993. Democratic Left later merged with the Labour Party.
154. *An Phoblacht/Republican News* 4 Nov. 1993.
155. *The Irish Times* 6 Nov. 1993.

156. Fergus Finlay, Spring's advisor who drafted the speech, said that despite this mistake the speech made a considerable impact both on the opinion of unionists and on the British government:Finlay, *Snakes and Ladders,* p. 196.
157. *The Irish Times* 5 Nov. 1993.
158. *Dáil Éireann Debates* Vol. 435, Col. 2188, 18 Nov. 1993.
159. Major, *An Autobiography,* p. 451.
160. The SDLP's Séamus Mallon confirmed that three of the points included in the six principles proposed by Spring had originated from the Hume–Adams document, *Newsletter* 30 Oct. 1993.
161. *Newsletter* 29 Oct. 1993.
162. Ibid.
163. *Dáil Éireann Debates* Vol. 437, Cols 774–5, 15 Dec. 1993.
164. Albert Reynolds addressing The Irish Association, *The Irish Times* 11 Jan. 1994.
165. Bourke, *Peace in Ireland,* p. 291.
166. *Dáil Éireann Debates* Vol. 437, Col. 741, 15 Dec. 1993.
167. *The Irish Times* 13 Dec. 1993.
168. Mansergh, 'Mountain-Climbing Irish Style: The hidden challenges of the peace process', p. 111.
169. *Newsletter* 23 Dec. 1993.
170. *The Irish Times* 18 Dec. 1993.
171. Interview with Albert Reynolds 8 Aug. 2003. Sinn Féin submissions to the Forum were generally well received. Interview with Mary O'Rourke, 15 Nov. 2005.
172. Arthur, P. 'The Anglo-Irish joint declaration: Towards a lasting peace', *Government and Opposition,* 29, 2 (1994), p. 225.
173. See Sunday *Business Post* 19 Dec. 1993.
174. Interview with Noel Treacy, 1 Dec. 2005.
175. John Coakley has pointed out that the veto given to the Republic's electorate on any settlement may have consequences for any future referendum on a united Ireland. Coakley, J. 'Conclusion: New strains of Unionism and Nationalism', in J. Coakley (ed), *Changing Shades of Orange and Green: Redefining the Union and the Nation in contemporary Ireland* (Dublin: University College Dublin Press, 2002), p. 151.
176. Interview with Aengus Ó Snodaigh, 12 June 2003.
177. Interview with Martin Ferris, 12 June 2003.
178. McCartney, R. 'The McCartney Report on Consent', Belfast: UK/Unionist Party, 1997, as reproduced in McCartney, R. *Reflections on Liberty, Democracy and the Union* (Dublin: Maunsel and Co., 2001), p. 119.
179. McCartney, *Reflections on Liberty, Democracy and the Union,* pp. 122–3.
180. Interview with Albert Reynolds, 8 Aug. 2003.
181. *The Irish Times* 23 Dec. 1993.
182. Ibid.
183. *The Irish Times* 17 Dec. 1993.
184. *The Irish Times* 11 Jan. 1994.
185. Dick Spring, *The Irish Times* 14 Jan. 1994.
186. *The Irish Times* 21 Jan. 1994.
187. *The Irish Times* 29 Jan. 1994.
188. *The Irish Times* 2 Feb. 1994.
189. Hennessey, *The Northern Ireland Peace Process,* p. 84.
190. Statement released by Northern Ireland Office 19 May 1994, Linenhall Library, Hume/Adams Box 4.
191. Moloney details a 14-point proposal sent by the Reynolds' government to the IRA. The commitments contained within this would be implemented in the event of an IRA ceasefire, Moloney, *A Secret History of the IRA,* pp. 424–5.
192. Adams, *Hope and History,* pp. 174–6.
193. Adams, *Hope and History,* p. 144.
194. Dick Spring, *The Irish Times* 5 May 1994.
195. *Irish News* 1 July 1994.
196. Sunday *Business Post* 28 Aug. 1994.
197. Sunday *Tribune* 28 Aug. 1994.
198. *The Irish Times* 1 Sept. 1994.

199. Ibid.
200. *Derry Journal* 2 Sept. 1994.
201. *Irish Press* 1 July 1994.
202. *Irish News* 14 July 1994.
203. *Derry Journal* 2 Sept. 1994.
204. *Irish Press* 20 July 1994.
205. *The Irish Times* 3 Sept. 1994.
206. Northern Ireland Information Service, *Statement by Prime Minister on Northern Ireland,* 16 Sept. 1994.
207. *The Irish Times* 7 Sept. 1994.
208. Ibid.
209. Mary O'Rourke referred to the new business-like approach which Reynolds brought to the peace process. Interview with Mary O'Rourke, 15 Nov. 2005.
210. *Irish News* 26 July 1994.
211. Interview with Albert Reynolds, 8 Aug. 2003.

CHAPTER FOUR

Bertie Ahern: From opposition leader to peacemaker 1994–8

INTRODUCTION

Bertie Ahern succeeded Albert Reynolds as leader of Fianna Fáil on 17 November 1994. He also became leader of the opposition when Fine Gael, Labour and Democratic Left reached agreement and formed what became known as the Rainbow Coalition. However, Ahern became Taoiseach in June 1997 and he oversaw the renewal of the IRA ceasefire, just weeks after his election as Taoiseach, and the conclusion of the Good Friday Agreement in April 1998. This chapter not only offers an investigation of the significance of the Good Friday Agreement for Fianna Fáil but also demonstrates that Reynolds' view of Fianna Fáil's role in the peace process and towards the republican movement was inherited by Ahern and his party. An examination of the period of opposition for Fianna Fáil between December 1994 and June 1997 provides an interesting insight into how Fianna Fáil under Ahern viewed its own role within the peace process, but also into how it saw the centrality of Sinn Féin within that process. However, it will become apparent that once Ahern came to power his government faced a struggle between the need to fulfil the commitments of pan-nationalism and the desire to find agreement with unionism, which required a more balanced approach. Ahern ultimately decided to move from the position which he strongly advocated in opposition, and this allowed for the completion of the Good Friday Agreement. The implications for Anglo-Irish relations are also discussed. The chapter fills a gap in the academic literature, which has tended not to examine in any great depth the factors influencing the Irish government's role in the negotiations leading to the Good Friday Agreement.

FIANNA FÁIL IN OPPOSITION, DECEMBER 1994–JUNE 1997

On his departure from office Reynolds was praised for his contribution to Northern Ireland[1] and there was much speculation as to how the process would proceed in light of the change of government.[2] The absence of Martin Mansergh meant that party political changes were accompanied by a break in continuity in officials working on Northern Ireland.[3] Ahern vowed that he would continue to give prominence to Northern Ireland, and as the leading opposition party Fianna Fáil broke the cross-party consensus and was critical of the Rainbow Coalition's policy on Northern Ireland.

The Framework Documents of February 1995

While the relationship between Fianna Fáil and the government during its period in opposition was characterized by hostility and disagreement, there was a marked agreement within the Dáil when the Framework Documents were accepted. This was mainly due to the fact that Fianna Fáil had been heavily involved in the negotiations with the British government relating to the Documents while in government in 1994. Speaking at the Forum for Peace and Reconciliation, Mary O'Rourke welcomed the Framework Documents on behalf of Fianna Fáil both for their commitment to the three-stranded approach and also on the basis that the 'balance of constitutional issues is consistent with the position we had negotiated'.[4] John Bruton presented the Framework Documents to the Dáil on 22 February 1995 and explained that the Documents represented 'a shared understanding between the two governments to assist discussion and negotiation involving the Northern Ireland political parties … it is not a blueprint rigidly to be imposed on the people of Northern Ireland'.[5] The publication of the Framework Documents heralded a period of consensus in the Dáil[6] and confirmed that Fine Gael had not diverged from the approach adopted by the Reynolds administration.

Ahern's speech in the course of the Dáil debate illustrated the nature of the debate taking place within Fianna Fáil at that time on issues relating to Articles Two and Three and how the prospect of changing these articles could be reconciled with Fianna Fáil's republican roots and traditional definition of the nation. It also highlighted the lack of concern within Fianna Fáil at the implications of the Framework Documents. Ahern claimed that an acceptance of the principle of consent by Fianna Fáil was not new, as Charles Haughey formally conceded it in his summit with Margaret Thatcher in 1980. The Downing Street Declaration, Ahern said, represented 'a new development', given that 'self-determination and consent were the twin pillars'.[7] For Fianna Fáil, the Framework Documents represented the continuation of a crucial process both of reconciling the principle of consent with the concept of self-determination and of ensuring that self-determination was given equal recognition. So, while there had been no agreement as to the wording of constitutional change,[8] there was obviously a cross-party consensus now as to the need for such change, and Fianna Fáil was apparently debating the extent to which it could shift from the original articles. Accepting that 'constitutional balance' was essential to any overall settlement,[9] Ahern linked any constitutional changes to the ideology of the leading 1916 figure, Patrick Pearse. According to Ahern, Pearse saw the Irish people as sovereign and called for the right of the Irish people to govern themselves without external interference.[10] This, he argued, was reflected in the 1937 Constitution. Ahern argued that the principle of consent was consistent with this because, 'as a result of balanced constitutional change, the ultimate sovereignty on whether to remain in the Union or join a united Ireland will also be rested in the people of the North ... British territorial sovereignty over Northern Ireland will be gone. We will have helped to place sovereignty unequivocally in the hands of the people.'[11] This argument is indeed very compelling; the principle of consent represented a concession, but the transfer of sovereignty from the British government to the people of the island, to be decided in concurrent referenda, was very clearly in harmony with traditional Fianna Fáil republican doctrine.

Ahern also made it clear that any constitutional change would not alter the 'wording in its present form in order to maintain the integrity of the Irish nation ... we are entitled to say that the whole of Ireland belongs to the Irish nation in all its diversity'.[12] This was the position maintained by Fianna Fáil in the negotiations which led to the Good Friday Agreement and this enabled the party to claim it had not abandoned its republican roots, given that this formula did not affect the integrity of the nation. Having outlined his position on the articles and the definition of the nation as a pluralist one, Ahern and other Fianna Fáil deputies made it clear that the party was not prepared to shift from this stance.[13] Ahern evoked the legacy of Wolfe Tone as guiding his party's desire to achieve his ideal of 'substituting for Protestant, Catholic and Dissenter the common name of Irishman' but declared that he would not be prepared to accept a '26 county definition of the Irish nation, which would exclude Northern nationalists'.[14] He reiterated this line of reasoning when later challenged on his party's approval of plans to change Articles Two and Three. Having restated his point on the transfer of sovereignty, he extended the argument by utilizing an analysis originating from Martin Mansergh; the principle of consent amounted to 'a self-limitation on the manner in which that right [to self-determination] is to be exercised' and was in essence the Irish people's right to decide their own volition.[15] Fianna Fáil could therefore comfortably reconcile itself to the ideological implications of the Framework Documents.

The contrasting reactions from nationalism and unionism to the Framework Documents would seem to confirm an impression that the Framework Documents were one-sided. Despite assurances from the Minister of Foreign Affairs, Dick Spring, that, 'if the document creates difficulties, which it may well do on all sides, that is a matter to be sorted out in negotiations',[16] both the DUP and UUP reacted angrily.[17] Members of the Ulster Unionist Party appeared angry at their leader's perceived inability to alter the mindset of the British government.[18] This related to a major cause of concern among unionists that they were being isolated from the realms of decision-making at Westminster.[19] David Trimble said that the Documents had been produced without consultation with his party: 'The government promised to consult with us but in fact didn't do so. We were not consulted on this document and it's been produced clearly going against the representations that we made.'[20] Nigel Dodds, DUP, made a similar point about the lack of consultation with unionist opinion and claimed that, because the Irish government under Bruton had remained in consultation with Hume and Adams, the Framework Documents were the latest 'off-spring' of the Hume–Adams agreement and were the result of British government efforts to meet the demands of Hume–Adams.[21] Ian Paisley confirmed that his party would be rejecting the Documents and would be actively working against them, while the UUP promised a backlash of the kind witnessed in the aftermath of the Anglo-Irish Agreement.[22] A statement by the Progressive Unionist Party (PUP) described the feelings of isolation felt by unionists as a result of the Framework Documents and claimed that the Documents contained 'a blatant bias towards Irish nationalism and this perception is reinforced by the lack of criticism from that quarter'.[23]

Beyond the obvious fury at not being properly consulted and the perception of a nationalist bias on the part of both governments, unionists had a number of specific ideological objections to the Framework Documents. They centred on the proposed provisions relating to North–South bodies. In the course of the Commons debate on the Framework Documents, UUP MP, Ken Maginnis, challenged John Major on the proposed North–South bodies: 'How can you endorse harmonisation of policies between Northern Ireland and the Irish Republic when Northern Ireland is part of the United Kingdom by the will of its people, demonstrated at the ballot box?'[24] The proposed North–South institutions were viewed by unionists as having the potential to bring about a united Ireland without their consent. The wording of the consent principle within the Framework Document was seen to possess the same danger. This particular criticism was voiced by the UUP and represented the main source of unionist concern:

> The Framework Document [sic] undermines the principle of consent. Mr Major's assertion that the consent of the majority is a guarantee of Northern Ireland remaining within the United Kingdom is meaningless. The whole purpose of the document is ultimately to render such consent unnecessary through a process of 'harmonisation' which will lead inexorably to joint authority between Belfast and Dublin, and ultimately a united Ireland.[25]

The UUP statement also referred to paragraph 47 of the Framework Documents as encompassing a threat to unionists: 'If the Assembly collapses, joint authority would be imposed by the two governments [who] would ensure that the functions of the North–South body continue to develop, whatever the will of the people.'[26]

A joint statement issued by a large number of unionist organizations, including the UUP, DUP, PUP and the UDP, declared: 'Representatives of the broad family were unanimous in their rejection of the framework document. The aims and objectives of these documents have nothing positive to offer to unionists. The representatives interpreted the documents to be a vehicle towards the destruction of the Union and the ultimate achievement of a united Ireland.'[27] In short, unionists objected to the Framework Documents because they argued that the concentration upon institutions aimed at 'harmonisation' across the island rendered the principle of consent obsolete, since such a process would result in a *de facto* united Ireland. The principle of consent had been further undermined by what Peter

Robinson referred to as a process whereby: 'The self-determination rights, possessed by "the people of Northern Ireland alone", have been plundered, carried off and expropriated by "the people of the island of Ireland alone".'[28] The feeling that the Framework Documents illustrated a lack of interest on the part of the British government in upholding the rights of the unionist community, in direct contrast to the active interest displayed by the Irish government on behalf of northern nationalists, exacerbated the unionist community's worries about consent and North–South bodies.[29] As a result of the publication of the Framework Documents, James Molyneaux declared that the understanding between his party and the British government had now been concluded and that his party was now planning to vote against the government in appropriate circumstances because Major had 'rejected our policy ... what the two governments are now doing is to sentence Northern Ireland to division'.[30]

Richard English has since argued that the Framework Documents, like the Downing Street Declaration, sought to 'create a symmetrical political balance in relation to Northern Ireland [through] respectful references and rhetorical guarantees of equal legitimacy'.[31] Paul Dixon has maintained that this symmetry was never possible since 'the British government cannot be both an advocate of the unionist cause and a neutral arbiter between the parties in Northern Ireland', and that the Framework Documents 'underlined further the isolation of Ulster Unionism'.[32] Brendan O'Duffy has claimed that the major innovation in the Framework Documents was the British government's recognition that the two opposing sovereign claims over Northern Ireland are 'comparable, if not equivalent' and that this concession was won as a result of the establishment of an alliance within constitutional nationalism which had effected this 'fundamental change in constitutive sovereignty'.[33] This, however, brings us back to Dixon's point that viewing the two opposing causes as equal is impossible. This has meant that the peace process, rather than managing to reconcile both causes, has simply concentrated on one to the exclusion of the other. The Framework Documents clearly illustrated the exclusion of unionism. The reiteration to unionists that the principle of consent was in place to protect them was not sufficient to compensate for such advances by the Irish government and nationalists in both ideological terms and, most importantly, in terms of the proposed North–South bodies. Thus, attempts by both Bertie Ahern and John Bruton to assuage unionists' fears that they would be coerced into a united Ireland by pledging that 'a durable arrangement' would have to be fair in its respect for both traditions[34] did not ease unionist anger. The contrast between the extensive consultation with Hume and Adams and the lack of consultation with unionists did nothing to undermine the belief that the main concern of both governments at this stage was to ensure the continuation of the IRA ceasefire.

The publication of the Framework Documents in February 1995 confirmed Bruton's adherence to the approach laid down by Reynolds in negotiations with the British government in the first part of his time in office. Having earlier labelled Bruton's policy on Northern Ireland 'rubbish',[35] Sinn Féin changed its view of that administration.[36] However, the response of both governments to the unionist reaction led to stalemate over decommissioning and ultimately broke the consensus on Northern Ireland within the Dáil. This also disguised the fact that Bruton had adopted Fianna Fáil's approach to the peace process, and also the fact that it was Fianna Fáil that endorsed a significant move away from the ethos of the Framework Documents in the course of the 1998 negotiations.

The Collapse of Bi-partisanship

Although the publication of the Framework Documents had mended relations between Sinn Féin and the Fine Gael-led government and enabled agreement within the Dáil, this was short lived. This was due to the shift by Bruton away from his attempts to overcome his reputation as hostile towards republicans in favour of a new concentration upon unionist concerns. Soon after the Framework Documents were released, the government set about assuring the 'unionist population that we understand their concerns and are ready to seek ways of allaying them in frank discussion with their elected representatives'.[37] Dick Spring told unionists that he identified 'a keen sense of the importance of a responsible and balanced approach to the most delicate and vital process on this island' among Dáil delegates who took part in the debate on the Documents. He confirmed his government's willingness to hear 'counter-proposals for the achievement of the same objective'. He also called on the Dáil to continue to 'reach out to the unionist community and to dispel their misunderstanding' regarding the meaning of the Documents.[38] Dick Spring did not, however, agree with the British government on decommissioning. The dispute between the British government and Sinn Féin on this issue was hindering progress. Spring argued that the concentration on decommissioning was 'a formula for disaster'.[39] Though he agreed that it was an important issue, he stressed: 'I don't think it should be put up as a totem pole, that, unless you solve this one first, nothing else can happen.'[40] However, it became clear that John Bruton took a different view and aligned his government with the view of the British government. Bruton pleaded with Sinn Féin to make a unilateral attempt to end the deadlock by offering a substantial move on the arms issue[41] and Major remained firm on the issue of prior decommissioning.[42] This lack of flexibility on the part of the British government, which was acquiesced in by John Bruton (much to the consternation of Fianna Fáil), was a direct response to the unionist reaction to the Framework Documents.[43] The statement by Patrick Mayhew in Washington (the conditions set out by Mayhew became known as 'Washington 3') that decommissioning must take place before talks as an act of goodwill on the part of paramilitaries has been described as a deliberate attempt by the British government to 'compensate' for the nationalist sentiments echoed in the Framework Documents.[44] It was from this point on that the process began to stall and was only later salvaged by the intervention of the Clinton administration in America, which agreed to appoint Senator George Mitchell as chairman to the International Body on Decommissioning.[45]

It is a matter of contention whether prior decommissioning had been clearly stated as a precondition to talks in advance of the ceasefire. There is some evidence that both the Reynolds and the Major government stressed the need for decommissioning at different times, leading to confusion about the issue. According to Hauswedell and Brown, the Irish government discussed with Sinn Féin in May 1993 the need to ensure that 'every effort would be made to deal expeditiously [with] arms and equipment'.[46] Bew and Gillespie have pointed to speeches made by Spring and Adams as proof that decommissioning was clearly discussed prior to the ceasefire. They cite Spring's declaration in the Dáil in December 1993 that 'the handing up of arms' would be necessary to 'determine a permanent ceasefire'.[47] Adams complained in January 1994 that the British government was only interested in discussing 'how the IRA will hand over their weapons'.[48] This, according to Bew and Gillespie, is evidence that 'there was, therefore, no truth, in the claim ... that the British had slurred over this matter'.[49] However, this is blurred by the fact that the British government did not emphasize the point in discussions with republicans prior to the ceasefire and by the fact that the Irish government softened on the issue in order to ensure the ceasefire.[50] The main problem for Sinn Féin and the IRA was the fact that John Bruton allowed the British government to place this issue top of the agenda and to employ it as a precondition to Sinn Féin's inclusion in talks. Gerry Adams has stated that the Rainbow Coalition provided the British government with the 'breathing space and allowed the subversion of the process to continue':

> [O]nce the British Government saw that the new Bruton Government was soft on the issue, that allowed them that entire year almost. Even though Mr Bruton, I think, came round to the right position, it was after the summer [of 1995], and I think what Albert Reynolds understood totally was that you had to keep running at the Brits, you had to keep jigging at them, you had to keep moving them forward.[51]

Fianna Fáil clearly agreed that the débacle surrounding decommissioning represented a breach of faith on the part of the British government, in particular, and an error of judgement on the part of the Rainbow Coalition. Bertie Ahern criticized the government's deviation from the essence of the Framework Documents as well as the British government's 'unjustified attempt ... to impose a precondition prior to talks, which was not mentioned in the Downing Street Declaration, the British government's formal clarification or the many appeals to Sinn Féin made by the British Prime Minister and Secretary of State prior to the ceasefire'.[52] Dermot Ahern concurred: 'Decommissioning is, in my opinion, a Unionist agenda. It was, surprisingly enough, a middle class unionist agenda and came from those who, while involved in politics, were not directly involved in the strife.'[53] Fianna Fáil deputies continued to make their frustration clear at the British government's stance. They also attacked the Fine Gael government for not applying pressure on the British government to alter their position. Criticism levelled at the government from the opposition benches illustrated, once again, Fianna Fáil's perspective that the maintenance of the pan-nationalist alliance was a vital element of the peace process.

While questioning John Bruton in November 1995 about proposals which had been sent to London in an attempt to overcome the decommissioning impasse, Fianna Fáil TD and later Minister for Foreign Affairs, Ray Burke, asked:

> Will the Taoiseach explain why he presented separate proposals to the British government to those published by the SDLP and Sinn Féin ... it would have been better to put the proposals of

the SDLP and Sinn Féin to the British, rather than having a division within the nationalist consensus ... as had been done by his predecessor and which eventually led to the Downing Street Declaration?[54]

In the subsequent debate Bruton made clear that he felt compelled to meet the needs of both nationalists and unionists in Northern Ireland and not, as Burke had suggested, only one party or section of opinion in the North. Dermot Ahern responded that the latter approach had 'got us where we are today'.[55] In a very interesting and illuminating speech to the Dáil, Dermot Ahern explained that: 'The major dynamic in the peace process has always been what is disparagingly called the pan-nationalist front which we regard as a nationalist consensus, with Sinn Féin, the SDLP, and the greater body of Nationalist Ireland ... this was the major dynamic which brought about this peace process.'[56] Ahern confirmed that it was this point that was now the cause of differences between Fianna Fáil and the government.[57] The announcement of the twin-track approach, which envisaged the commencement of talks and decommissioning simultaneously in November 1995, had been too late to save the IRA ceasefire, since the deadlock had continued long enough to 'strengthen the militants within the [republican] movement'.[58] The IRA argued that the opportunity presented by the ceasefire had not been grasped by the British government, which had acted in bad faith by introducing preconditions to talks at a late stage.[59]

When the IRA plan to end its ceasefire and return to violence was made manifest in the Canary Wharf bomb in February 1996, Bertie Ahern reacted by referring to the understanding that had been reached through the Downing Street Declaration:

> The only precondition for participation in dialogue and negotiations with other parties is a permanent end to violence. We on this side of the house and many others have been saying for more than a year that the basis for a move to all-party negotiations had already been provided by the sustained ceasefires. The two governments have now vindicated that point of view.[60]

The Fianna Fáil leader believed that the Taoiseach's announcement that a date had now been set for all party talks and that Sinn Féin could participate in the event of a renewed ceasefire vindicated his party's warning to Fine Gael that Sinn Féin must be included and that decommissioning must not be a precondition to this. Ahern assured Sinn Féin that, in the event of a new IRA ceasefire, his party would be willing to treat them fairly in relation to their place within the talks and negotiating processes.[61]

John Bruton declared that it was his intention to devote the necessary 'dedication and imagination' in order to save the peace process, while Major adopted a hardlined stance by claiming this had vindicated his government's view that the issue of decommissioning illegal weapons needed to be dealt with promptly.[62] The government appeared not to know how to act to resolve the problems facing the peace process but reacted by cutting off direct contact with Sinn Féin, and Bruton refused to meet with Adams. Ahern immediately condemned this move by the government and proposed the appointment of Senator George Mitchell as a special envoy who would meet with all the parties in the search for a way forward.[63]

In an article in *The Irish Times* in the aftermath of the Canary Wharf bombing, Bertie Ahern outlined the importance of the Irish government's role in bringing about the initial ceasefire and the role that it had agreed to play in order to maintain that ceasefire. He argued that John Bruton's government had failed to uphold this responsibility and that this had contributed to the breakdown of the ceasefire:

> The IRA in August 1994 made peace with the Irish Government and people, not with the British government. The present Taoiseach has been fully briefed on what passed between the Irish Government and Sinn Féin as the basis for peace. All the specific practical items and commitments were fulfilled by the Irish Government following the ceasefire, to the best of our ability, and Fianna Fáil, both in government and since, have acted at all times to maintain the spirit of the nationalist consensus, a consensus now broken.[64]

Ahern restated in this article what his party had been indicating to the government since Bruton took office: that the maintenance of the ceasefire was dependent on the maintenance of the pan-nationalist alliance. Ahern revealed that the commitment given by the Fianna Fáil government to act as a voice for the wider nationalist community, heavily influenced by Sinn Féin and the IRA, was crucial to the IRA's decision to forsake violence. Ahern continued to explain the importance of such agreements between the Irish government and Sinn

Féin, given the party's decision to reject the Downing Street Declaration: 'Republicans chose not to accept the Downing Street Declaration, and preferred instead to seek to tie down agreement on those matters that were within the power of the Irish government, such as meetings with the government, the timetable for the Forum, attitude to prisoners, as well as the degree to which political positions among Nationalists coincided.'[65]

Adams has also outlined why the Bruton government created problems for the peace process and the ceasefire: 'That stability and leadership [provided by the Reynolds government] had been crucial to persuading the IRA that the peace process, and the nationalist consensus that had created it, was a viable alternative to the armed struggle. Now this important element was gone.'[66] Mansergh claimed that the failure of Fine Gael to regain office in 1997 was due to the perception that that party had 'mismanaged the peace process'.[67] That the ceasefire ended while Fine Gael was in office highlights the importance of the Irish government's role in sustaining the ceasefire, which Ahern said (above) was the culmination of agreement between the republican movement and the Irish government. It also shows the function carried out by Fianna Fáil in the process. Ahern clearly believed that the problems in the peace process were due to the failure of the Rainbow government to preserve the pan-nationalist approach that had been adhered to by Fianna Fáil. The Fine Gael-led government had acted as an advocate of nationalist Ireland until the extent of unionist dissatisfaction became clear after the publication of the Framework Documents. This meant that the pan-nationalist alliance, which had been so appealing to Sinn Féin, was no longer operating.

There is speculation as to whether the IRA deliberately postponed reinstating the ceasefire until the election in the Republic was over. It has been suggested that Fianna Fáil encouraged the republican movement not to call a ceasefire prior to the election fearing Fine Gael would be re-elected on that basis.[68] Apart from the ethical question that this raises about Fianna Fáil's conduct, it suggests that Bruton may have been making some ground in retreating from his stance on decommissioning through his announcement of the twin-track approach and of a date for all-party talks.[69] But there is little doubt that Sinn Féin and the IRA preferred dealing with Fianna Fáil. Fianna Fáil's success in the peace process was, in the main, attributed to their concentration on republican concerns. The return of Fianna Fáil, the re-election of Clinton and the change in government in Westminster meant that 'the wider political context was now more favourable to political negotiations'[70] and this view was supported by the restoration of the IRA ceasefire in July 1997.

The new Secretary of State for Northern Ireland in the Blair government, Mo Mowlam, intimated a willingness to allow Sinn Féin join the renewed talks in the event of a ceasefire.[71] She also changed the British government's position on decommissioning: 'decommissioning is secondary to actually getting people into talks'.[72] Both governments made it clear that the impasse could not continue and indicated their intention to sponsor a joint approach which would propose concurrent decommissioning and talks processes, with decommissioning taking place on the commencement of dialogue.[73] David Trimble hinted at a change in the Ulster Unionist Party's position by stating that in principle he would not object to such an approach to decommissioning.[74] There were also signs that the possibility of a new Fianna Fáil–Progressive Democrats coalition government in the Republic would herald a change in policy by the Irish government towards the peace process when Ahern held a meeting with Gerry Adams prior to the election and without the reinstatement of the IRA ceasefire. Speaking after that meeting, Adams referred to the 'pivotal role' played by Fianna Fáil in the peace process, in obvious contrast to his view of the Bruton government. Adams intimated his preference for the newly elected government to be led by Fianna Fáil.[75] The election of the Fianna Fáil–Progressive Democrats government in June 1997 was lamented by unionists who pointed to the fact that Fianna Fáil would be in power with the aid of what David Trimble described as 'extreme republicans',[76] Sinn Féin TD, Caoimhghín Ó Caoláin and Independent Fianna Fáil TD, Harry Blaney.[77]

A number of conclusions can be made about Ahern's policy and rhetoric on Northern Ireland during his time as leader of the opposition. First of all, Ahern and Fianna Fáil reiterated Reynolds' view of the peace process and the centrality of the pan-nationalist alliance to that process. Secondly, Ahern's policy and language while in opposition highlights the centrality of that consensus and commitments made by the Irish government to the continuation of the ceasefire. It also strengthens the view that the strains within the pan-nationalist alliance during the Rainbow government contributed to the collapse of the ceasefire, and this can be seen to at least partly vindicate the argument that the peace process is grounded on the appeasement of violent republicans which has been voiced by people including Conor Cruise O'Brien, Jeffrey Donaldson and Robert McCartney.[78]

AHERN AS TAOISEACH: NEGOTIATIONS AND AGREEMENT

Ahern was elected Taoiseach in June 1997, supported by the Progressive Democrats and a number of Independents. The statement of a new ceasefire by the IRA in July 1997 boded well for his government; the ceasefire had been the product of many months of talks between Fianna Fáil and the republican movement. Despite the sympathy among the Progressive Democrats towards unionists there was an informal agreement prior to going into government that the Progressive Democrats would not 'seek to interfere, be it rhetorically or otherwise, in the development of the peace process'.[79] This meant that the government's approach to the peace process was led by Fianna Fáil and illustrates that Fianna Fáil attached such importance to the Northern Ireland issue that it formed part of pre-government negotiations. It also explains why there was little public evidence of any disagreement between the two coalition partners on Northern Ireland, as had been the case in the past. It is also evidence of the degree of consensus among the political parties in the Republic on issues relating to the North as a result of the peace process and ceasefire.[80] This consensus between Fianna Fáil and the Progressive Democrats was made easier by the fact that Ahern was keen, despite his speeches whilst in opposition, to provide the conditions for agreement with unionism.

Ahern's government provided no real innovation in relation to issues on Northern Ireland since the boundaries within which negotiations would be set had already been established; the important issues had already been decided upon and debated in previous years. Most significantly, despite Ahern's protestations while in opposition, once substantive negotiations began his government placed less emphasis on relations with Sinn Féin and, in fact, was constrained by the interests of achieving agreement. The dynamics of the Irish government's role altered once Sinn Fein's position at the table was secure and negotiations began. The concern at that point was to reach agreement, and that necessitated keeping both unionist and nationalist representatives involved. It is at this point that Fianna Fáil began to view the peace process as one managed jointly by both governments and the interests of unionism become equal to those of nationalists. So, while the origins of Fianna Fáil's role in the peace process are found within pan-nationalism, the agreement that Ahern sponsored with unionism in 1998 was a balanced one. The joint governmental approach adopted by the two governments has aimed at keeping both unionists and republicans on board the peace process. This has necessitated that both governments alternate between a unionist- or republican-friendly position rather than attempt to reconcile the interests of both. The post-Good Friday Agreement period sees both governments working together to implement the agreement through the use of such an approach with the Irish government, emphasizing the inclusion of Sinn Féin.

Issues of Contention: North–South institutions

The all-party talks commenced in June 1997 and, when Sinn Féin joined in September, the DUP and the UK Unionist Party representatives boycotted the process.[81] The negotiations on Strand Two began in October. Martin McGuinness immediately angered unionists by claiming that Sinn Féin were engaging with the talks process with the aim of 'smashing the Union' between Britain and Ireland.[82] Mitchel McLaughlin stressed the need for the multi-party talks to address the question of a united Ireland.[83] Séamus Mallon of the SDLP emphasized issues relating to Strand Two as being 'at the heart of our problems' since they are 'most important in terms of redefining relationships between the two main political traditions on this island'.[84] In his presentation at the Strand Two talks, the Minister for Justice, Equality and Law Reform, John O'Donoghue, stressed the importance of agreement on the establishment of North–South bodies:

> The creation of dynamic North–South institutions or bodies is an essential element to any solution, to express and cater for the many natural inter-connections on this island, be they the political and cultural links with the South felt and desired by Northern nationalists, or the potential for a productive intensification of common efforts across a wide range of practical issues that could in principle be welcomed across the community.[85]

For the Irish government the significance of the cross-border bodies was to 'allow Northern nationalists the chance to share along with unionists the sense that their aspirations and identity are reflected in the governance and administration of their own place'.[86] These institutions were referred to in successive submissions made by the Irish government to the talks. They were to take the form set out in the Framework Documents and 'promote the goal of bridging divisions and promoting agreement between the communities on the island of Ireland in an institutional framework for dialogue'.[87] Bertie Ahern has since confirmed that it was essential that the 'settlement provided real partnership and equality on an inclusive basis in the North and meaningful North–South institutions' in order to win both Fianna Fáil and northern nationalist support for the agreement and for fundamental constitutional change.[88] Similarly, Gerry Adams argued that Strand Two was critical to finding a solution to the conflict. He placed the onus upon the Irish government, who he said had 'a historic responsibility to pro-actively promote Irish national interests in an inclusive but assertive way'.[89] At this stage the three main nationalist parties were in agreement and, despite talk of a split within republican ranks due to a number of resignations from Sinn Féin and defections from the IRA, Adams claimed that there was no cause for concern about the IRA ceasefire.[90]

In the early stages of the talks there remained considerable tension among the parties. The challenge facing both governments was to ensure that all parties remained at the table.[91] This meant that the Irish government could not push Trimble on the issue of the North–South bodies, and also that care would be taken to ensure that defections from Sinn Féin and the IRA were kept to a minimum. So, while Ahern's official stance on a number of issues, including constitutional change and the working of North–South bodies, remained firm,[92] there is no doubt that from November 1997 Ahern was contemplating compromise. He held a meeting with David Trimble on 20 November 1997 and, after discussions which lasted over two hours, both claimed they had attained a 'better understanding' of the other's position.[93] While no agreement was reached, it was reported that the Irish government was 'actively considering' potential changes to Articles Two and Three of the Constitution.[94] Emphasis was placed on the East–West dimension of the talks in a deliberate attempt to placate Trimble and his party.[95] It was inevitable that once Ahern entered substantive discussions with Trimble compromise would be necessary. There was a definite shift in emphasis away from relations with Sinn Féin in order to reach agreement with Trimble. Continued concentration on the demand for executive North–South bodies together with the lack of movement on Articles Two and Three disguised this fact. It would appear that the language used by the Irish government was merely paying lip service to Sinn Féin's demands in order to keep the republican movement on board. Moves by Ahern in relation to prisoners were useful assurances for republicans while Ahern concentrated on finding common ground with Trimble. Despite this, it appears that the Irish government, through its concentration on prisoners, equality and North–South bodies, was still acting on behalf of nationalist interests. This was reflected in the depth of unionist and loyalist dissatisfaction with the process.

The multi-party talks faced breaking point in January, when loyal-ists made their frustration with the 'direction of the process and the lop-sided policy employed by our government' clear.[96] Many union-ists felt the process of embracing Sinn Féin was moving at an uncom-fortably rapid pace.[97] This was compounded by the British Prime Minister's decision to meet with republican leaders in early October 1997.[98] Unionists saw the Irish government's insistence that cross-bor-der institutions needed to be given executive powers as a direct advance towards a united Ireland.[99] They insisted that the cross-bor-der institutions would not have executive powers and instead sug-gested voluntary co-operation through bodies that would be linked to, and possibly subservient to, the Northern Ireland Assembly and the Dáil.[100] Sinn Féin strenuously objected to such a notion.

In order to compensate unionists for the proposed cross-border bodies, in January 1998 the two governments jointly presented a plan that envisaged a unionist inspired 'Council of the Isles' which would promote and symbolize the connection between the two islands.[101] A joint position was reached after discussions between Tony Blair, Bertie Ahern and David Trimble.[102] According to Hennessey, many of the demands made by the Irish government in its proposals presented at the beginning of the negotiations between the three leaders 'particu-larly on matters of power-sharing and British commitments on secu-rity and prisoners' were 'either deleted or watered down in order to secure Trimble's agreement'.[103] There is no doubt that Ahern made fundamental concessions on these issues in order to advance the nego-tiating process. The Heads of Agreement statement of January 1998 marked a distinct deviation away from the position established with-in the Framework Documents of 1995. Unionists had been isolated from the discussions which produced the Framework Documents. This time the leaders of the SDLP and Sinn Féin had not been con-sulted on this latest discussion document. As a result, the provision relating to North–South bodies referred to institutions that would be accountable to both the Northern Ireland Assembly and the Oireachtas, and it remained unclear as to how these would operate and with what powers. The unionist reaction was more positive than had been in February 1995. Jeffery Donaldson (UUP) now claimed that the Framework Documents had been rendered 'irrelevant'.[104] It is clear that, since the negotiations began in September, both govern-ments had been attempting to balance the interests of all participants to the talks in order to save the process from collapse.[105] This new Heads of Agreement document can be viewed in the context of efforts not only to keep the UUP on board but also to force the parties to engage in dialogue. The paper succeeded in these aims, though of course the parties interpreted the document differently.[106] While the aim was to lead Trimble into negotiations, it is clear, in the knowledge of the subsequent compromise reached on North–South bodies between Trimble and Ahern just prior to the Good Friday Agreement (see below), that the Irish government was ready to compromise on the scope of these institutions and that the Heads of Agreement accurately reflected the government's position.

Although Sinn Féin gave a cautious welcome to the British–Irish paper as 'a step in the right direction', which meant the governments had now reclaimed 'the leadership of this process',[107] Martin McGuinness accused the governments of giving into the 'Orange card'.[108] He committed his party to 'going into the talks to oppose the document'.[109] The IRA released a statement rejecting the proposition paper as 'a pro-unionist document [which] has created a crisis in the peace process'.[110] Both Adams[111] and Brid Rogers[112] (SDLP) were adamant that an internal settlement could not be contemplated by either of their parties. Former Taoiseach, John Bruton, met with a Sinn Féin delegation and agreed that the language of the Heads of Agreement document had departed from that of the Framework Documents. He insisted that, while the name given to the bodies was not important, the North–South institutions must have practical functions.[113] Adams met with Tony Blair in London to express his dissatisfaction with the joint governmental paper.[114] Despite the damage to the relationship between Sinn Féin and the Irish government, Sinn Féin decided to persevere with the talks.

Issues of Contention: Articles Two and Three

Outlining plans for a referendum in the Republic on Articles Two and Three, Bertie Ahern explained that his government was insistent that the proposed changes would not be published until agreement was reached in the talks process and only at that stage 'would it be appropriate to debate it in the house'.[115] It was a well-established Fianna Fáil stance that constitutional change would only take place as part of an overall settlement and can be seen in resolutions passed at the party's Árd Fheis in the early years of the Troubles. Having intimated that the contentious territorial claim would be removed in the context of an overall settlement, Ahern outlined the delicate nature of the modifications:

[Changes to the articles will] ensure that the birthright of anyone born on the island to declare themselves members of the Irish nation, if they chose so, will be strengthened and copper-fastened, as the current constitutional provisions are not very strong in this respect ... It is also our intention to ensure that the achievement of a united Ireland, by agreement and by consent, is, and remains, a legitimate goal, and the door to a peaceful evolution towards that will remain open.[116]

In accepting the Framework Documents, Ahern had made a convincing argument in favour of changing the constitutional provisions in question and once again portrayed the redefinition of the Irish nation in a positive light. He also suggested that it was more important that nationalists in the North were satisfied that issues of policing and equality were being addressed adequately.[117] The general consensus among Fianna Fáil deputies in the Dáil was that Articles Two and Three would not be an issue in the context of an overall settlement, which provided for strong North–South bodies. Fianna Fáil TD, Michael Moynihan, said that he had been surprised at the level of support for change within the party and described a 'wait and see attitude' among members.[118] Seán Ardagh, Fianna Fáil Dublin South Central TD, summed up the thinking within the party: '[If there are] changes in the Government of Ireland Act, a new structure in Northern Ireland and new North–South bodies, then I don't think we could but consider a change in Article 2.'[119]

John Bruton condoned the government's approach to constitutional change, endorsing Ahern's concentration on other issues such as the equality agenda, since 'there will be wide support across the Dáil for changes in Articles Two and Three if these form part of a fair overall settlement'.[120] However, unionist politicians expressed dissatisfaction with the Irish government's attempt to make a final trade off for the articles. Reg Empey stated that unionists would not contemplate agreeing to 'an embryonic all-Ireland government' in return for a change in the Irish Constitution, which he explained would have the overall effect of 'partially implement[ing] Articles Two and Three'.[121] The lack of progress on the issue had already caused a UUP delegation to abandon a meeting with the Minister for Foreign Affairs, David Andrews, in October 1997.[122] Dick Spring had attempted to persuade Andrews to accept constitutional change as 'a matter of fact'.[123] The Minister remained deliberately coy on the matter.[124]

A number of organizations lobbied in favour of keeping the articles intact. In a plea to the Irish people these organizations accused the Fianna Fáil government of seeking to win support for a deal which afforded 'second class citizenship for the Irish people'.[125] Among the groups were the Ancient Order of Hibernians and a number of American based organizations such as Irish American Unity Conference, American Irish Political Education Committee and the Irish American Business Organization. They called for the Irish people to reject any changes to Articles Two and Three which would dilute the 'sacred right of the Irish people to self-determination'.[126] However, according to the opinion polls, support for change had increased but the public's view reflected the government's commitment to the need for an overall settlement encompassing compromise on both sides.[127] Interestingly, the outcome of the poll showed that Fianna Fáil opinion remained evenly divided on the issue. The final wording of the revised articles was published on April 10 and agreement looked possible despite many reservations within Sinn Féin about the negotiations. Mitchel McLaughlin claimed that the process was edging 'closer and closer … to the point of collapse'[128] and, when agreement was finally reached on Friday 10 April, Sinn Féin supporters were apprehensive about the outcome. Martin Ferris, Sinn Féin Árd Chomhairle member from Kerry and later TD for the area, believed that the rank and file had 'enormous reservations' about the agreement, while a Sinn Féin Tralee councillor suggested that Sinn Féin members in the Republic would find it very difficult to relinquish Articles Two and Three since they 'are the essence of republicanism'.[129]

The domestic importance of the talks became apparent in the final stages of negotiations and threatened the possibility of a settlement. Independent TD Harry Blaney declared his intention to rethink his support for the coalition if he was not satisfied with the government's handling of the constitutional issue.[130] Bertie Ahern was forced to plan a nationwide tour to meet party organizations in an effort to quell fears over constitutional change.[131] This followed reports of 'great concern' about the movement towards constitutional change within certain sections of the Fianna Fáil party. Fianna Fáil backbencher, Liam Aylward, warned the Taoiseach that the wider party would need advance notification about proposed changes and that they wanted to be part of the debate concerning the articles. Fianna Fáil's Louth TD, Séamus Kirk, echoed these sentiments and pointed to the concern within the parliamentary party at the lack of debate on the issue.[132] David Andrews, Minister for Foreign Affairs, stressed that, while it was difficult for Fianna Fáil to contemplate changing de Valera's con-

stitution since it and 'Articles Two and Three are central to the core
and spirit of Fianna Fáil', the party must face this challenge and 'take
account of the need to bring about a permanent peace'.[133] He pointed
to the fact that commitments to change the constitution had already
been undertaken in the Downing Street Declaration and the
Framework Documents and will only materialize 'in the context of a
balanced and comprehensive overall agreement which brings about
fundamental change and a new beginning in all our relationships'.[134]

The Negotiations

Negotiations entered the final and substantive stage in mid March
1998, when Sinn Féin re-entered the talks after a temporary exclusion
because of IRA activity. David Andrews, the Minister for Foreign
Affairs, presented a very firm stance on the issue of North–South bodies: 'My government has at all times been very clear on where it stood
in relation to cross-border institutions. North and South with executive powers.'[135] The minister remained publicly resolute about this
point right up to the final stages of negotiations.[136] However, when
the talks resumed there was no certainty about the possibility of
agreement. The Irish government made it clear that they expected
that David Trimble and the Ulster Unionists would have to significantly alter their position if agreement was to be reached. Together
with the SDLP, the Irish government applied pressure on Trimble to
accept the notion of cross-border bodies with executive powers and
promised the removal of the territorial claim from the Constitution.[137]

Speaking at the Unionist Party's AGM, David Trimble agreed that
any settlement would make provision for a North–South element.
The UUP leader described the functions of the North–South bodies to
'facilitate consultation and co-operation' but which would operate on
the authority of and be accountable to the Northern Ireland
Assembly.[138] Ahern challenged Trimble to outline his party's position
on issues that were of great interest to nationalists, in essence to set out
their 'attitude to substantive and workable North–South structures,
including implementation bodies with meaningful powers, which we
regard as indispensable to an agreement'.[139] A suggestion by Ahern that
a regular poll on support for the union should be carried out in
Northern Ireland, as a mechanism to test the consent principle, was
received negatively by Fine Gael.[140] Opposition leader, John Bruton,
was vehemently opposed to this idea and questioned how it could add
'to the necessary stability to ensure the North–South and internal

arrangements work harmoniously in the initial difficult years'.[141] The suggestion was part of an attempt to make the final package more appealing to Fianna Fáil members. Ahern had held two meetings with Fianna Fáil TDs and senators over the previous weekend.[142]

In the final weeks of negotiations the UUP leader and Irish government officials were in disagreement over a number of issues. This led to confrontation between Trimble, David Andrews and the Minister of State at the Department of Foreign Affairs, Liz O'Donnell.[143] Irish government sources blamed the UUP's hardline approach, while the UUP claimed Ahern needed to rework the latest drafts of Articles Two and Three.[144] David Trimble was unhappy with the latest proposals which David Andrews explained were 'intended to incorporate the consent principle, to guarantee the citizenship rights of everyone born on the island of Ireland and to express the legitimate aspiration on national unity by peaceful means and based on the principle of consent'.[145] There was concern that, if the UUP did not concede to cross-border bodies with 'real and significant'[146] executive powers as envisaged by the Irish government, then the electorate in the Republic would not agree to the proposed constitutional change.[147] Gerry Adams insisted that any constitutional change must not have the effect of redefining the nation by excluding the North. He attended a meeting with the Taoiseach in Dublin prior to the planned summit between the two Prime Ministers and it was later suggested that Adams urged Ahern to take a strong stance in relation to the remaining unresolved issues.[148] Following two heads of government meetings, it was reported that movement had been achieved both with regards to the Assembly and also on the North–South bodies.[149] But the talks process came very near to absolute deadlock as a result of the joint paper presented to the delegates by the talks chairman, George Mitchell, on behalf of the two governments. In particular, the sections relating to North–South bodies and their respective powers and remit were contentious. The reaction from within the unionist camp forced both Ahern and Blair to take an active role in the talks and visit Belfast.

What is important in the overall context of the Irish government's approach was the fact that the eventual deal on North–South bodies was concluded between the Irish government and the UUP delegation with an input from the British government. Neither Sinn Féin nor the SDLP made an input at this point.[150] This was a very clear change in approach by Ahern, which originated from his acceptance of the need for a wider consultative base in order to fulfil the government's responsibilities as co-guarantor of the talks process. His role as co-guarantor was a more neutral one than that which he and his party had previously played in championing Sinn Féin's place in the process. Rather than simply act on behalf of nationalist Ireland, he now sponsored a compromise between nationalism and unionism. In order to do so, Ahern needed to engage with Trimble and unionism.

Various Irish government officials, including the Taoiseach and the Minister for Foreign Affairs, repeatedly referred to the importance of the North–South dimension in their public statements prior to the announcement that agreement had been reached. Despite this, the various accounts of how that agreement was reached have highlighted the manner in which Bertie Ahern struck a deal with David Trimble and his UUP delegation in order to ensure the negotiations would not collapse. Ahern conceded a dilution of the North–South bodies which was much closer to that envisaged in the Heads of Agreement paper of January 1998 than proposed in the Framework Documents of February 1995. Indeed, in the aftermath of the agreement, Bertie Ahern was credited with having enabled agreement by 'achieving the final break-throughs'.[151] In her assessment of Ahern's negotiating skills, Geraldine Kennedy speculated that Ahern had deliberately set an extremely high mark on North–South bodies in order to force Trimble to negotiate on the issue, which he had not done previously in the course of the talks process.[152] Whether this accurately depicts Ahern's thinking at the time is unclear; however, it may explain the remarkable distance between Ahern's initial demands and the eventual deal. It is probable that the proposals outlined in the Heads of Agreement proposition paper in January reflected the best that the Irish government felt it could get Trimble to accept and that the months of upping the ante on the issue were aimed both at reassuring nationalists and also at forcing Trimble and his party to commit itself to concrete provisions for North–South institutions. Significantly, Paul Bew, in an article in the *Sunday Independent* after agreement was reached, argued that the three main players in bringing this about were Blair, Ahern and Trimble.[153] It was this relationship, and not the one between the Irish government and Sinn Féin, which was of crucial importance to agreement in the end.

The Good Friday (Belfast) Agreement

The Belfast Agreement was presented to the Dáil for debate on April 21 1998. Bertie Ahern depicted the accord as 'a balanced constitutional settlement that provided a peaceful method of resolving fundamental differences in the future while creating a basis for practical partnership and co-operation'.[154] The Taoiseach claimed that the British government was now 'effectively out of the equation'.[155] He was re-enforcing his earlier point that the changes in Articles Two and Three had the effect of allowing the people of Ireland, North and South, to be sovereign and 'for the first time, formally recognises [consent] to be a two-way process. The importance of this cannot be emphasised enough.'[156] In his interpretation of consent, Ahern was suggesting that the agreement amounted to a reorientation of the principle in favour of nationalists. Not only did it protect the right of a majority of the population in Northern Ireland to determine the future of Northern Ireland, it also recognised that the consent of the nationalist community was required within Northern Ireland and also that the population of the southern state now had an input. He maintained that the proposed modifications to Articles Two and Three were 'sensible' and that it was realistic to have the North–South bodies dependent on the existence of the Northern Ireland Assembly since all parts of the agreement must be 'interdependent'.[157] Significantly, Ahern made this speech at Arbour Hill after the annual Fianna Fáil commemoration of the 1916 Rising.

The May 1998 Referenda

Writing in the immediate aftermath of the Good Friday Agreement, John A. Murphy, who had championed constitutional change for some time, portrayed the 'changes proposed [as] visionary and courageous, and reflect[ing] a spirit of true patriotism'. He predicted that 'they will require considerable explanation as part of an information and publicity campaign, aimed at getting an overwhelming endorsement in the forthcoming referendum on the whole Agreement'.[158] Ahern did subsequently mount a forceful campaign calling for a 'Yes' vote in the referendum to be held on May 22.[159] He called on the electorate to carry out its civic duty in the referendum. Constitutional change should be welcomed as part of 'defining our nation in generous and inclusive 32-county terms and by putting people before territory'.[160] He again endorsed the agreement as 'a historical breakthrough in terms of consolidating peace'. His main argument in favour of the changes to Articles Two and Three was as before; that it placed sovereignty firmly in the hands of the Irish people, allowing them to decide upon a united Ireland.[161] The initial feeling about the chances of a 'Yes' vote in the Republic was only 50:50, since peace was not guaranteed.[162] Labour Party leader, Ruairi Quinn,[163] argued that the compromises involved in the deal were worth it: 'The ceding of these powers [North–South bodies] and the restating of our national identity to recognise a *de facto* position are small prices to pay for the potential peace and economic prosperity which are embodied in this Agreement.'[164] Dublin West TD, Joe Higgins of the Socialist Party, welcomed the changes in Articles Two and Three:

> Regarding the debate on changing Articles Two and Three of the Constitution, it should be clearly stated that those articles as they stand are a fraud and amounted to a window dressing exercise by Mr de Valera and his Government in 1937. In concrete terms, the suggestion that the State in the Irish Republic could exercise jurisdiction over Northern Ireland is a sham.[165]

The Minister for Foreign Affairs, David Andrews, argued that the alterations to Articles Two and Three reflected debates which successive governments had been involved in: 'Successive Irish Governments have argued that lasting peace can only be achieved if underpinned by a balanced and comprehensive political agreement. The fundamental values and objectives of this and previous Governments are squarely reflected in the Agreement. The interlinked principles of consent and self-determination form the basis of the section on constitutional issues.'[166] The then Minister for the Marine and Natural Resources, Dr Michael Woods, also endorsed the balanced nature of changes to the Constitution and the 1920 Government of Ireland Act:

> The proposed reformulation of Articles Two and Three represent, in the context of the total constitutional package which includes repeal of the Government of Ireland Act, 1920, a generous reaching out to the traditions of those in Northern Ireland who regard themselves as British. At the same time, the proposed new Articles reaffirm and strengthen the fundamental Nationalist aspiration to Irish unity. They define the entitlement and birthright of every person born on the island of Ireland to be part of the Irish nation ... The Agreement recognises that it is for the people of Ireland alone, by agreement between the two parts respectively and without external impediment, to exercise their right of self-determination on the basis of consent, freely and concurrently given, North and South, to bring about a unit-

ed Ireland if that is their wish, subject to the agreement and consent of a majority of the people of Northern Ireland.[167]

Micheál Martin, then Minister for Education and Science, again illustrated the level of agreement within the parliamentary party on the issue of Constitutional Change:

> The proposed amendments [to Articles Two and Three] are consistent with the continued will of the significant majority of the Irish nation to be united in one State. However, they also recognise the strong will of the Irish nation that a united Ireland can only be brought about through peaceful means and by consent. The new wording is crucial in that it establishes a mechanism whereby the reunification of the country can come about without the interference of any person outside the island. This is a vital new element in the process when taken together with changes in British constitutional legislation and the Agreement accepted by Unionist parties.[168]

The endorsement of constitutional change by Fianna Fáil contributors to the debate on the Good Friday Agreement was noticeable. The contentious issues were not those of the North–South institutions or the constitutional implications of the agreement but instead related to policing, decommissioning and prisoner releases. This reflects the fact that much of the debates relating to Articles Two and Three had already been concluded in favour of change.[169] Because self-determination had been given a central position in the agreement and recognized as a principle of equal significance to that of consent, the Fianna Fáil party was able to accept the ideological basis of the agreement. As was illustrated in Chapter Two when the reformulation of the principles of consent and self-determination was assessed, the inclusion of self-determination in such a manner as to ensure the recognition of the integrity of the nation enabled the founding principles of Fianna Fáil to remain intact. The practical recognition that was given to Northern Ireland did not detract from this, since Fianna Fáil ideology has long since been distinguished from policy and so long as an ideological commitment to the integrity of the nation remained it did not matter that Northern Ireland was recognized as a political entity. The same principles that informed the party's decision to support Árd Fheiseanna resolutions in the 1960s in favour of unity, but not those which advocated action, now informed the party's attitude towards the Good Friday Agreement.

Sinn Féin debated the merits of the agreement at its Árd Fheis in Dublin on May 10. Gerry Adams told his audience that the Good Friday Agreement must be judged 'in the context of strategy and struggle'.[170] The presence of a number of prisoners urging a positive position on the Agreement aided the 'Yes' side.[171] Not all IRA members agreed with Sinn Féin's analysis; the Real IRA declared its intention to continue with the war and threatened to direct its 'war machine' against the British cabinet.[172] The threat from the splinter organization was, however, not thought to be significant. The general thinking was that, once Sinn Féin had endorsed the Agreement, it would make a 'Yes' vote in the Republic almost inevitable.[173] A poll published by *The Irish Times* predicted that 61 per cent of the electorate in the Republic would vote in favour of the agreement.[174] The low level of debate subsequent to the agreement did not reflect the enormity of the constitutional change which was contained in the Good Friday Agreement and which was accepted by the Irish government and the electorate. The fact is that the changes inherent in the agreement had been contemplated by Irish nationalism for some time. The Irish government, the SDLP and Sinn Féin had been preparing for such compromises long before the talks process began. The apparently easy conversion to the constitutional position contained in the agreement disguises the long conflict, which has been catalogued in the preceding chapters, within nationalism, Fianna Fáil and Irish society over such changes.

The general feeling within the party was that constitutional change was acceptable since it had been balanced by amendments to the Government of Ireland Act.[175] Ahern had also worked hard to keep the party on board to the changes that he was contemplating prior to the Good Friday Agreement. He consulted with party members and kept the cabinet and parliamentary party informed of developments during the talks. There does not appear to have been any real dissent within the cabinet or Fianna Fáil parliamentary party at this stage but reassurances, particularly on Articles Two and Three, were sought and given by Ahern.[176] This groundwork undertaken by Ahern, together with the context of peace and advanced debate, enabled a relatively easy acceptance of the Good Friday Agreement by the party. The emerging positive response from republicans, the electorate in the Republic and the Fianna Fáil party allowed Ahern to concentrate his efforts on convincing unionists to accept the deal.

UNIONISM AND THE GOOD FRIDAY AGREEMENT

The generally positive reaction within the republican movement and Fianna Fáil was contrasted by the reaction from unionists.[177] There was concern about the reaction within the unionist population to the agreement. It was felt that Trimble had not been doing enough to keep his party membership up to date with the progress of the talks and that he was 'the leader of the seemingly most fragmented support at the negotiating table'.[178] Trimble faced stiff opposition to the Agreement from within the wider unionist community. Ian Paisley labelled the Belfast Agreement the 'mother of all treachery ... worse than the Anglo-Irish Agreement, more treacherous than the Framework Document and posed far greater dangers to the Union with Britain than the Sunningdale Agreement'.[179] The party declared its intention to campaign vigorously for a 'No' vote in the referendum. Despite Trimble's success in winning some 70 per cent support from the Ulster Unionist Council, there was continuing unease within wider unionist circles and most UUP MPs opposed the agreement.[180] In an article which appeared in the *Daily Telegraph*, David Trimble outlined how concessions had been won from the Irish government in relation to North–South bodies and that assurances had been given on decommissioning.[181] He also argued in favour of the agreement as upholding the principle of consent, which, he argued, entailed recognition by the Irish government of British territorial sovereignty.[182] Trimble urged voters not to be swayed by Paisley and set out that: 'A "No" vote means no decommissioning; no end to the territorial claim; no end to Dublin interference in Northern Ireland's affairs; no end to Maryfield and no end to the Anglo-Irish Agreement.'[183] But grassroots unionists did not appear to be convinced with lukewarm responses reflected in opinion polls.[184] United Unionists, who were campaigning against the Belfast Agreement, claimed their case was enjoying 'a massive surge of support'.[185] UKUP leader, Robert McCartney, said the unionist public 'would not accept armed terrorists committed to violence governing them'.[186] Many unionists did not want to pay the price of having IRA and Sinn Féin members in government in the hope of peace.[187] Trimble's case was not aided by Ahern's claims that the British government was now irrelevant to Northern Ireland's future (see above).

Ahern and Blair stepped up efforts to win over undecided unionist voters.[188] Bertie Ahern took a very firm line on continued terrorism and committed his government to 'firmly crushing' any renewed violence.[189] Blair paid a last minute visit to Northern Ireland, endeavouring to secure unionist backing for the agreement.[190] During his visit, Blair guaranteed legislation relating to decommissioning and paramilitary clampdowns, which, he claimed, would render the IRA's war at an end.[191] Ahern offered his support: 'People are entitled to an absolute assurance that the conflict is over, that weapons will not be used again by either the parties owning them or allowed to fall into the wrong hands'.[192] On the eve of the referenda, Ahern appealed to unionists to vote 'Yes'. Assuring unionists that he respected their fears, he called on them to embrace a new kind of Northern Ireland that respected the diversity of its communities in the interests of stability.[193] He called for the debate about whether the agreement strengthened or weakened the union to cease, since it was misguided and would ultimately be determined by the people in Northern Ireland.[194] Trimble was clearly delighted to have won the support of his Ulster Unionist Council, hence silencing critics within the party.[195] It appeared that Blair's last minute assurances were successful as support from within the unionist community was said to be recovering. Trimble was confident of a 70 per cent endorsement of the agreement.[196] The agreement was endorsed on both sides of the border on May 22, by 94.4 per cent in the Republic and 71.1 per cent in Northern Ireland.[197]

CONCLUSION

The aim here is not to offer a complete examination of the nuances of the Belfast Agreement. However, it is clear that the agreement reflected extensive constitutional reformulation. Conclusions can be reached on two levels: Firstly, regarding the constitutional implications for Fianna Fáil and the Republic and secondly in relation to the role played by the Fianna Fáil-led government in bringing about the agreement. On the first point, there is little uncertainty that Ahern presided over Fianna Fáil's official acceptance of major constitutional and attitudinal change. The general lack of dissent within Fianna Fáil is explained by Ahern's consultations at cabinet and parliamentary party level during the talks and by the fact that debate within Fianna Fáil, the Dáil and the media on issues relating to Northern Ireland was well advanced by 1998. Previous chapters have argued that from an ideological point of view the Good Friday Agreement, through its endorsement of the concept of self-determination, represented an advance for Irish republicanism. Much of the ideological framework for agreement had been set out prior to Ahern's accession to power. As Ivory has shown: 'The protracted nature of the political debate in the Republic of Ireland over the issue of Northern Ireland prepared the constituency of southern Irish nationalism for the political compromises eventually struck, thus providing a coherent explanation as to why over 94 percent of that constituency voted in favour of the 'Good Friday' Agreement on 22nd May 1998.'[198] The Irish electorate had already accepted both the necessity of constitutional change and the principle of consent. Thus, on constitutional issues, Fianna Fáil had reconciled itself to change and Ahern had presented a strong argument in portraying these changes as a positive move for constitutional republicanism.

However, while Ahern had a strong case from an ideological point, he did make concessions when negotiating the North–South bodies. It may be that Trimble and his party could never have compromised on these institutions, but it is notable that there was practically no debate or dissent within Fianna Fáil in the aftermath of the deal. This is explained by the willingness to see these concessions as benevolent gestures towards peace and reconciliation, and also by the party's historical preoccupation with maintaining its ideology and ability to distinguish between ideology and policy formation. That the party's policy formation and concessions on North–South bodies appear at odds with its ideology is justified by the fact that the core points of its ideology remain intact in the aftermath of the Good Friday Agreement. Fianna Fáil's immediate policy and language on Northern Ireland has been revised significantly as a result of the party's role within the peace process. However, its ideology has not been subject to such profound revision, even though it has given recognition to the reality of Northern Ireland. The distinction that has historically existed between Fianna Fáil's ideology on Northern Ireland and its actual policy on the matter was also key to understanding the party's acceptance of the Good Friday Agreement. It is the fact that the party's fundamental commitment to the integrity of the nation remained unaltered through the central role given to national self-determination that explains the party's seemingly stress-free endorsement of the Good Friday Agreement.

On the second issue, relating to Ahern's role in the peace process, a number of points are stressed. Firstly, Ahern's time in opposition was characterized by the persistence within Fianna Fáil of a view of the party's role in the peace process which saw its members advocate the strengthening of the pan-nationalist alliance. The importance of this alliance to the achievement and continuation of the IRA ceasefire and to the peace process in general was also underlined. Bruton's departure from the pan-nationalist consensus serves to vindicate the interpretation that the peace process had pan-nationalism as its basis. Secondly, while the Anglo-Irish Agreement of 1985 meant that both governments remained in contact, it did not signify the instigation of good Anglo-Irish relations nor a joint governmental approach, both of which have their origins in the negotiations of late 1997 and 1998. The Blair–Ahern rapport is perhaps a more significant Anglo-Irish relationship in the context of the peace process than that between Reynolds and Major.

Finally, and perhaps most importantly, in understanding the achievement of agreement in April 1998, Ahern's stewardship of the peace process involved a shift away from giving priority solely to the interests of the participants of the pan-nationalist alliance. The onset of substantive negotiations witnessed a movement towards the development of a joint governmental approach and has resulted in what Brian Cowan, the then Minister for Foreign Affairs, referred to as 'joint-sponsorship' of the agreement and its implementation.[199] Fianna Fáil had been resolute about the need to have Sinn Féin at the negotiating table and had placed Sinn Féin's participation at the core of the process. Once Sinn Féin's place was secured in the final stages of negotiations there was a definite shift in emphasis away from relations with Sinn Féin towards the search for agreement with unionism. While the Irish government sought to keep the republican movement on board through its concentration on policing, prisoners and so forth, the Heads of Agreement document and the final deal on the North–South institutions were designed to be 'unionist friendly'. A change in approach by the Fianna Fáil-led government instigated by the onset of the negotiations culminated in a final pact between the Irish government and the UUP delegation.

The new role assumed by the Irish government as a co-sponsor of the negotiations has informed the post-agreement approach of both governments with circumstances dictating whether the emphasis is placed on republican or unionist concerns. This approach has taken the form of an alternation between addressing unionist and republican concerns, in an attempt to keep both sides on board. It has not involved any meaningful attempt at reconciliation between the two communities. This has been underpinned by the fact that securing and maintaining Sinn Féin's involvement has been a dominant element of Ahern's approach to the peace process, both before and after the Good Friday Agreement. Despite the fact that Adams has stated that the nationalist consensus, which had been so central to the foundation of the peace process, has been broken in the aftermath of the agreement,[200] the Irish government has remained committed to Sinn Féin's continued presence within the process. The difference in the post-agreement context is that this has taken place in a joint governmental setting. This was evident in Ahern's words when he dedicated his government to the terms of the Good Friday Agreement: 'Let me make it clear that the Irish and British governments will not allow anyone to wreck a properly endorsed agreement or to overturn the clearly expressed will of the greater number.'[201] The role of the Irish government in the peace process since the signing of the Good Friday Agreement has been conducted within the context of a combined British–Irish governmental approach aimed at both implementing the Good Friday Agreement and keeping Sinn Féin involved.

NOTES

1. *The Irish Times* 17 Nov. 1994.
2. See Robin Wilson's discussion in *The Irish Times* 15 Nov. 1994.
3. Eamon Delancy, an ex-official at the Department of Foreign Affairs, has pointed to the fact that Reynolds' work on the North was made easier by the continuity in staff both in the Department of Foreign Affairs, where Seán Ó hUiginn was head of the Anglo-Irish section, and in the Taoiseach's office, where Martin Mansergh remained the key person on Northern Ireland. Delaney, E. *Accidental Diplomat: My years in the Irish Foreign Service, 1987–1995* (Dublin: New Island, 2001), p. 341.
4. Mary O'Rourke in *Paths to a Political Settlement in Ireland: Policy papers submitted to the forum for peace and reconciliation* (Belfast: Blackstaff Press, 1995), pp. 99–100.
5. *Dáil Éireann Debates* Vol. 449, Col. 1332, 22 Feb. 1995.
6. For Bertie Ahern's reaction, see *Dáil Éireann Debates* Vol. 449, Col. 1342, 22 Feb. 1995.
7. *Dáil Éireann Debates* Vol. 449, Col. 1353, 22 Feb. 1995.
8. *Irish Press* 22 Feb. 1995.
9. *Dáil Éireann Debates* Vol. 449, Col. 1354, 22 Feb. 1995.
10. For a study of Padraig Pearse, see Edwards, R.D. *Patrick Pearse: The triumph of failure* (Dublin: Poolbeg Press, 1990, 1st Edition, London: Victor Gollancz, 1977).
11. *Dáil Éireann Debates* Vol. 449, Cols 1,355–6, 22 Feb. 1995.
12. *The Sunday Business Post* 26 Feb. 1995.
13. Bertie Ahern and James McDaid, *Dáil Éireann Debates* Vol. 449, Col. 1356, 22 Feb. 1995.
14. *The Irish Times* 23 Feb. 1995.
15. *The Irish Times* 28 Feb. 1995.
16. *Irish Press* 8 Feb. 1995.
17. See *Irish Press* 21 Feb. 1995.
18. *The Irish Times* 3 Feb. 1995.
19. See Ronan Fanning's column, Sunday *Independent* 5 Feb. 1995.
20. *Newsletter* 23 Feb. 1995.
21. *Belfast Telegraph* 23 Feb. 1995.
22. *Irish Press* 22 Feb. 1995.
23. *Newsletter* 23 Feb. 1995.

24. Ibid.
25. *Ulster* Unionist Party, *Response to Frameworks for the Future*, available at http://www.uup.org/current/fraMr.esp.html, accessed August 2003.
26. Ibid.
27. *Belfast Telegraph* 23 Feb. 1995.
28. Robinson, P.D. *The Union Under Fire: United Ireland framework Revealed* (Belfast: Peter D. Robinson, 1995), p. 53.
29. See arguments made in Robinson, *The Union Under Fire*, p. 25.
30. *Irish Press* 25 Feb. 1995.
31. English, R. 'The State and Northern Ireland', in R. English and C. Townshend (eds), *The State: Historical and Political Dimensions* (London: Routledge, 1997), p. 102.
32. Dixon, P. 'Internationalization and Unionist Isolation: A response to Feargal Cochrane', *Political Studies*, XLIII (1995), p. 499.
33. O'Duffy, B. 'British and Irish Conflict Regulation from Sunningdale to Belfast, Part II: Playing for a draw 1985–1999', *Nations and Nationalism*, 6, 3 (2000), p. 418.
34. *The Irish Times* 3 Feb. 1995.
35. Sinn Féin councillor, Mary Nelis, speaking at the Forum for Peace and Reconciliation, *The Irish Times* 3 Dec. 1994.
36. See *Irish Press* 29 March 1995.
37. *Irish Press* 24 Feb. 1995.
38. Ibid.
39. *Irish Independent* 1 March 1995.
40. *Irish Press* 1 March 1995.
41. *Irish Press* 14 March 1995.
42. *Irish Press* 20 March 1995.
43. See Ruane, J. and Todd, J. 'Peace Processes and Communalism in Northern Ireland', in W. Crotty and D.E. Schmitt (eds), *Ireland and the Politics of Change* (London and New York: Longman, 1998), p. 185.
44. O'Duffy, 'British and Irish conflict regulation from Sunningdale to Belfast, Part II', p. 418.
45. See Mitchell, G. *Making Peace: The inside story of the making of the Good Friday Agreement* (London: William Heinemann, 1999) for his memoirs on this period.
46. Hauswedell, C. and Brown, K. *Brief 22 Burying the Hatchet: The decommissioning of paramilitary arms in Northern Ireland* (Bonn International Center for Conversion, INCORE, no date), p. 10.
47. Dick Spring quoted in Bew and Gillespie, *Northern Ireland: A chronology of the Troubles, 1968–1999*, p. 284.
48. Gerry Adams quoted in Hauswedell and Brown, *Brief 22 Burying the Hatchet*, p. 13.
49. Bew and Gillespie, *Northern Ireland: A chronology of the Troubles*, p. 294.
50. Hauswedell and Brown, *Brief 22 Burying the Hatchet*, p. 13.
51. Gerry Adams quoted in Rowan, B. *The Armed Peace: Life and death after the ceasefires* (Edinburgh and London: Mainstream Publishing, 2003), p. 74.
52. *Dáil Éireann Debates* Vol. 459, Col. 199, 29 Nov. 1995.
53. *Dáil Éireann Debates* Vol. 462, Cols 966–7, 29 Feb. 1996.
54. *Dáil Éireann Debates* Vol. 458, Col. 486, 15 Nov. 1995.
55. *Dáil Éireann Debates* Vol. 458, Col. 487, 15 Nov. 1995.
56. *Dáil Éireann Debates* Vol. 462, Col. 968, 29 Feb. 1996.
57. *Dáil Éireann Debates* Vol. 462, Col. 968, 29 Feb. 1996.
58. Ruane and Todd, 'Peace Processes and Communalism in Northern Ireland', p. 185.
59. See English, R. *Armed Struggle: A History of the IRA* (Oxford: Macmillan, 2003), p. 290.
60. *Dáil Éireann Debates* Vol. 462, Cols 902–3, 28 Feb. 1996.
61. *Dáil Éireann Debates* Vol. 462, Col. 905, 28 Feb. 1996.
62. *The Irish Times* 10 Feb. 1996.
63. *The Irish Times* 12 Feb. 1996.
64. *The Irish Times* 16 Feb. 1996.
65. Ibid.
66. Adams, G. *Hope and History: Making Peace in Ireland* (Kerry: Brandon, 2003), p. 197.
67. Interview with Martin Mansergh, 12 Dec. 1996. In an opinion poll of Sept. 1995, 58% of

those questioned approved of Bruton's handling of Northern Ireland; however, in June the following year an opinion poll showed that 40% thought that the Irish government did not reflect nationalist opinion strongly enough. While Bruton's policy differed little from that of Fianna Fáil, the collapse of the ceasefire and the murder of Garda McCabe by the IRA in Limerick provided Fianna Fáil with an advantage over Bruton's government and enabled Ahern to argue that his party was the best one to deal with the peace process. See, M. Marsh and P. Mitchell (eds), *How Ireland Voted 1997* (Oxford: Westview Press and PSAI Press, 1999), pp. 19–21.

68. De Bréadún, D. *Far Side of Revenge: Making peace in Northern Ireland* (Cork: The Collins Press, 2001), p. 31.
69. See John Bruton TD, *Dáil Éireann Debates* Vol. 462, Cols 893–4, 28 Feb. 1996.
70. Ruane and Todd, 'Peace Processes and Communalism in Northern Ireland', p. 185.
71. *The Irish Times* 5 May 1997.
72. *The Irish Times* 10 May 1997.
73. *The Irish Times* 6 June 1997.
74. *The Irish Times* 7 June 1997.
75. *The Irish Times* 15 May 1997.
76. *The Irish Times* 9 June 1997.
77. Caoimhghín Ó Caoláin was Sinn Féin's only TD in the Dáil after the election in 1997; he was the first TD the party had elected to the Dáil. Harry Blaney was the brother of Neil Blaney and maintained the Blaney dynasty in Donegal by regaining Neil's seat in 1997.
78. For an outline of the argument that the peace process has been based on appeasement, see Skelly, J.M. 'Appeasement in our time: Conor Cruise O'Brien and the peace process in Northern Ireland', *Irish Studies in International Affairs*, 10 (1999), pp. 221–36.
79. Interview with Conor Lenihan, 16 Nov. 2005.
80. This consensus is in fact central to the experience of the peace process in the Republic. The next chapter will deal with the implications of this consensus and lack of dissent for Fianna Fáil and the peace process and illustrate the way in which this consensus has been challenged in recent times.
81. The UUP delegation decided to stay in the talks as a result of an opinion poll which was conducted to gauge public support for the talks process. The opinion poll revealed that 93% of UUP supporters were in favour of the party's continued involvement in the talks. See Irwin, C. *The People's Peace Process in Northern Ireland* (Hampshire: Palgrave Macmillan, 2002), pp. 16, 17, 155, 56.
82. *The Irish Times* 7 Oct. 1997.
83. See his article in *The Irish Times* 31 Oct. 1998.
84. *The Irish Times* 8 Oct. 1997.
85. Multi-Party Talks, submissions to Strand Two, *Address on Behalf of Irish Government by Mr John O'Donoghue TD, Minister for Justice, Equality and Law Reform,* 7 Oct. 1997, Linenhall Library, Belfast.
86. Ibid.
87. Multi-Party Talks, *Nature, Form and Extent of New Arrangements – Irish Governments,* 24 Oct. 1997, Linenhall Library.
88. Bertie Ahern quoted in Whelan, K. and Masterson, E. *Bertie Ahern: Taoiseach and peacemaker* (Edinburgh: Blackwater Press, 1998), p. 203.
89. *The Irish Times* 8 Oct. 1997.
90. *The Irish Times* 7 Nov. 1997.
91. Deaglán de Bréadún, *The Irish Times* 1 Nov. 1997. Note that the UKUP and the DUP did not join the talks process, despite this commitment.
92. See article in *The Irish Times* 20 Nov. 1998 by Robin Wilson criticizing Ahern's approach to the peace process as the cause of continued division.
93. *The Irish Times* 21 Nov. 1997.
94. Ibid.
95. *The Irish Times* 22 Nov. 1997.
96. Gary McMichael, leader of the Ulster Democratic Party, explaining the decision of the UFF and UDA to withdraw their support from the talks process, *Irish Independent* 5 Jan. 1998.
97. See Steven King's article in *The Irish Times* 14 Oct. 1997.

98. *The Irish Times* 14 Oct. 1997.
99. See Sunday *Independent* 4 Jan. 1998.
100. Ruane, J. and Todd, J. 'The Belfast Agreement: Context, content, consequences', in J. Ruane and J. Todd (eds), *After the Good Friday Agreement: Analysing political change in Northern Ireland* (Dublin: University College Dublin Press, 1999), p. 10.
101. *Irish Independent* 10 Jan. 1998. The idea for a Council of the Isles came from Trimble.
102. Hennessey, T. *The Northern Ireland Peace Process: Ending the Troubles?* (Dublin: Gill and Macmillan, 2000), p. 117.
103. Hennessey, *The Northern Ireland Peace Process*, p. 117.
104. *The Irish Times* 28 Jan. 1998.
105. George Mitchell, the talks chairman, has described the way in which the two governments balanced the gains on both sides throughout the talks. Mitchell, *Making Peace*, p. 134.
106. See Rachel Donnelly's report in *The Irish Times* 28 Jan. 1998, and see Gerry Moriarty's report in *The Irish Times* 20 Jan. 1998.
107. *The Irish Times* 28 Jan. 1998.
108. *The Irish Times* 19 Jan. 1998.
109. *Irish Independent* 19 Jan. 1998.
110. *Irish Independent* 22 Jan. 1998.
111. *The Irish Times* 20 Jan. 1998.
112. *The Irish Times* 22 Jan. 1998.
113. Ibid.
114. *The Irish Times* 20 Jan. 1998.
115. *The Irish Times* 4 March 1998.
116. *The Irish Times* 7 March 1998.
117. Ibid.
118. *The Irish Times* 7 March 1998.
119. Ibid.
120. *The Irish Times* 8 March 1998.
121. *The Irish Times* 7 March 1998.
122. *The Irish Times* 21 Oct. 1997.
123. *Dáil Éireann Debates* Vol. 482, Col. 404, 4 Nov. 1997.
124. In reply to Dick Spring, David Andrews stated that he did not 'want to give a direct answer to his question at present'. *Dáil Éireann Debates* Vol. 482, Col. 404, 4 Nov. 1997.
125. As referred to in John A. Murphy's article in *The Irish Times* 9 April 1998.
126. *The Irish Times* 9 April 1998.
127. Sunday *Independent* 29 March 1998.
128. *Irish Independent* 10 April 1998.
129. *The Irish Times* 8 May 1998.
130. *The Irish Times* 12 March 1998.
131. Sunday *Independent* 22 March 1998.
132. *The Irish Times* 18 March 1998.
133. Sunday *Independent* 19 March 1998.
134. *Dáil Éireann Debates* Vol. 489, Col. 711, 1 April 1998.
135. *The Irish Times* 3 March 1998.
136. See *The Irish Times* 27 March 1998.
137. *The Irish Times* 6 March 1998.
138. Sunday *Independent* 22 March 1998.
139. *Irish Independent* 31 March 1998, *The Irish Times* 31 March 1998.
140. *The Irish Times* 31 March 1998.
141. *Dáil Éireann Debates* Vol. 489, Col. 418, 31 March 1998.
142. Conor Lenihan, *Irish Independent* 31 March 1998.
143. *The Irish Times* 1 April 1998.
144. Ibid.
145. *Irish Independent* 1 April 1998.
146. Bertie Ahern, *Irish Independent* 1 April 1998.
147. David Andrews, *Irish Independent* 1 April 1998.
148. *The Irish Times* 3 April 1998.

149. Ibid.
150. For an account of the events leading up to the final agreement on Strand Two and the agreement itself see Mallie, E. and McKittrick, D. *Endgame in Ireland: The search for peace in Northern Ireland* (London: Hodder and Stoughton, 2001), Chapters 15–16. See also Hennessey, *The Northern Ireland Peace Process,* Part II; Mitchell, *Making Peace.*
151. *Irish Independent* 11 April 1998.
152. *The Irish Times* 11 April 1998.
153. Sunday *Independent* 12 April 1998.
154. *Dáil Éireann Debates* Vol. 489, Col. 1028, 21 April 1998.
155. *Irish Independent* 27 April 1998.
156. *Dáil Éireann Debates* Vol. 489, Col. 1029, 21 April 1998.
157. *Irish Independent* 27 April 1998.
158. Sunday *Independent* 12 April 1998.
159. Fianna Fáil allocated a budget of IR£200,000 to its 'Yes' campaign, *The Irish Times* 30 April 1998.
160. *The Irish Times* 2 May 1998.
161. *The Irish Times* 1 May 1998.
162. *Irish Independent* 18 April 1998.
163. Ruairi Quinn; Labour Senator, 1976–7, 1981–2; elected to the Dáil in 1977 and again in 1982; Minister for Finance, 1994–1997; Deputy leader of the Labour Party, 1990–7; elected leader of the Labour Party in 1997.
164. *Dáil Éireann Debates* Vol. 489, Col. 1049, 21 April 1998.
165. *Dáil Éireann Debates* Vol. 489, Col. 1064, 21 April 1998.
166. *Dáil Éireann Debates* Vol. 489, Col. 1068, 21 April 1998
167. *Dáil Éireann Debates* Vol. 489, Cols 1105–6, 21 April 1998.
168. *Dáil Éireann Debates* Vol. 489, Col. 1132, 21 April 1998.
169. This was mirrored in the unionist community, see Farrington, C. 'Ulster Unionist Political Divisions in the Late Twentieth Century', *Irish Political Studies,* 16 (2001), pp. 49–72.
170. *The Irish Times* 20 April 1998.
171. See report by Barry White in the *Irish Independent* 12 May 1998 for unionist and loyalist reactions to the presence of ex-prisoners.
172. See Tom Brady's column in the *Irish Independent* 11 May 1998.
173. Denis Coghlan, *The Irish Times* 30 April 1998.
174. As quoted in the *Irish Independent* 18 April 1998.
175. Interview with John O'Donoghue, 7 Feb. 2006.
176. Interviews with Mary O'Rourke, 15 Nov. 2005; Conor Lenihan, 16 Nov. 2005; Noel Treacy, 1 Dec. 2005; Tom Kitt, 12 Jan. 2006.
177. For a study of unionist responses to the Good Friday Agreement, see Farrington, C. 'Ulster Unionist Political Divisions in the Late Twentieth Century'. See also Farrington, C. *Ulster Unionism and the Peace Process in Northern Ireland* (Basingstoke: Palgrave Macmillan, 2006).
178. Maire Geoghegan-Quinn, *The Irish Times* 11 April 1998.
179. *Irish Independent* 16 April 1998.
180. *Irish Independent* 25 April 1998.
181. As reprinted in the *Irish Independent* 17 April 1998.
182. *The Irish Times* 18 May 1998.
183. *Irish Independent* 21 May 1998.
184. As referred to by John A. Murphy in the Sunday *Independent* 19 April 1998.
185. *The Irish Times* 19 May 1998.
186. Ibid.
187. See Nuala Haughey's article in *The Irish Times* 5 May 1998.
188. The 'Yes' campaign in Northern Ireland is widely credited with shoring up the unionist vote in favour of the agreement. This campaign was organized by a number of non-partisan third sector groups, to win support for the agreement, and particularly targeted undecided unionist voters. See Couto, R.A. 'The Third Sector and Civil Society: The case of the 'Yes' campaign in Northern Ireland', *Voluntas: International Journal of Voluntary and Non Profit Organisations,* 12, 3 (Sept. 2001), pp. 221–8.
189. *Irish Independent* 18 May 1998.

190. Sunday *Independent* 17 May 1998.
191. *Irish Independent* 15 May 1998.
192. Ibid.
193. *The Irish Times* 21 May 1998.
194. *Sunday Independent* 17 May 1998.
195. *The Irish Times* 20 April 1998.
196. *Irish Independent* 21 May 1998.
197. The turnout in Northern Ireland was 80.98% and in the Republic it was disappointingly low at 56.1%. Figures available to http://cain.ulst.ac.uk/issues/politics/election/ref1998.htm, accessed May 2004.
198. Ivory, G. 'Revisions in Nationalist Discourse among Irish Political Parties', *Irish Political Studies*, 14 (1999), p. 102.
199. Brian Cowen on *Hearts and Minds,* BBC1 Northern Ireland, 12 June 2003.
200. Adams, *Hope and History,* p. 380.
201. *The Irish Times* 21 May 1998.

'The Monster of the Peace Process'[1]: Fianna Fáil and Sinn Féin after the 1998 Good Friday Agreement

INTRODUCTION

Fianna Fáil views the peace process and its contribution to it as a source of enormous pride. It took the risk of encouraging a process which included Sinn Féin, and this paid off for the party with the signing of the Good Friday Agreement in 1998, which gained cross-party and public support. The downside of this process became apparent in the course of the 2002 general election campaign, when Fianna Fáil faced similar problems to those also faced by the SDLP in elections in the North. The previous chapters saw Fianna Fáil deal with issues relating to pan-nationalism, the principle of consent and Articles Two and Three and reaching agreement with unionists. But the issues at the heart of the Sinn Féin–Fianna Fáil relationship, in the aftermath of the 1998 Good Friday Agreement, are in the main Republic of Ireland-based and relate to Sinn Féin's place in politics in the Republic. The peace process placed Sinn Féin at the centre of politics in Northern Ireland and encouraged Sinn Féin progression's into politics in the Republic as well. As a republican party with a traditionally distinctive voice on Northern Ireland, Fianna Fáil had the potential to clash with Sinn Féin and was most affected by the ideological challenge that Sinn Féin posed. This ideological challenge also had electoral implications. In addition, the normalization of Sinn Féin's position within the political arena in the Republic created problems for Fianna Fáil's policy on the peace process. In order to counter the challenge posed by Sinn Féin, Fianna Fáil had to ensure that it was not 'outflanked' by the republicanism espoused by Sinn Féin. Yet the Good Friday Agreement and the peace process placed a limit on traditional republican rhetoric and discussions about unity. Fianna

Fáil, as we will see, responded by claiming a direct link from the republicanism of its party and the 1916 and War of Independence era to the peace process. In addition, Fianna Fáil faced questions as to why it would not contemplate coalition with Sinn Féin when it had encouraged Sinn Féin's inclusion in the devolved institutions in Northern Ireland. Fianna Fáil had to be careful that it did not criticize the peace process or Sinn Féin's inclusion in government in Northern Ireland when it criticized Sinn Féin in the course of the 2002 general election.

This chapter takes a different approach to that adopted in the previous chapters. It does not concentrate on the policy of the Fianna Fáil leadership but looks at a public political debate surrounding Sinn Féin's suitability for government in the course of the 2002 general election campaign. It will assess the implications of Sinn Féin's presence in the political arena in the Republic and its ability to mount an electoral challenge for both Fianna Fáil and the peace process. Secondly, the approach adopted by Fianna Fáil in rejecting Sinn Féin as a coalition partner will be shown to be based on a distinction made on a North–South basis. It will become clear that, while Fianna Fáil rejected Sinn Féin in government in the Republic, it did not question Sinn Féin's place in the peace process. Thirdly, the chapter will outline the criticisms made of Sinn Féin by journalists, unionists, opposition members and members of the government parties. The differences in the criticisms made by each are crucial to understanding attitudes towards the peace process and Sinn Féin at this point. They also indicate the extent to which the political parties were willing to go in criticising Sinn Féin and the peace process in 2002. Finally, the chapter examines the shifts which occurred in the debates about Sinn Féin and the peace process in the aftermath of the Northern Bank robbery in December 2004, the murder of Robert McCartney by IRA members in January 2005, IRA criminality and the lack of completed decommissioning. The final section will assess the extent to which criticism of Sinn Féin (as opposed to the peace process itself) by the Irish government, including Fianna Fáil, heralded a new approach to the peace process.

These two points of focus in the post-Good Friday Agreement period enable an examination of the relationship between Fianna Fáil and Sinn Féin, Fianna Fáil's approach to the peace process and its use of rhetoric on Northern Ireland and unity. It also offers an opportunity to reflect on the implications of the peace process for constitutional republicanism and rivalry between Fianna Fáil and Sinn Féin.

A DUAL APPROACH TO SINN FÉIN

Prior to the 2002 General Election there was speculation about the possibility of a post-election coalition between Fianna Fáil and Sinn Féin, but the Taoiseach, Bertie Ahern, ruled it out immediately. A Fianna Fáil parliamentary party decision was taken not to enter into such a coalition and the party maintained that line throughout the election campaign.[2] The Taoiseach declared that: '[E]ven if the IRA were disbanded, all weapons put beyond use and there was a complete end to vigilantism and punishment attacks, North and South, and full support given to the Police Service of Northern Ireland, there would be insufficient time to establish confidence for government participation to be realistic.'[3] He also explained that 'parliamentary dependence on Sinn Féin by government through any formal or informal arrangement in the next Dáil would place an unacceptable burden on North–South and British–Irish relations'.[4] Not only would the peace process be adversely affected by a government in the Republic involving Sinn Féin, so too would relations with the British government. Ahern was consistent in his rejection of a coalition with Sinn Féin. The Taoiseach referred to a very practical reason why Fianna Fáil would not be able to contemplate a coalition with Sinn Féin. He stated that, while he felt Sinn Féin had progressed, they had still to move further to distance themselves from the past.[5] The then Fianna Fáil Minister for Justice, John O'Donoghue, agreed that: 'They [Sinn Féin] cannot be in government and I don't believe that any legitimate government can have the support of any organisation that has an illegal army attached to it. We are a long way from the stage where Sinn Féin can participate in any sensitive security matters in this state.'[6]

Reiterating what John O'Donoghue had already said, the Minister for Foreign Affairs, Brian Cowen, confirmed that he too would object to the formation of government supported by Sinn Féin. Calling for 'more progress in the peace process', in which Sinn Féin 'has a very important part to play', he outlined that 'it is [also] a question of synergy and policy position. Sinn Féin policies are not in line with ours, for a start their economic policies'.[7] The Progressive Democrats leader, Mary Harney, also rejected Sinn Féin on similar grounds when she proclaimed that 'Sinn Féin [needs to] abandon their left-wing policies'.[8] Willie O'Dea, the then Minister of State at the Department of Education and Science, alleged that Sinn Féin's success was not 'due to [their] policy platform'. He proceeded to say: 'While many might admire both Adams and McGuinness and may even express this in opinion polls, that esteem soon evaporates when they see the antics of their local activists. In many areas Sinn Féin is synonymous with what might be most politely described as extra-legislative activities.[9] Willie O'Dea reconciled the fact that the Irish government had been pivotal to Sinn Féin's entrance into the political arena with the fact that the mainstream political parities now disowned them: 'We have brought Sinn Féin into the political arena. Chaperoning duties have ended. Normal political rules now apply.'[10] Despite the firm rejection of Sinn Féin as a coalition partner, Fianna Fáil continued to support Sinn Féin's place within the peace process and politics in Northern Ireland. While not accepting that Sinn Féin was suitable for government in the Republic, the Taoiseach accepted the IRA's reassurances that its ceasefire was intact and accepted its denial of any involvement in the then recent raid at the Castlereagh Special Branch offices.[11] In the aftermath of the first act of decommissioning by the IRA, Bertie Ahern welcomed this as 'unparalleled'.[12] He referred to a later act of decommissioning prior to the 2002 election as a 'significant move' and said he was 'extremely happy'.[13] Ahern remained supportive of the peace process and the involvement of Sinn Féin in that process. Other members of Fianna Fáil also defended the peace process from attack, even though they had been involved in the negative campaign against Sinn Féin in the Republic. Brian Cowen berated those who appeared pessimistic about the move as 'carpers and naysayers'. He said: 'regrettably there was, as ever, a queue of those ready to diminish this achievement and to question the motivation of those who brought it about', but added: 'Their carping will not distract us from acknowledging the scale of what we have achieved.'[14] The government gave unqualified support to the peace process and Sinn Féin's involvement in the Northern Ireland Assembly but maintained that this could not be repeated in the Republic, on a number of grounds that related to security and democratic values.

Mary Holland of *The Irish Times* claimed that Bertie Ahern was justifying the support he gave to Sinn Féin in government in Northern Ireland but not in the Republic on the basis that 'the executive in the North was especially devised for the political purpose of conflict resolution and that, anyway, it is under the jurisdiction of the British government'.[15] Indeed, Fianna Fáil TD Noel Treacy explained that 'Northern Ireland is a different environment' and therefore different considerations apply.[16] Making a distinction between Sinn Féin's suitability for government North and South on the basis that Sinn Féin have still further to go before they can be involved in issues of security of the state exposes the fact that Fianna Fáil has supported a peace process that had put a 'slightly-constitutional' party in government in Northern Ireland. While rejecting Sinn Féin as a coalition party, Ahern and his party continue to give support to Sinn Féin's position in government in Northern Ireland by pointing to acts of decommissioning as evidence of the distance travelled by Sinn Féin and the IRA.

ISSUES OF SECURITY, DEMOCRACY AND DECOMMISSIONING

It is clear that concerns relating to democracy and security were at the heart of objections to Sinn Féin in government in the Republic. Many controversies with which Sinn Féin became associated provided ample opportunity for such points to the made. One of those was the arrest of a Sinn Féin director of elections who faced allegations of involvement in vigilante-style activities in Martin Ferris's North Kerry constituency.[17] At the same time Sinn Féin's existing TD, Caoimhghín Ó Caoláin, faced criticism for his failure to encourage members of the public to assist the Gardaí in their efforts to convict republicans. Attempts were made in the Dáil to suspend the TD from the Dáil because his stance was deemed to be 'reprehensible' and an 'insult to every member of the Garda Síochána'.[18] The bad publicity affected Sinn Féin's showing in the polls. Adams' satisfaction rating had dropped ten points to 49 per cent, no doubt a result of the fact that one in two believed Sinn Féin to be involved in vigilantism.[19] Adding to Sinn Féin's electoral problems was the determination of the US government to detail the exact connection between Sinn Féin and Colombian terrorists FARC.[20] Former Taoiseach and leader of Fine Gael, John Bruton, suggested that, since Adams appeared unable to travel to the US to answer questions on IRA and Sinn Féin links to FARC, he should be allowed to do so in the Republic. He envisaged that the Oireachtas Foreign Affairs Committee would ask Adams questions on this matter. In The Irish Times on Wednesday 3 April 2002 Bruton confirmed that he had contacted the committee's chairman, Des O'Malley, and had made a suggestion to that end.[21]

Subsequently a meeting of the Dáil's Foreign Affairs Committee was planned and a dispute was reported between Gerry Adams and Des O'Malley on the matter. The Irish Independent reported that a series of 'sharp letters' had been exchanged between Adams, Ó Caoláin and O'Malley. Sinn Féin called for a clarification of the objective of the meeting but, having only asked for such an explanation on the morning of the intended meeting, O'Malley responded: 'I doubt if you seriously expected this to happen.'[22] The controversy relating to the Colombia Three remained an issue throughout the election campaign. Former Fine Gael leader, John Bruton, criticized Sinn Féin's refusal to help the US 'in its enquiry into sources of terrorism' and asked: 'How will anybody ever take him [Adams] seriously in Washington again? What will Americans make of Sinn Féin's continuing links with the IRA now?'[23] The Minister for Foreign Affairs, Brian Cowen, berated Sinn Féin over its 'US Congress snub' and asserted that Sinn Féin had 'no prospect of being in any coalition government in the Republic until the IRA disbanded'.[24] Criticism had come consistently from Progressive Democrats Dáil candidate, Michael McDowell, and therefore he did not hesitate to reiterate his objection to Sinn Féin as causing others to 'decommission democracy to accommodate those who must decommission weapons'.[25]

Because reservations existed about Sinn Féin's commitment to democracy and as a result of the party's involvement in such controversies, the decommissioning gesture by the IRA in April 2002 was received with scepticism in some areas. The response from the White House was cautious. The development was welcomed but the sentiment that 'decommissioning is an on-going process, not a single event'[26] was reiterated. Members of the opposition parties in the Republic remained critical of Sinn Féin. The Labour leader, Ruairi Quinn, viewed the decommissioning gesture by the IRA as a political stunt with an aim 'to revive Sinn Féin's flagging election campaign'[27] and Fine Gael TD, Jim Mitchell, expressed the hope that voters would not be 'fooled by such a cynical ploy'.[28]

In the weeks prior to the election in June 2002, regular Sunday *Independent* columnists Ruth Dudley Edwards, Eoghan Harris, Alan Ruddock, John A. Murphy and Éilis O'Hanlon argued that the 'the gap between the sexy political rhetoric and the brutal reality of the Sinn Féin party'[29] had become apparent. Ruth Dudley Edwards attacked Sinn Féin for its disregard of democracy and compared the situation to the success of Jean-Marie Le Pen in France.[30] She claimed that Sinn Féin and the IRA 'hate democracy, unless it delivers the results that suits them'. She also cited the 'discipline' around which the party is run and which had seen 'republicans who challenged the leadership ... beaten, shot and murdered'[31] as a reason to rethink any inclination to vote for the party. This was the first comparison made with the right-wing challenge in France, although the same columnist had referred to Sinn Féin as a 'fascist movement'.[32]

Sinn Féin's success in five constituencies in the 2002 general election caused Ruth Dudley Edwards to declare an almost doomsday scenario: 'our democracy is now in peril'.[33] She claimed that a 'democratic boost' had been given 'to neo-Nazis'.[34] While she accepted that their increased vote highlighted the numbers who feel neglected by the Celtic Tiger and reflected a certain level of anti-government sentiment, she feared Sinn Féin's reliance on 'propaganda, thuggery and intimidation'.[35] Alan Ruddock concurred and berated the electorate's decision to vindicate men 'who have served their time on the IRA's Army Council' allowing them now to 'bask in the acclamation of the Irish electorate'.[36] Éilis O'Hanlon reiterated her objection to Sinn Féin's northern-based priorities and chastized the fact that it had not diminished the party's vote. She too, like McDowell and Brian Hayes (see next section), bemoaned the lack of a 'moral edge' in dealing with Sinn Féin.[37]

CRITICISMS OF THE PEACE PROCESS

We have seen that a range of sources was critical of Sinn Féin. In the course of the 2002 general election the peace process also came under attack. Such attacks on the peace process at this point were generally confined, with the exception of some opposition members, to certain newspaper columnists and anti-agreement unionists. There were two related objections to the peace process. The first was the view that the process was one of appeasement. The second objection was based on the argument that the peace process entailed an assault on democratic values; it enabled a party linked to an armed group to enter politics without any real evidence that it had moved away from violence and has seen both the Irish and British governments ignore illegal activity or acts of violence such as punishment attacks.

The main issue of contention for those critical of the peace process was the view that the process was aimed at producing the political conditions that would satisfy Sinn Féin and the IRA to the extent that they would renounce the militant tradition of republicanism and embrace politics. The peace process is therefore seen as one of appeasement in favour of republicans and, to an extent, loyalists. This has been summed up as follows: 'It is a classical case of the appeasement of the violent by those who crave for peace: Chamberlain at Munich, but at a much smaller scale and in a more sordid manner ... the logic of the peace process which has been based from the begin-

ning on the expedience of appeasement.'[38] The exponents of this
school of thought describe the peace process as 'corrupt'.[39] At the time
when there was speculation as to the possibility of an act of decommissioning from the IRA, Kevin Myers made it clear that he was not
convinced by the IRA's supposed jettisoning of the armed struggle and
condemned the peace process as 'a benign sea of appeasement …
There are no general punishments for these casual homicides [by 'dissident' IRA groups], no political consequences, because none is
allowed.'[40] Kevin Myers has vigorously presented this perspective of
the peace process. In the course of the election campaign in 2002 he
outlined his objection to Sinn Féin's involvement in government and
also the problems created for political democracy by the peace
process:

> [T]he peace process, not merely has created a corrupt political
> dispensation in Northern Ireland, but it has also given those
> associated with terrorism utterly unreal expectations of what
> they are naturally entitled to, and what they must do in return.
> The peace process has created a world without consequences for
> the IRA … Is it really surprising that Martin Ferris is so indignant
> that Fianna Fáil won't consider a coalition with Sinn Féin? How
> can such as he be expected to know our rules, when we have sys-
> tematically corrupted them to make them fit the requirements?[41]

Myers was not only disapproving of the possibility of Sinn Féin entering government in the Republic but also of the manner in which, as
he saw it, the principles of democracy in Northern Ireland were also
being undermined by the entire peace process because it was premised
upon the inclusion of all parties including Sinn Féin. This is a recurring theme within the wider debate about Sinn Féin's position both in
the politics of the Republic and the peace process. Alan Ruddock,
writing in the Sunday *Independent*, referred to the manner in which
'democracy in Northern Ireland has been debased in the name of
peace' through the participation of Sinn Féin.[42]

This tendency to criticize Sinn Féin for its conditional support of
democracy was a constant feature in the case against Sinn Féin's participation in government. As we have seen, these political columnists
and politicians have criticized the peace process, which had as its
basis, in their view, the tolerance of an undemocratic party in
Northern Ireland as a matter of expedience, in the hope of peace and
stability. In their view this has undermined democratic values in

Northern Ireland, which Myers especially was not convinced was warranted by its results. In this sense the columnists are displaying a consistency not visible in the position of the political parties that have chosen to view the two jurisdictions on the island in different terms. Of course, for these columnists this is exactly what is at the very heart of the problem. A number of politicians displayed irritation at the silence imposed upon them by the peace process; the success of the peace process was contingent upon Sinn Féin's participation and the parties in the Republic were compelled, through their support for the peace process, to be careful in their criticisms of Sinn Féin so that they would not highlight the double standards of the peace process. In his criticism of RTÉ's 'lack of political balance' in the handling of Sinn Féin, Fine Gael TD, Brian Hayes, referred to a 'hush-puppy type of coverage [being] afforded to Sinn Féin'. Sinn Féin was cited as the 'monster that has been created by the peace process'.[43] In the days after the election, Labour's Pat Magner made a similar criticism; he blamed Sinn Féin's success on what he called the 'soft focus'[44] approach inherent in the peace process. The Attorney General and Progressive Democrats election candidate, Michael McDowell, also criticized the complacency inherent in the peace process that has meant 'blind[ing] us to the huge dangers of adopting a naïve and uncritical approach to what they really stand for'. Speaking at the Progressive Democrats convention, McDowell rebuked Sinn Féin on the grounds that 'any person or party who owes a loyalty to the IRA, to its Army Council, to its 'court martials', to its claimed right to inflict murder and torture as a system of discipline or punishment, or to any putative sovereign authority which is not the Irish State, simply has no business in the Dáil or the Seanad'. He also maintained that Sinn Féin represented 'obvious threats to democracy and human rights'.[45] McDowell's point about the lack of criticism of Sinn Féin inherent in the peace process hinted again at the fact that the 2002 election campaign witnessed, not only criticism of Sinn Féin, but also of the peace process. Despite this the opposition parties have gener ally supported the peace process.

It is interesting to note the manner in which the main participants in the peace process on behalf of the Irish government and Sinn Féin have rejected such criticisms. Mansergh labelled suggestions that the peace process was based upon appeasement to republicans as 'absurd given how far republicans have moved. [The peace process operated] not in the spirit of appeasement but one of trying to get people to accept democratic principles.'[46] In Chapter Three we saw Reynolds describe how important the establishment of a pan-nationalist alliance was to the peace process and to his approach to it. However, he too has rejected the insinuation that his role amounted to appeasing republicans:

> No, no, I never approached it as a situation that you'd appease one to the expense of the other. You have to be fair and balanced and of course you'd never satisfy everybody, you can never satisfy all of the people all of the time so you make your best effort. So they had their own rights as they saw them and they wanted recognition for them ... When you start out to set something right in either community the other community tended to view it as appeasement, no matter which side, so you had to be fair and be fair on both sides and move forward from there. I think that the Agreement, the Good Friday Agreement, was a balance between both and that's what the Downing Street Declaration and that's what the Frameworks Document [sic] was and finally negotiated between all of the parties themselves, they all signed up to it.[47]

Martin Ferris does not accept that the peace process is premised upon appeasement:

> I don't accept that ... I think what it is, it is a mechanism where we can resolve the reasons why we have conflict, where we can build trust and understanding, for all our people, where we can promote equality for all our people, irrespective of their religious and their political background. And I think the events of the last ten years, in particular, is [sic] testimony to what has been achieved.[48]

Ferris also suggested that the process ought to be judged on the basis that ordinary people have benefited and not in terms of appeasement.[49] Ferris' colleague in the Dáil, Aengus Ó Snodaigh, responded to accusations of appeasement in a similar manner:

> Usually they all come from the same agenda and they were an agenda who [sic], when the peace process was initiated, attacked, not the republicans, because they do that anyway, but attacked the likes of John Hume for having the gall to meet with Gerry Adams initially. I think they're short-sighted ... the concessions

that republicans have now, if you want, are in the main no other than rights that would be enjoyed in any other society around the world. And most of them in the Good Friday Agreement are no threat to either society; they're a threat to an ethos maybe, superiority ethos that was there. They're not a threat to their livelihood or their existence as such.[50]

THE 2002 GENERAL ELECTION

One of the main characteristics of the 2002 general election campaign was the rivalry between Fianna Fáil and Sinn Féin. Sinn Féin attacked the government on a number of issues and this added to the sense of rivalry between the two parties. Sinn Féin supported a campaign to force the government to compensate taxi drivers who were affected by increased taxi licences. In the same week Sinn Féin heralded the plight of those who had voted against the ratification of the Nice Treaty, when Adams alleged that the 'Taoiseach and Tánaiste have not implemented the decision of the people and have not respected their democratically expressed will' and called for the formation of 'a Europe of equals'.[51] In seeking to canvass on these issues, Sinn Féin was only further alienating the main political parties. These topics were extremely unfavourable and the government did not want them to be raised. As a rebuttal, the Minister for Foreign Affairs presented his position and asserted that Adams' views on Europe 'do not reflect a clear understanding of the facts of where Ireland's real national interests lie ... Ireland's future prosperity is linked to a strong, prosperous and enlarged European Union'.[52] The government was not prepared to allow Sinn Féin to seize the moral high ground and ardently defended its position on the issues which the party raised.

Reports in the *Irish Independent* of a huge 'swing to Fianna Fáil and Bertie Ahern', with the possibility 'that Mr Ahern could win the first outright Dáil majority since 1977',[53] were not realized and Fianna Fáil eventually agreed to a programme for government with the Progressive Democrats. Sinn Féin improved its showing with the party's first preference share of the vote increasing by 3.96 per cent. The party gained an extra four seats in the Dáil. Martin Ferris received 24 per cent of the first preference vote in Kerry North. Both Sean Crowe and Caoimhghín Ó Caoláin topped the poll and were elected on the first count. Aengus O Snodaigh was elected in Dublin South Central and Arthur Morgan was elected in Louth, causing Fine

Gael, Fianna Fáil and Labour to lose out. Sinn Féin finished with five seats and there were a number of other constituencies where Sinn Féin made considerable inroads but were hampered by the lack of transfers, such as Joe Reilly in Meath and Dessie Ellis in Dublin North East. In Bertie Ahern's constituency, Dublin Central, the Taoiseach's running mate faced a strong challenge from Sinn Féin's candidate Nicky Kehoe, who eventually lost out by some 75 votes, saving Ahern considerable embarrassment.

THE IMPLICATIONS FOR FIANNA FÁIL AND THE PEACE PROCESS

Former deputy leader of Fianna Fáil, Mary O'Rourke, referred to the party's determination not to be 'outflanked' by Sinn Féin.[54] O'Rourke's statement reflects a determination that was clearly evident in 2002. The decision by the government to authorize the state funerals of ten IRA men executed during the War of Independence was the first in a number of attempts by Bertie Ahern and Fianna Fáil both to dethrone Sinn Féin as the apparent heirs of the 1916 and War of Independence legacy and to present the Good Friday Agreement as representing a continuation of that era and claim the agreement to be the final working out of these ideas.[55] The party argued that Fianna Fáil, rather than Sinn Féin, represented continuity with the republican roots of the state and also had successfully settled the issue through its part in the peace process. These attempts to reclaim the republican mantle saw Ahern state that:

> We in Fianna Fáil represent the honourable, living and inclusive Republican tradition of this State. We have a particular responsibility, which we have been exercising since the peace process began, to give leadership to those in Northern Ireland who share our sense of nationhood, our outlook and our values. But our most urgent task is to strengthen the accommodation and co-operation between our two main traditions on this island ... the issue of political legitimacy, for the future at least, because the past cannot be altered, has been settled by the Good Friday Agreement.[56]

As well as asserting a link between Fianna Fáil and the republican foundations of the state, Ahern also disputed the legitimacy of the IRA and any other republican violence post 1921. At a 1916 Rising commemoration ceremony at Arbour Hill he called on the IRA to disband: 'The fundamental question is this: Eight years on, what is the necessity of having a well-trained, well-drilled, well-equipped private army?'[57]

The level of agreement that Sinn Féin was unsuitable for government in the Republic reflects a consensus that the current peace process involved the only realistic mechanism of managing, if not yet solving, the Northern Ireland problem. Efforts by Sinn Féin to place issues of Northern Ireland and Irish unity at the centre of politics in the Republic contravened the political parties' view that acceptance of the Good Friday Agreement meant that these issues could be viewed in some way as settled. Sinn Féin's interpretation of the Good Friday Agreement as an immediate pathway to unity demonstrates the rhetorical differences between Sinn Féin and the other parties.[58] A fear existed that a government dependent on Sinn Féin would mean a change in emphasis and agenda. Mitchel McLaughlin's call for a new emphasis upon the issue of Irish unity[59] provided the basis for an ideological objection to Sinn Féin in government in the Republic. The debate about Sinn Féin's participation in government reveals the lack of space for debate regarding unity within the political discourse in the Republic in the years following the Good Friday Agreement. Support for and acceptance of the Good Friday Agreement removed unity from the equation, in an attempt to solidify the principles and institutions resulting from the agreement.

The absence of the issues of Northern Ireland and the peace process from the official election campaign further underlined this. On the issue of Northern Ireland the Taoiseach simply reiterated his view that the Good Friday Agreement represented 'an unprecedented term of peace, prosperity and progress' and stated that this was the area in which the government was most proud of its 'historical breakthrough'.[60] His immediate priority on re-election would be 'bringing together the two Governments and all of the party leaders for a serious debate on what we need to do collectively to push forward the implementation of the Agreement and to address the problems which exist'.[61] The Fianna Fáil manifesto asserted the party's priority to 'secure lasting peace in Ireland through the full implementation of the Good Friday Agreement' without 'prejudice to the ultimate goal of achieving a united Ireland'.[62] This was a contradictory position; there is a conflict between the acceptance of the Good Friday Agreement as closing the chapter on unity and stating that unity is the ultimate goal. The desire by Fianna Fáil to halt debate on unity, in contrast to Sinn Féin, again underlined the level of ambiguity adopted by Fianna Fáil on the issue through its support for the Good Friday Agreement and the peace process.

The muted response to the publication of Sinn Féin's manifesto was perhaps explained by the fact that by that stage it was clear that Sinn Féin would probably not be in coalition. But the lack of engagement with the ideas contained in the manifesto, which Sinn Féin labelled as a 'blueprint for a united Ireland',[63] was again indicative of the lack of debate generally about the possibility of a united Ireland. Thus a striking conclusion from the 2002 general election campaign is that the Good Friday Agreement has placed limits upon debate about unity in the Republic of Ireland.

Sinn Féin's presence and continued references to unity highlighted the fact that Fianna Fáil's language on Northern Ireland was no longer anti-partitionist and irredentist. Since Fianna Fáil and the other parties in the Republic support the peace process, the continued involvement of Sinn Féin at its centre essentially prevents any real criticism of Sinn Féin/IRA activity in Northern Ireland. However, the success of the peace process and the importance of maintaining the existing position on Northern Ireland requires the exclusion of Sinn Féin from politics in the Republic because of its destabilizing effect. The need to expose Sinn Féin's unsuitability for government in the Republic reveals the tension between policy North and South, as well as the contradictions upon which the peace process relies. Fianna Fáil overcame this problem by adopting a dual approach to Sinn Féin in Northern Ireland and in the Republic.

2005: A NEW APPROACH OR THE SIN-BINNING OF SINN FÉIN?[64]

Sinn Féin has continuously argued that responsibility for the peace process rests with the Irish and British governments. At moments of crisis in the process Sinn Féin has pointed to the governments to act to resolve the difficulties. This was the case in April 2004, when Gerry Adams, at a rally in Dublin, claimed that the challenge of getting the peace process back on track lay with Tony Blair and Bertie Ahern.[65] Fianna Fáil has generally appeared happy to accept the responsibility for the peace process in the way in which Sinn Féin has claimed it should. In the months before Christmas 2004 it seemed as though some kind of agreement between the DUP and Sinn Féin might be possible, with Bertie Ahern hosting separate meetings with DUP leader Ian Paisley[66] and Gerry Adams and Martin McGuinness.[67]

The most overt attempt by Fianna Fáil to assist progress in the peace process at this point was seen in a speech by Dermot Ahern at Hillsborough. In the speech, which was reportedly encouraged both by the DUP and by Sinn Féin,[68] the Minister for Foreign Affairs suggested that a coalition government in the Republic involving Sinn Féin was 'only a matter of time'. While he said decommissioning would have to be complete, he envisaged Sinn Féin in government in both the Republic and the North.[69] When criticizing this statement, Fine Gael Senator Brian Hayes argued that putting Sinn Féin in government in the Republic would be wrong, on the basis that the 'Republic is not the North. We don't have divided allegiance in this part of the island. The Northern Ireland Assembly is a regional parliament, established with the purpose of bringing together the divided and sectarian society that is Northern Ireland.'[70] This followed the North–South distinction that had been laid down at the time of the 2002 election, as seen above. How much was this changed by the Northern Bank robbery at the end of 2004, the murder of Robert McCartney in Belfast in January 2005 by IRA members and, more generally, continued IRA criminality? Did the Irish government's approach to the peace process alter in the midst of severe criticism of Sinn Féin and the IRA? Were there changes in the debates relating to the peace process and Sinn Féin's position within this process?

The massive robbery of about £26.5m from the Northern Bank in Belfast's city centre in December 2004 became a central issue in the peace process throughout much of 2005. Speculation as to whether the IRA had carried out the robbery ceased when the PSNI Chief Constable, Hugh Orde, stated his belief that the IRA was responsible.[71] With immediate effect, the opposition parties in the Republic were critical of Sinn Féin. Fine Gael's spokesperson on Justice, Jim O'Keefe, called on the Taoiseach and the Minister for Justice to state whether they believed the IRA had been involved. He called on Sinn Féin to accept the rule of law.[72] The leader of the Labour Party, Pat Rabbitte, explicitly stated that it was now time for a reassessment of the peace process. He admitted that the political parties in the Republic had tended in the past to 'turn a blind eye' to IRA activities in the hope that republicans would make the transition into full democratic politics. According to Rabbitte, this had not happened and he believed it was now time for Sinn Féin fully to engage in democratic politics.[73] He later welcomed the fact that the bank robbery provided the opportunity to expose the ambiguity within the peace process and that it had forced the issues of criminality and decommissioning to the centre of debate.[74] Fine Gael's spokesperson on Education and Science was critical of the government's track record on Sinn Féin and of the fact that it had been a bank robbery that finally prompted the government to raise the bar in terms of Sinn Féin. Speaking on RTE's 'Questions and Answers', Olwyn Enright also criticized the peace process, which made her sceptical about whether Sinn Féin would now face any consequences as a result of the bank robbery, since 'they [Sinn Féin] haven't had to take a whole lot of medicine in the past and perhaps they think they won't have to in the future'.[75] The leader of Fine Gael, Enda Kenny, also questioned the sustainability of a peace process that, he argued, had allowed the republican movement to corrupt the democratic process. He accused the government of allowing a 'sovereign Government [to be] held to ransom by an illegal terrorist organisation'. He argued that that process had seen both the Taoiseach and the Minister for Justice, Equality and Law Reform 'capitulate to its [IRA] demands for the early release of the murderers of Detective Garda Jerry McCabe in return for the fulfilment of IRA commitments under the Good Friday Agreement'.[76] The publication of a report by the Independent Monitoring Commission in February 2005 caused Kenny to call on the government to make adequate resources available to the Criminal Assets Bureau, so that it could focus on seizing IRA assets.[77] The Green Party leader, Trevor Sargent, argued that Sinn Féin needed to engage in policing in Northern Ireland.[78] Sargent and Rabbitte were again critical of Sinn Féin when arrests were made in Cork and Dublin, apparently related to IRA money laundering.[79]

The murder of Robert McCartney from the Short Strand area of Belfast by IRA members outside a public house in the city on 31 January 2005 further fuelled anti-Sinn Féin rhetoric among political parties in the Republic. The campaign by the sisters of Robert McCartney had an even greater impact on opinion in the Republic than the bank robbery. The two events together served to underline the issue of IRA criminality. Fine Gael's Jim Higgins suggested that the trustworthiness of Sinn Féin should be measured by the inability of its leaders to call on those responsible for the murder to go to the police. He questioned the sincerity of the two governments' efforts to bring the IRA to an end.[80]

There is little doubt that Bertie Ahern's response to the Northern Bank robbery was critical, like that of the other political parties in the Republic. His statement in response to the Chief Constable's claim of IRA involvement referred to the bank robbery as 'a serious set-back for

the political process in Northern Ireland and is corrosive of the public confidence that we have been seeking to create'. He went on to
outline the consequences: 'It underscores the need for compelling
commitments – both in word and deed – that the full spectrum of IRA
paramilitary activities and capability has been brought to a definitive
closure. This must include the necessary assurance in regard to all
forms of criminal activity which, following the Northern Bank robbery, clearly remains a major concern.'[81] Ahern made it clear that he
accepted the word of Hugh Orde, supported by Garda intelligence,
that the Northern Bank robbery 'was a Provisional IRA job. This was
a job that would have been known to the political leadership.'[82] The
British government was also adamant that the IRA had been involved
in the robbery and agreed with the stance of the Irish government that
the issues of IRA criminality and decommissioning would have to be
resolved before progress could be made in the peace process.[83] Tony
Blair made it clear that he believed that the IRA had carried out the
bank robbery. He stated the impact that this had on his government's
position: that Sinn Féin could not now be involved in a devolved
assembly in Northern Ireland until IRA decommissioning was complete.[84] This was the stance of both governments, despite statements
by the IRA and Sinn Féin members that the IRA had not been involved
in the robbery.[85] In fact Ahern described repeated denials by Sinn Féin
leaders of IRA involvement in the robbery as 'childish'.[86] Intense pressure was exerted on Sinn Féin on the issues of criminality and decommissioning. The Minister for Foreign Affairs, Dermot Ahern, insisted
that Sinn Féin and the IRA must now decide whether 'they [are] up
for full politics or are they not? We need an end to the criminal acts
associated with the IRA. They need to state categorically, once and for
all, there is to be an end to criminal acts associated with the activities
of the IRA.'[87] Mary Harney also said that Sinn Féin now had serious
questions to answer and that it must make it clear that the Provisional
IRA had ceased all criminal activity and violence. She also dismissed
claims by the Sinn Féin leadership that it did not know of the plans to
rob the Northern Bank, as well as claims by Martin Ferris that he was
not currently in the IRA.[88]

This is the first episode of the peace process where the Irish govern-
ment and, more significantly, Fianna Fáil explicitly placed the onus for
progress with Sinn Féin and the IRA. This was made clear to the Sinn
Féin leadership at a meeting at Government Buildings, when both
Dermot Ahern and Michael McDowell called on Adams and
McGuinness to 'reflect' on the government's insistence that criminality

must end.[89] Dermot Ahern called on the IRA to 'take a major initiative' to restore confidence in the political process and stated that the government would not take on a 'business as usual' approach towards the 'Provisional movement'. He alleged that the impasse in the peace process was due to the Provisional leadership's failure to decommission and to end criminality.[90]

Relations between Sinn Féin and the Irish government were obviously affected, with Sinn Féin claiming that 'many nationalists and republicans will be deeply disappointed that the Taoiseach has chosen to believe the British and to jump on to the DUP bandwagon of blame'.[91] Martin McGuinness responded to pressure from Dermot Ahern by warning that both governments were moving 'onto dangerous ground' if they were to attempt to exclude Sinn Féin.[92] Relations between Sinn Féin and the Irish government were characterized at this stage by a number of public disputes between Sinn Féin members and government ministers. For example, Sinn Féin members clashed with a number of Fianna Fáil ministers as a result of the refusal by Sinn Féin to state whether it believed the IRA murder of Jean McConville to have been a crime. Willie O'Dea and Seamus Brennan attacked Sean Crowe and Mary Lou McDonald on this issue.[93] There was also a series of bitter disputes in the course of Dáil debates. Bertie Ahern consistently reiterated the breach of trust which had resulted from the Northern Bank robbery and placed the issues of criminality and decommissioning as central to further progress.[94] Sinn Féin TD, Caoimhghín Ó Caoláin, reacted angrily to Ahern's accusations about Sinn Féin involvement in criminality. He said that Ahern 'has a neck trying to label any other political party with the criminality tag'. He rejected Ahern's allegations and accused Ahern of damaging the peace process by making these allegations in relation to the Northern Bank robbery. He called on him to withdraw the allegations, which he claimed had been made by the Taoiseach for electoral reasons.[95] As had been the case in the past, the Minister for Justice, Equality and Law Reform, Michael McDowell, was outspoken in his attacks on Sinn Féin. McDowell argued that: 'The Provisionals have a single set of beliefs. That set of beliefs involves the rather fanciful view, but it is the one held by all of them, that the Army Council is the supreme lawful authority on this island. As long as they are stuck in that mindset and that time warp they have a serious problem.'[96] He also caused controversy when he claimed that the Sinn Féin TD for Kerry North, Martin Ferris, was a member of the IRA Army Council along with Gerry Adams and Martin McGuinness.[97] This soured relations between Sinn

Féin and the Irish government even further and McGuinness responded by arguing that McDowell had merely identified a 'window of
opportunity to attack our party, to criminalise our party in the best
tradition of Margaret Thatcher'. Gerry Adams also made it clear that
Sinn Féin was determined to 'weather the storm' that had resulted
from recent events.[98]

The Taoiseach, Bertie Ahern, did hint that he was adopting a new
approach to Sinn Féin and the peace process. When Enda Kenny challenged him in the Dáil for following what he termed 'a path of
appeasement',[99] Ahern admitted that 'there was a view that for some
time this was tolerated in order to try to move the process forward.
However, ten years on, we cannot continue to do that.' Ahern went on
to criticize Sinn Féin for believing that it could continue to develop its
involvement in democratic politics while continuing to engage in criminality. He also referred to specific criminal acts which the IRA were
believed to have committed and claimed to be offended at the ability
of the IRA to 'turn-off' punishment beatings when Sinn Féin was
involved in negotiations with the Irish government. He argued that a
breach of trust had been committed because of Sinn Féin's knowledge
of the bank robbery plans while in talks with the governments.[100]
Ahern stressed that the two governments and the parties in the North
could not trust Sinn Féin in negotiations until clarity was achieved on
the issues of criminality and decommissioning.[101] He reiterated this
stance in the aftermath of his meeting with Tony Blair and the PSNI
Chief Constable, Hugh Orde, when he said that 'the position is clear
... If we get a definitive answer from Sinn Féin, for which both of us
have asked, about how to deal with decommissioning ... it would be
helpful to the process now and into the future. The second issue is an
end to paramilitarism and the related issues of criminality. That is the
position.' He said that progress could only be made 'if we get a clear
position, which means a road that brings us to the end of criminality,
decommissioning and paramilitarism. It is not a question of the
Government being able to move forward. There is no possibility of
getting anywhere until we get answers to those questions.'[102] Ahern and
Blair both stated that an inclusive process could not continue without
a definitive resolution of the issues of criminality and decommissioning.[103] In the weeks after the murder of Robert McCartney, Ahern again
stressed that Sinn Féin must offer more than words to convince people that they could be trusted. He wanted a comprehensive end to
criminality coupled with decommissioning: 'We want no ambiguity, no
fudge and no messing. Let us be straight and let us get to the bottom

line ... We can try to restart the process if that is achieved. We will not be able to do so if that is not achieved.'[104]

The Northern Bank robbery and the murder of Robert McCartney placed the issues of criminality, paramilitarism and decommissioning as central, not just to questions raised by opposition parties or in journalistic debates, but to the approach of both governments. This represented a short-term change in the discourse relating to the peace process and Sinn Féin. As we have seen in the previous sections, criticism of Sinn Féin was most prominent among certain sections of the media, opposition parties and some government members at election time. This criticism became widespread in the early months of 2005.

What did distinguish the language of the government, both Fianna Fáil and the Progressive Democrats, from that of others was the absence of criticism of the peace process itself. Both government parties concentrated heavily on criminality and decommissioning and were critical of Sinn Féin because of this. Fianna Fáil members also attacked Sinn Féin's idea of republicanism. For example, the Minister for Foreign Affairs, Dermot Ahern, accused Sinn Féin and the IRA of having ...

> ...besmirched the term republicanism. A true republican would adhere to and follow the will of the people as expressed democratically. The people expressed that will democratically in 1998 and the only impediment to the further implementation of the Good Friday Agreement on our side, the nationalist side, is the issue of the full decommissioning and the end of paramilitarism in the name of republicanism. No Irish republican can oppose that will ... How can we ever have Irish unity down the barrel of a gun, through punishment beatings or robbing banks.

He went on to describe the Provisional movement as 'the single greatest impediment to Irish unity' and restated the Taoiseach's view that 'what really matters is that core of the issue ... are Sinn Féin and the IRA going to take the quantum leap to become fully and exclusively democratic to promote their political ideals or not?'[105] John O'Donoghue made a similar attack on Sinn Féin's Conor Murphy on RTE's 'Questions and Answers'.[106]

Yet from an early point the Irish government explained that it remained committed to the long-term inclusion of Sinn Féin in the peace process. The Labour Party leader, Pat Rabbitte, was scornful of Ahern's view that Sinn Féin should remain included since exclusion in the past had brought thirty years of violence.[107] Despite such criticism and the tough stance adopted by Ahern in relation to IRA criminality and decommissioning, there is little doubt that the Taoiseach believed that Sinn Féin must remain included. While making clear that issues of criminality and decommissioning were now key to progress, Ahern dismissed accusations made in an IRA statement that both governments had changed their approach to the peace process.[108] The Irish government did not respond with enthusiasm to the Northern Ireland Secretary of State Paul Murphy's suggestion that, in the absence of pledges from the party of its commitment to democracy, the British and Irish governments now adopt an approach that did not include Sinn Féin.[109] Fianna Fáil ministers remained convinced that the IRA had no intention of returning to violence, despite the impasse facing the peace process.[110] This encouraged the party to remain committed to the inclusion of Sinn Féin. As a result, Bertie Ahern repeatedly stated his judgement that engagement remained the only possible option for his government. He believed that the stalemate could not be broken in a vacuum and that he must therefore continue to try to reach an agreement involving Sinn Féin.[111] The Irish government emphasized its continued commitment to the implementation of the Good Friday Agreement with the conclusion of decommissioning and criminality as a core part of this.[112] Ahern and Blair outlined that they were 'rock solid in their determination to implement all aspects of the Good Friday Agreement'.[113]

This informed the government's policy towards Northern Ireland and the peace process: the Good Friday Agreement was paramount and Sinn Féin would remain involved in the peace process. This meant that there was no change in policy on the part of the government. The government insisted that the impetus for progress must come from Sinn Féin, since it needed to address central questions of criminality and decommissioning. This was a new element in the government's approach to the peace process in this period.

While this was evidence of the government's claim that it would be setting the bar higher as a result of the robbery, Ahern remained open to continued negotiations with Sinn Féin. This was despite threats by the White House to revoke Gerry Adams' visa to the US as well as the party's right to fundraise there.[114] The Irish government opposed the imposition of any sanctions against Sinn Féin by either the British or the American government.[115] McDowell also agreed that sanctions should not be imposed since this would then allow Sinn Féin to present itself as a victim.[116] Dermot Ahern held a meeting with Mitchel McLaughlin in Derry amidst the controversy and criticism and also said that the government did not want Sinn Féin to be excluded from the White House St Patrick's Day celebrations and believed that Sinn Féin leaders needed 'to be given the space to deal with those [issues]'.[117] He said that 'cool heads' were needed and the Taoiseach confirmed the government's intention to engage with the British government and all the parties in the North.[118] Bertie Ahern made it explicit that the Irish government did not intend to be diverted from its traditional commitment to a process including Sinn Féin. He argued that Sinn Féin should not be excluded despite IRA criminality, as a comprehensive deal must include republicans. However, he did clarify that Sinn Féin needed to fully accept democratic means.[119] In response to President Bush's decision to curtail White House St Patrick's Day celebrations by not inviting any of the northern parties, including Sinn Féin, Ahern again stated that 'exclusion is a hopeless exercise'.[120] By early March, Ahern was suggesting that he might soon resume discussions with Sinn Féin. He said he did not believe that Adams and McGuinness 'would have put so much into the peace process ... not to see it through'. He also said that both he and Tony Blair 'were always happy to work with the Sinn Féin leadership' while working to resolve outstanding issues.[121]

There was much criticism of Sinn Féin in the US, where the sisters and partner of Robert McCartney were guests of honour at many St Patrick's Day events. Ted Kennedy, who was usually supportive of Sinn Féin's presence in the peace process, was also critical and called on the IRA to disband. Amidst this criticism, which was unprecedented since the signing of the Good Friday Agreement, Ahern urged Irish America to remain committed to the peace process 'until the job was done'.[122] Both Ahern and Blair said that a 'clear and decisive' IRA statement of decommissioning and criminality was needed.[123] They were uncharacteristically cautious, in the context of the peace process, when the IRA stated that its members were not to be involved with any activities and that its armed struggle was over. Ahern described the statement as 'a momentous and historical development' but a joint Ahern–Blair statement stressed that independent verification of full decommissioning was still required and that IRA words would have to be borne out with deeds.[124] Despite this caution and the fact that the DUP leader, Ian Paisley, was unconvinced[125] by what Adams described as a 'hugely courageous' statement,[126] the Northern Ireland Secretary of State, Peter Hain, announced plans to decrease troop levels in Northern Ireland and also to end non-jury Diplock Courts.[127] Emphasis remained attached to the issue of decommissioning, the need for criminality to be seen to have ended and the need for Sinn Féin to become involved with policing in Northern Ireland.[128] McDowell confirmed that the IRA would remain an outlawed organisation.[129] The final act of decommissioning[130] by the IRA, as witnessed by two clerics from Northern Ireland, was received very positively by Fianna Fáil. The Taoiseach spoke of his desire 'not to dwell on a past that is all too familiar' at what he described as 'a real moment in Irish history'. He accepted that decommissioning had been completed, not on the word of the IRA, but because it had been verified by the Independent International Commission on Decommissioning (IICD) and the two independent witnesses, Reverend Harold Good and Father Alex Reid. He referred to the need for a process of security normalization to be completed in Northern Ireland and for the restoration of devolved institutions to take place. He also suggested that full negotiations should now commence.[131]

CONCLUSION

The debates that took place about Sinn Féin's suitability for government in the Republic prior to the 2002 election and the discourse between Sinn Féin and the other political parties in the Republic offer a number of conclusions. Criticism of the peace process and Sinn Féin was consistently made by a number of journalists. Sinn Féin was viewed as a threat to the democratic nature and security of the state and the peace process was criticized as rewarding violence, for being immoral, appeasing terrorists and allowing Sinn Féin a central place in Irish politics. Some members of the opposition also objected to aspects of the peace process and to Sinn Féin. Fianna Fáil's criticism of Sinn Féin was confined generally to electoral campaigns and not extended to the peace process.

The 2002 general election saw Fianna Fáil continue to redefine the boundaries of its republicanism by linking the Good Friday Agreement and the peace process to the era of 1916–21. The election campaign witnessed Fianna Fáil lay claim to the ethos of 1916–21 as legitimizing the party's commitment to the Good Friday Agreement. Ahern's addresses at the burials of Kevin Barry and the other War of Independence IRA members and at the Fianna Fáil Árd Fheis were eloquent acts in bridging the gap between his party's roots and the ideological implications of the Good Friday Agreement and also in refuting any correlation between the 1916 Rising and Sinn Féin and the IRA campaign between 1970 and 1994.

On an ideological basis the competition between Fianna Fáil and
Sinn Féin does revolve around who has ownership of the ideals of
1916, but their joint commitment to the peace process and the Good
Friday Agreement means that they cannot compete over who has the
best policy on Northern Ireland or on bringing about a united Ireland.
What they compete over instead is who is most able to manage that
peace process. Fianna Fáil argues that Fine Gael in government would
be damaging for the peace process and makes the same argument
about the implications of Sinn Féin in government in the Republic. It
is in this way that Northern Ireland and the peace process feature in
electoral politics in the Republic at this stage. It is in the same way
that it was an issue in the 1970s and 1980s, as a question of competency.

The government's pursuance of a contradictory approach of
attempting to render Sinn Féin's position illegitimate in the Republic
while accepting its centrality to the continuation of the peace process
in Northern Ireland was seen most clearly at that point. The 2002
election highlighted the inconsistency in the government's treatment
of Sinn Féin as a 'northern party' suitable only for government in
Northern Ireland, where the journey to complete democracy has not
yet been concluded.

The 2002 election campaign offers a useful point of comparison in
assessing whether 2005 and the fallout from the Northern Bank robbery and the murder of Robert McCartney heralded significant
changes. The bank robbery served as a reminder of the type of criminality that the IRA was still involved with[132] and 'derailed confidence'[133] in Sinn Féin, and there were a number of crucial changes.
However, the government's approach and commitment to the peace
process, Sinn Féin's inclusion and the implementation of the Good
Friday Agreement remained. The major change was seen in the widespread criticism of Sinn Féin. What this did was draw attention to the
failings and ambiguities in the peace process, which thus far had only
been highlighted by members of the media, anti-agreement unionists
and some members of the opposition. A second crucial change was
the insistence by both the Irish government and the British government that the onus for progress rested with Sinn Féin and the IRA.
Government ministers reiterated the need for IRA decommissioning
and an end to IRA criminality before the political process could proceed and devolution could be restored.

One point of continuity between the 2002 election campaign and the
2005 debates was that the Irish government did not engage in criticism

of the peace process itself in the way in which opposition leaders such as Enda Kenny and Pat Rabbitte did. Fianna Fáil remained committed to the implementation of the Good Friday Agreement and an inclusive process with Sinn Féin involved. Ahern, in the face of criticism of Sinn Féin from the US government, argued that Sinn Féin must remain involved. Mary O'Rourke described this as Ahern's commitment to the 'long game',[134] while Conor Lenihan explicitly distinguished between the opposition's criticism of Sinn Féin's inclusion in the peace process and Fianna Fáil's criticism of Sinn Féin on issues of criminality and decommissioning. He stressed that the Progressive Democrats and, specifically, Michael McDowell, had been in tune with Fianna Fáil on this.[135] While McDowell was highly critical of the republican movement, he did not attack the peace process. McDowell's role as Minister for Justice, Equality and Law Reform has allowed a 'good-cop, bad-cop' scenario to develop. Lenihan also referred to the fact that certain sections of his party's voters do not like it when the leadership are critical of Sinn Féin.[136] Instead, McDowell has taken on the role, on behalf of the government, of criticising Sinn Féin in order to get movement on such issues as decommissioning.

The intense criticism that was visited upon Sinn Féin for most of 2005 yielded significant results. The statement by the IRA that its armed struggle was over, together with a final act of decommissioning witnessed by two independent observers, has proven this. This might all have been achieved at an earlier date, had the Irish and British governments adopted such a tough stance on these issues in the past. The resolution of these issues has seen a return to the traditional operation of relationships and roles within the peace process. Sinn Féin has once again placed the onus for progress with the two governments and with unionists.[137] Martin Ferris' statement also illustrates this:

> There are a number of things that need to happen and on which the two governments have already made commitments – the political institutions need to be restored; the British government need to come forward with legislation on policing and justice; the Equality Commission and Human Rights Commission need additional resources and powers; Northern representation for all MPs – nationalist, unionist and republican – in the Oireachtas; and the completion of the process of demilitarisation.[138]

2005 has also seen the resolution of a number of issues for Fianna Fáil. The party has perfected its stance on the possibility of coalition with Sinn Féin. At the 2002 election, Ahern made a distinction, like many others, between North and South in justifying his decision not to contemplate government with Sinn Féin. He also stated that Sinn Féin had further to go before it could be considered a suitable coalition partner. In November 2005, however, Ahern stressed differences in relation to economic policies as the reason why he did not want to go into government with Sinn Féin.[139] This is a particularly expedient use of an uncontroversial issue to allow Fianna Fáil to justify not going into government with Sinn Féin. This allows the party to avoid issues such as the security of the state and criminality, which are surely among the reasons for rejecting government with Sinn Féin. This way Fianna Fáil avoids highlighting the contradictions in approach to the peace process, the absence of a conversion to democracy by Sinn Féin and also the alienation of voters.

NOTES

1. Brian Hayes, then Fine Gael TD, *Sunday Independent* 10 Feb. 2002.
2. Interview with Dermot Ahern, 1 Nov. 2002.
3. Sunday *Independent* 20 Jan. 2002.
4. Ibid.
5. *Irish Independent* 17 April 2002.
6. *The Irish Times* 12 Jan. 2002.
7. *The Irish Times* 25 Jan. 2002. This is a reference to the socialist nature of policies which Sinn Féin has adopted.
8. Sunday *Independent* 20 Jan. 2002.
9. Sunday *Independent* 10 Feb. 2002.
10. Ibid.
11. Bertie Ahern accepted that the IRA had not been involved in the raid at the Special Branch offices, when a number of documents were stolen. However, it was subsequently claimed that the raid was connected to accusations against members of Sinn Féin and the IRA of an alleged spy ring, which eventually caused the suspension of the Assembly in Oct. 2002.
12. *Belfast Telegraph* 24 Oct. 2001.
13. *Irish Independent* 9 April 2002.
14. *The Irish Times* 10 April 2002.
15. Mary Holland, *The Irish Times* 8 May 2002.
16. Interview with Noel Treacy 1 Dec. 2005.
17. *The Irish Times* 2 March 2002.
18. Séamus Brennan, then Government Chief Whip, Sunday *Independent* 3 March 2002.
19. Sunday *Independent* 10 March 2002. In the same poll, Bertie Ahern's personal rating remained steady at 69 per cent, Mary Harney's rating was high at 63 per cent while Michael Noonan's was low at 32%.
20. Conor Cruise O'Brien's column, *Irish Independent Weekend Review* 23 March 2002.
21. *The Irish Times* 3 March 2002.
22. *Irish Independent* 12 April 2002.
23. *The Irish Times* 24 April 2002.
24. *Irish Independent* 29 April 2002.
25. Sunday *Independent* 12 May 2002.
26. White House statement, *Irish Independent* 9 April 2002.
27. *Irish Independent* 9 April 2002.
28. Ibid.
29. Ruth Dudley Edwards, Sunday *Independent* 5 May 2002.

30. Jean Marie Le Pen's party, the National Front, is widely viewed as right-wing, fascist and xenophobic. The party has secured between 15 and 20 per cent of the national vote in France. See Bruce Crumley's article in *Time Magazine*, 159, 23, 10 June 2002.
31. Sunday *Independent* 5 May 2002.
32. Sunday *Independent* 14 April 2002.
33. Sunday *Independent* 19 May 2002.
34. Ibid.
35. Ibid.
36. Ibid.
37. Ibid.
38. *Irish Independent* 10 Jan. 1998.
39. Ibid. Columnists writing in the Irish media who have presented this argument have done so along similar lines as a number of anti-agreement unionists such as Ian Paisley, leader of the DUP, and Robert McCartney of the UKUP.
40. *The Irish Times* 26 March 2002.
41. *The Irish Times* 9 Jan. 2002.
42. Sunday *Independent* 20 Jan. 2002.
43. Sunday *Independent* 10 Feb. 2002.
44. *RTÉ Election 2002* 18 May 2002.
45. *The Irish Times* 22 Feb. 2002.
46. Interview with Martin Mansergh, 12 Dec. 2002.
47. Interview with Albert Reynolds, 8 Aug. 2003. Reynolds did acknowledge that the DUP did not accept the Good Friday Agreement.
48. Interview with Martin Ferris, 12 June 2003.
49. Ibid.
50. Interview with Aengus Ó Snodaigh, 12 June 2003.
51. *The Irish Times* 20 Feb. 2002. Sinn Féin and the Green Party were the only parties to oppose the Nice Treaty.
52. Brian Cowen, *The Irish Times* 21 Feb. 2002.
53. *Irish Independent* 8 May 2002.
54. Interview with Mary O'Rourke, 15 Nov. 2005.
55. O'Brien has referred to Ahern's attempts to claim a 'continuity with the self-sacrifice of the past, [and] the party would simultaneously lay to rest any suspicion that it had relegated principle to pragmatism'. O'Brien, J. *The Modern Prince: Charles J. Haughey and the quest for power* (Dublin: Merlin Publishing, 2002), p. 174.
56. Bertie Ahern's presidential address to the Fianna Fáil Árd Fheis, 13 Oct. 2001, as quoted in O'Brien, *The Modern Prince*, p. 177.
57. *Irish Independent* 22 April 2002.
58. Ferris, for example, was very clear in his view that the Good Friday Agreement would not be the final settlement; Interview with Martin Ferris, 12 June 2003. Fianna Fáil also stresses the ultimate goal of a united Ireland but the implementation of the Good Friday Agreement is its immediate focus.
59. Mary Holland's column, *The Irish Times* 24 Jan. 2002.
60. *The Irish Times* 26 April 2002.
61. Speech by Bertie Ahern: 'Northern Ireland–Building the Peace', 16 May 2002, available at http://www.fiannafail/archive_article.php4?id=661, accessed August 2003.
62. *The Irish Times* 26 April 2002.
63. *Irish Independent* 8 May 2002.
64. Criticism by Fine Gael Leader, Enda Kenny, that the government's response to the Northern Bank robbery and continued criminality by the IRA would merely be to 'sin bin' Sinn Féin before returning to its normal approach to the peace process, *Dáil Éireann Debates* Vol. 597, No. 2, 8 Feb. 2005.
65. *News Letter* 12 April 2004.
66. *The Irish Times* 1 Oct. 2004.
67. *The Irish Times* 5 Oct. 2004.
68. Sunday *Independent* 17 Oct. 2004.
69. *The Irish Times* 13 Oct. 2004.
70. Sunday *Independent* 17 Oct. 2004.
71. *Irish Independent* 8 Jan. 2005.

72. Sunday *Independent* 2 Jan. 2005.
73. *Irish Independent* 17 Jan. 2005.
74. *Dáil Éireann Debates* Vol. 598, Col. 514, 23 Feb. 2005.
75. Questions and Answers, RTE 1 17 Jan. 2005.
76. *Dáil Éireann Debates* Vol. 596 Col. 27, 26 Jan. 2005. Garda Jerry McCabe was murdered in Limerick in June 1996 by IRA members in the course of an armed robbery. The question of whether those convicted in relation to his murder ought to be considered for early release under the Good Friday Agreement has been a continuing issue. John O'Donoghue, who was Minister for Justice, Equality and Law Reform at the time of the Good Friday Agreement, has claimed that they were never part of the agreement and that Sinn Féin knows this. Interview with John O'Donoghue, 7 Feb. 2005.
77. *Dáil Éireann Debates* Vol. 597 No. 5, 4647/05, 15 Feb. 2005.
78. *The Irish Times* 11 Feb. 2005.
79. *The Irish Times* 18 Feb. 2005; see also *Irish Independent* 18 Feb. 2005.
80. *Dáil Éireann Debates* Vol. 598, Cols 517–19, 23 Feb. 2005.
81. Statement by An Taoiseach, Bertie Ahern 7 Jan. 2005, available at http://cain.ulst.ac.uk/issues/politics/docs/dott/ba070105.htm, accessed August 2003.
82. *The Irish Times* 10 Jan. 2005.
83. Ibid.
84. *Irish Independent* 29 Jan. 2005.
85. *The Irish Times* 19 Jan. 2005.
86. *The Irish Times* 12 Feb. 2005.
87. *Irish Independent* 17 Jan. 2005.
88. *The Irish Times* 24 Jan. 2005.
89. *The Irish Times* 26 Jan. 2005.
90. Ibid.
91. Mitchel McLaughlin, *The Irish Times* 10 Jan. 2005.
92. *Irish Independent* 17 Jan. 2005.
93. *Irish Independent* 24 Jan. 2005.
94. *Dáil Éireann Debates* Vol. 596 Col. 28, 26 Jan. 2005.
95. *Dáil Éireann Debates* Vol. 596 Col. 33, 26 Jan. 2005.
96. *The Irish Times* 7 Feb. 2005.
97. *The Irish Times* 21 Feb. 2005.
98. Ibid.
99. *Dáil Éireann Debates* Vol. 596, Col. 29, 26 Jan. 2005.
100. *Dáil Éireann Debates* Vol. 596, Col. 30, 26 Jan. 2005.
101. *Dáil Éireann Debates* Vol. 598, Col. 510, 23 Feb. 2005.
102. *Dáil Éireann Debates* Vol. 596, No. 4, 2 Feb. 2005.
103. *The Irish Times* 2 Feb. 2005.
104. *Dáil Éireann Debates* Vol. 598, Col. 513, 23 Feb. 2005.
105. Sunday *Independent* 6 March 2005.
106. Questions and Answers, RTÉ 1 21 Feb. 2005.
107. *Dáil Éireann Debates* Vol. 598, Col. 514, 23 Feb. 2005.
108. *The Irish Times* 4 Feb. 2005.
109. *Irish Independent* 12 Jan. 2005.
110. Eamon Ó Cuiv, *Irish Independent* 24 Jan. 2005.
111. *The Irish Times* 19 Jan. 2005.
112. Bertie Ahern, *Dáil Éireann Debates* Vol. 596, Col. 28, 26 Jan. 2005.
113. *The Irish Times* 28 June 2005.
114. *Irish Independent* 19 Jan. 2005.
115. Dermot Ahern, *The Irish Times* 26 Jan. 2005.
116. Sunday *Times* 6 Feb. 2005.
117. *Irish Independent* 8 Feb. 2005.
118. *The Irish Times* 8 Feb. 2005.
119. *The Irish Times* 22 Feb. 2005.
120. *Irish Independent* 9 Feb. 2005.
121. *The Irish Times* 4 March 2005.
122. *The Irish Times* 17 March 2005.
123. *The Irish Times* 28 June 2005.

124. *The Irish Times* 29 July 2005.
125. *News Letter* 29 July 2005.
126. *Daily Ireland* 29 July 2005.
127. *The Irish Times* 2 Aug. 2005. The controversial non-jury Diplock Courts were introduced to Northern Ireland by the British government in 1972 in an attempt to prevent intimidation of witnesses.
128. *The Irish Times* 17 Sept. 2005.
129. *Irish Independent* 29 Aug. 2005.
130. See *Derry Journal* 27 Sept. 2005.
131. *Dáil Éireann Debates* Vol. 606, No. 1, 28 Sept. 2005.
132. Correspondence with Frank Fahey, 4 Jan. 2006.
133. Interview with Noel Treacy, 1 Dec. 2006.
134. Interview with Mary O'Rourke, 15 Nov. 2005.
135. Interview with Conor Lenihan, 16 Nov. 2005.
136. Ibid.
137. Gerry Adams, *The Irish Times* 11 Oct. 2005, Martin McGuinness, *Derry Journal* 15 Nov. 2005.
138. *The Irish Times* 11 Oct. 2005.
139. Sunday *Independent* 13 and 20 Nov. 2005.

Revising Republicanisms?

REPUBLICANISMS: FIANNA FÁIL AND THE PEACE PROCESS

The relationship between Fianna Fáil and Sinn Féin has been described as one of 'wayward cousins'[1] and Fianna Fáil's relationship with northern nationalism and republicanism is central to understanding its approach to Northern Ireland since the outbreak of the Troubles. Chapter One illustrated that, rather than engage with the debates generated by the Northern Ireland Troubles as epitomized in works by, among others, Conor Cruise O'Brien and Garret FitzGerald, Fianna Fáil continued to utilize traditional republican rhetoric throughout the 1970s. Chapter Two also demonstrated that debate within Fianna Fáil on the same issues was prevented throughout the 1980s by the party's need to respond to continued IRA violence, the growth of Sinn Féin in the North and the potential of Sinn Féin to cost Fianna Fáil government in the Republic.

While Jack Lynch and Charles Haughey indicated acceptance of the principle of consent and willingness to think about constitutional change, both leaders espoused an anti-partitionist position based on their belief in a united Ireland. They also held the view that the British government must take the initiative in advancing that solution. The anti-partitionism that formed the basis of both Lynch's and Haughey's rhetoric on Northern Ireland reflected the beliefs and interpretations of the party and its leaders. Since the outbreak of the Troubles in Northern Ireland Fianna Fáil has consistently sought, as part of a solution to the Troubles, to undermine support for the IRA by removing the reasons for its campaign. In order to do this, both Lynch and Haughey adopted a policy of unification and made use of anti-partitionist language. Fianna Fáil has always believed that unionists are Irish and, if the British government could give a statement in favour of unity, it would remove the reasons for IRA violence and force unionists into an early realization of their Irishness and that their interests lie in unity. Once this happens, reconciliation could occur. As long as IRA violence continued Fianna Fáil was not likely to revise its traditional republican language since it formed part of its approach to undermining the IRA's campaign. It was also a key part of the party's response to electoral competition from FitzGerald, to the extent that the rivalry between Haughey and FitzGerald related to Northern Ireland, and from H-Block or Sinn Féin candidates.

The decision by Haughey to open contacts with Sinn Féin in 1988 was crucial to altering Fianna Fáil's language and informed its subsequent policy. Haughey's willingness to respond to shifts within the republican movement created the peace process and underscored Fianna Fáil's role within it. The openness of key republican leaders to compromise was exposed in the various 1988 talks between Sinn Féin, the SDLP and Fianna Fáil and represented the catalyst for change in Fianna Fáil's language. From this point on both parties debated the correlations between self-determination and consent and changes to Articles Two and Three.

The book has highlighted that Fianna Fáil has traditionally been concerned with maintaining its ideological commitments to unity and national self-determination. It is for this reason that such ideological concepts were central to the peace process. Self-determination became a central issue because it was a 'republican concept' and was therefore vital in securing Fianna Fáil, Sinn Féin and IRA acceptance of the process. Sinn Féin had a very clear view of the role which the Irish government would play in creating a strong pan-nationalist alliance which would act as an alternative to the violent campaign by extending the republican struggle. Fianna Fáil's Tom Kitt has explained that, under Reynolds, Fianna Fáil's approach to the peace process was 'to facilitate and to give leadership to the pan-nationalist movement, the Hume–Adams initiative, to give recognition to that, to give substance to that' by working with the nationalist community and subsequently the British government.[2] Chapter Three therefore demonstrated that Fianna Fáil's function within the peace process was to ensure the continued operation of the pan-nationalist alliance in an effort to provide the conditions for a ceasefire. The Downing Street Declaration was the most obvious manifestation of the Irish government's role in securing an IRA ceasefire. Commitments made by the Reynolds government were crucial in persuading the IRA to call a ceasefire. Once the ceasefire was reached, the Irish government sought to ensure Sinn Féin's position at the negotiating table. The importance of the pan-nationalist alliance and commitments made by the Irish government was illustrated again in Chapter Four by the collapse of the ceasefire during the Bruton administration. Fianna Fáil, in opposition in this period, was very clear in its criticisms of the Rainbow Coalition for departing from the pan-nationalist alliance.

Chapter Three also demonstrated that the Anglo-Irish Agreement was not key to the Irish government's role in the peace process. Anglo-Irish relations offered a natural arena for the process which emanated from pan-nationalism to proceed once agreement was reached within nationalism. The institutions of the Anglo-Irish Agreement merely complemented this movement forward but did not spawn the peace process. Reynolds envisaged a wider process involving the British government and unionists but agreement within nationalism took precedence in the early stages.

There are a number of reasons why Fianna Fáil, under Reynolds and subsequently Ahern, placed the pan-nationalist alliance and the inclusion of Sinn Féin at the centre of its approach to the peace process. They were both guided by two principles of Fianna Fáil policy on Northern Ireland dating back to the Lynch era. The first of these was the belief that the Irish government and Fianna Fáil had a natural affinity with nationalists in Northern Ireland. The second was the view held by Fianna Fáil since the outbreak of the Troubles that the key to a solution to the Northern Ireland Troubles was to remove the reasons for IRA violence. This, according to Fianna Fáil, remained the arena within which progress needed to be made and Fianna Fáil, because of its natural affinity with northern republicans, had it within its power to do something to move the logjam created by IRA violence. It was exactly this that Reynolds sought to achieve when he committed himself to the pan-nationalist alliance and Sinn Féin's inclusion in constitutional politics. Reynolds was guided by these two long-standing principles of Fianna Fáil policy on Northern Ireland. His success means that effectively the peace process reflects Fianna Fáil's ideological and policy positions on Northern Ireland.

Fianna Fáil's objective in the peace process throughout the 1990s was to secure Sinn Fein's place at the negotiating table. This is crucial in understanding the motivations of Fianna Fáil throughout the peace process. The manner in which the principle of consent has been correlated with national self-determination to enable an honourable entry into politics by the republican movement is indicative of this.

Fianna Fáil only adopted an approach that enabled it to engage with unionism in late 1997 when substantive negotiations had begun.

Hence, in understanding the peace process, it is useful to make a distinction between that process and the Good Friday Agreement which it spawned. The Good Friday Agreement was a balanced agreement in that concessions were made on all sides. Yet the peace process has not been so balanced. It had its origins in a decision by the republican movement to extend its struggle to the political arena and was advanced by the willingness on the part of the SDLP and Fianna Fáil to support this by providing the necessary favourable conditions. Thus, its origins are in pan-nationalism. The negotiations and post-agreement period have witnessed an alteration between addressing nationalist and unionist concerns. While this has altered the operation of the pan-nationalist alliance, concessions continue to be made to republicans. Anti-agreement criticisms surround the issue of rewarding violence and the continued threat of a return to violence and are in fact much more critical of the peace process and the process of implementing the Good Friday Agreement than of the agreement itself.

The peace process has significantly altered the relationship between Fianna Fáil and Sinn Féin. The acceptance of the Good Friday Agreement by both Sinn Féin and Fianna Fáil marked an agreement between the two parties.[3] The level of variance between the two parties does not relate to an ideological difference regarding partition but rather to the pace at which the Good Friday Agreement should move towards achieving a united Ireland. The rivalry between the two parties has been translated onto an electoral plane in the Republic and is defined by the distinction which Fianna Fáil has applied to the question of Sinn Féin's suitability for government on a North–South basis. This shows that Fianna Fáil's approach to the peace process in the aftermath of the Good Friday Agreement has been defined by the need to reconcile the central principle of the peace process, the inclusion of Sinn Féin, with Sinn Féin's electoral and ideological threat to the traditional constitutional nationalist parties in both states in Ireland. It is in this manner that Sinn Féin has continued to influence Fianna Fáil's northern policy and this has been illustrated throughout.

THE NATION

Speaking in October 2003, Sinn Féin president, Gerry Adams, defined what the term 'republicanism' entailed for him: 'Being an Irish repub-

lican means more than paying lip service to the 1916 Proclamation or
to the ideal of "the republic". It means refusing to stand still. It means
taking risks. It means reaching out to others. It means moving forward.'[4] Adams' reference to 1916 shows that he needed to portray
this 'movement forward' as a continuation of the ideals of that period. Yet the peace process has meant a significant movement *away*
from the historical position of classic Irish republicanism. What
Adams outlined as being central to that movement characterizes the
extent to which the peace process has shifted his party from its traditional language. He continued: 'The Good Friday Agreement, with its
vision of a fair and just society operating exclusively democratically
and peacefully, was democratically endorsed by the people of both
states on the island of Ireland.'[5] This subtle reference to the 'two
states on the island of Ireland' reflects the ideological implications
which the peace process has entailed for republicanism. Bertie Ahern
has espoused a similar recognition of the two states on the island:

> Maintaining the integrity of the nation as set out in Article Two
> is vital ... At the same time, our citizenship laws do not force
> anyone in the North who does not want it to accept Irish citi-
> zenship. Equally, we could not ask any nationalist, North and
> South, to accept the proposition that Armagh, Antrim or Down
> or the other counties are no longer Irish as far as we are con-
> cerned. It is another matter to claim that the whole island is or
> should be under the jurisdiction of Twenty Six county state insti-
> tutions.[6]

Maintaining a thirty-two county definition of the nation but also
accepting the continued existence of two states on the island represented the key formula employed by Fianna Fáil in terms of constitutional change. That both Fianna Fáil and Sinn Féin should speak in a
similar language on this issue is indicative of the level of consensus
which has been established between the two republican parties in the
course of the peace process. Once again, this stresses the need to
understand the dynamics of the peace process and the role of Fianna
Fáil within it through the study of the relationship between these two
parties, and this has been the central framework of the book.

The ability of the Sinn Féin leader to speak in terms which were
alien to the party's doctrinaire position of over a decade ago suggests
significant revisions in the party's ideology. The party's abandonment
of its traditional demand for a declaration on the part of the British

government of its intention to withdraw and its acceptance of a devolved Assembly in Northern Ireland are testament to this.[7] However, it is too simplistic to view the Fianna Fáil experience of the peace process in this way. Another prominent conclusion drawn from this study is the need to draw a distinction between the party's decision to revise its approach and day-to-day language on Northern Ireland and its ability to reconcile, as opposed to revise, its ideology with the existence of Northern Ireland. There is clearly a new body of language utilized by the party. A cursory look at Fianna Fáil's vocabulary in the course of the implementation of the Good Friday Agreement highlights this point. Bertie Ahern has depicted the Good Friday Agreement as producing 'a new era in the history of British–Irish relations', which has transformed the future direction of politics on the island.[8] He referred to 'the enhanced quality of the relationship between Ireland and Britain', which has witnessed both governments undertake the role 'as co-sponsors and guarantors' of the agreement.[9] Both governments have continued to 'reaffirm our individual and collective commitment to the Good Friday Agreement and to its full and complete implementation'.[10] At individual times of crisis, both governments have stressed the 'collective responsibility'[11] of implementing the agreement and have sought a joint approach. The northern parties have looked to the governments to undertake their responsibilities in such a way.[12] A concentration on the Good Friday Agreement as representing the opportunity for a final settlement, the desire for the peaceful reunification of the island and an emphasis on functioning with the British government to ensure the implementation of the 1998 agreement characterizes the new language and revised approach which Fianna Fáil has adopted as part of the peace process.

However, our ability to conclude whether the ideology at the core of the Fianna Fáil party has been dramatically revised in a similar way to that of its language is not so apparent. While the rhetoric utilized by the modern Fianna Fáil party has been transformed, the party has succeeded in maintaining a consistent link with the ideology of its founding fathers. The introduction to this book outlined the core elements which have traditionally been central to the party's republicanism. They included an acceptance of some form of federalism, a distinction between recognition and consent, the use of republicanism as a tactic in the definition of the party and, most importantly, the priority that the integrity of the nation should be maintained. The institutions established at Stormont represent a form of devolution inherently different from that which was envisaged by de Valera, as he sought to have them devolved from Dublin rather than from London, thus breaking the union with Great Britain. The acceptance of a continued British connection would suggest a fundamental departure from the founding ethos of the party. However, it has been argued in the academic literature that de Valera's reluctance to remove the state from the British Commonwealth, together with his decision not to declare the state a republic in the 1937 Constitution, is evidence of his recognition of the need for a continued link with Britain.[13] The distinction between the party's acceptance of the existence of the northern state and its refusal to sanction it has been blurred. However, the party has portrayed its role in a process which ultimately gave recognition to Northern Ireland as the search for 'a just and lasting accommodation' which had the potential to overcome 'the deeply-rooted psychological and historical realities of identity and political tradition'.[14] The party has been able to argue that the peace process and the Good Friday Agreement have been attempts to resolve 'the conflicts and conundrums that history bequeathed us',[15] without accepting responsibility for that historical legacy.

Fundamental to understanding the way in which Fianna Fáil ideology has been reconciled with the reality of Northern Ireland, rather than revised radically, are the issues of national self-determination and consent. The manner in which these principles have been resolved does not represent a radical alteration to the party's ideology since a recognition of the existence of Northern Ireland was inherent in de Valera's and Fianna Fáil's endorsement of a federal solution. Accepting that the consent of the majority of the population of Northern Ireland is required before any constitutional change can be effected sits easily with de Valera's declaration that the North cannot be coerced into a united Ireland. The ideological prerequisite for Fianna Fáil has always been that the definition of the Irish nation must extend towards the thirty-two counties of the island. Thus, Ahern's argument that the inclusion of self-determination ensured that sovereignty now lies with the Irish people and not the British government was central to acceptance of the Good Friday Agreement by the party and voters.[16] The Good Friday Agreement has endorsed a formula which can be summed up as a 'two states within one nation' theory.[17] Maintaining the cohesion of the nation has left the Fianna Fáil ideology relatively intact. Consequently, the Good Friday Agreement is compatible with the idea of maintaining the unity of the Irish nation on an ideological basis. Thus, what the Good Friday

Agreement and the peace process have meant for Fianna Fáil has been a process whereby its language and approach have been revised, enabling its ideology to be reconciled with the existence of partition and Northern Ireland. This has been the central achievement of the party's place within the peace process. The lack of tension within the Fianna Fáil and Progressive Democrats coalition from 1997 about Northern Ireland policy underlines the extent to which Fianna Fáil has adopted a body of language as well as an approach which have been acceptable to the other parties in the Dáil.

Accepting that the peace process has not affected the party's ideology to the same extent that it has impacted upon its language is not to undermine the significance of the changes which Fianna Fáil's rhetoric has undergone, since this is central to the party's ethos. In terms of an ideological commitment, both to unity and to the Good Friday Agreement, the level of contradiction within Fianna Fáil's republicanism has remained. Hence the distinction between policy and ideology, which was clearest in the pre-peace process era, has returned. Fianna Fáil has justified its concessions on the North–South institutions and its recognition of Northern Ireland by the maintenance of its ideological commitment to the integrity of the nation. Promoting the Good Friday Agreement as a settlement, together with reiterating the objective of unity, once again illustrates that the party's priority is maintaining an ideological commitment to unity rather than adopting a policy that might achieve it. It was this concentration on ideology that made acceptance of the Good Friday Agreement easier for Fianna Fáil. As long as the party ensured a continued ideological commitment to unity and the integrity of the nation, the fact that its policy contradicted this did not matter.

UNIONISM

A recurring theme throughout the book has been the inability of Fianna Fáil to reassess its understanding of the unionist community in Northern Ireland. This has stunted the creation of favourable North–South relations for decades. Conor Cruise O'Brien wrote in 1988 that 'the *Irish Mind* has no room for Ulster Protestants',[18] and there is little evidence that at the turn of the twenty-first century Irish nationalism has provided sufficient space within its ideology for unionism. Richard English has demonstrated that republicanism in 1930s Ireland can best be understood in terms of the concept 'solipsism'; that republicans lived as though their own circumstances, political beliefs and culture were the only ones which existed.[19] This goes a long way towards explaining why republicans have failed to assess the experiences, beliefs and politics of unionism. Sinn Féin TD Martin Ferris' statement that unionists are Irish 'because they were born in Ireland' epitomizes the extent to which the peace process has not witnessed a reassessment of unionism on Sinn Féin's part.[20] The same is true of Fianna Fáil. While the gulf between the leaders of unionism and republicanism in the Republic is not as profound as had been in the 1930s (the unprecedented meeting between DUP leader, Dr Ian Paisley, and Bertie Ahern in London on 29 January 2004 is a most recent manifestation of this), a fundamental impediment to a true reconciliation between Fianna Fáil and unionism remains. This is reflected in the ideology of Fianna Fáil, which can be summed up as a commitment to reunification by non-violent means. A desire for unity has been a constant feature for Fianna Fáil and has been periodically married with anti-partitionist language, depending on the political dynamics within the party and the party's position in power or in opposition or, as in Lynch's case, in the highly emotive time when the Troubles first erupted. It has been this use of anti-partitionist language as an expression of the party's continued fundamental ideological commitment to reunification that has raised questions about the party's commitment to reconciliation. Fianna Fáil's eventual engagement with the debate on Northern Ireland and with what has been termed 'revisionist' arguments, as outlined in the works of O'Brien and FitzGerald, in the late 1980s resulted in the reformulation of Articles Two and Three of the Constitution, an acceptance of the principle of consent through its appendage to self-determination and building trust with unionists. It did not include a rejection of unity as the ultimate aim or a revision of interpretations about unionists or about the history and problems facing Northern Ireland.

So, even in the course of the peace process of the 1990s, and in particular the post-Good Friday Agreement period, when anti-partitionist language was abandoned, the ideology remained unchanged. The appearance of reconciliation between unionism and Dublin has been a most striking result of the peace process, but this has been enabled by the context of peace. The republicanism of Fianna Fáil and the desire for reunification should not be underestimated. All four leaders assessed in this book espoused that republican ideology with Lynch, in particular, adopting a policy of reunification at inter-governmental level. It is the context that determines the language used in conjunction with that policy of reunification. For example, Haughey's position in opposition saw much anti-partitionist language whereas the context of the peace process means Ahern has abandoned such language. The belief and desire for unity nevertheless remains. In addition, the belief that one day unionists will realize that their interests are within a united Ireland remains within the party, particularly given recent economic success in the Republic. The Good Friday Agreement, as a mechanism for bringing the two parts of Ireland together, will play an important part in this.

The most striking obstacle to real reconciliation with unionism is the nature of the peace process and the fact that the role played by the Irish government, and in particular Fianna Fáil, has been conducted in relation to republicans. Fianna Fáil's commitment to a powerful pan-nationalist alliance with reunification as its central objective, its glee at what it has termed the removal of the British government from the equation, its strong advocacy of national self-determination and inclusion of Sinn Féin, even in the absence of decommissioning and an end to criminality, undermine the party's commitment to reconciliation with unionists, the principle of consent and its pledge not to force unionists into a united Ireland. The difficulties reside in Fianna Fáil's inability to recognize that the establishment of a strong pan-nationalist alliance which has aimed at persuading republicans to enter constitutional politics (and we have seen how many believe that this has been done at the cost of democracy and justice) is contrary to the pursuit of a real reconciliation with unionists. All of this has contributed to the sense of dissatisfaction about the peace process within unionism. Fianna Fáil has undoubtedly rejected the use of force in bringing about a united Ireland but it appears happy, along with Sinn Féin, to create the political conditions that would mean that the only option left for unionists is to accept and negotiate a united Ireland. It is these contradictions that arise from Fianna Fáil's experience of the peace process.

This does not mean that Fianna Fáil has not been genuine in its desire to reach agreement with the unionist community and endorse a peaceful co-existence on the island. All Fianna Fáil interviewees for this book stressed the number of visits by unionists to Dublin and by members of Fianna Fáil to Belfast to meet with unionist delegations. John O'Donoghue argued that the party recognizes that it must reach out to unionism, otherwise it cannot realize its ambition of a united Ireland, and has stated the desire of Fianna Fáil to assure unionists that they have nothing to fear from the party.[21] Tom Kitt also stressed the safeguards in place, to ensure that unionists are not forced into a united Ireland.[22] The desire to make benevolent gestures to unionism was also demonstrated in the ratification of legislation enabling the establishment of the British–Irish Council and the British–Irish Inter-Governmental Conference[23] and through the concessions made in relation to North–South bodies. Once again, it has been on a more practical level as opposed to on an ideological basis that Fianna Fáil has conceded ground to unionists. The formula relating to self-determination and consent has not entailed an explicit acknowledgement of the unionist community as a second ethnic grouping on the island, but the creation of the Stormont government and the East–West institutions represent a practical manifestation of that recognition. The approach and language adopted by the party in the post-Good Friday Agreement period has given a practical expression to the acceptance of the unionist community, the British connection and the fact that unity is a distant hope. However, the party remains as ideologically committed to unity as was the case in the past and believes that two states, not two nations, exist on the island.

FIANNA FÁIL, NORTHERN IRELAND, UNITY AND THE FUTURE OF THE PEACE PROCESS

In November 2005 Sinn Féin successfully initiated debate in the Dáil on the issue of Irish unity. Dáil members endorsed a counter motion that had been submitted by the government. That counter motion stressed a commitment to unity, but also that unity was a future project.[24] Despite the emphasis placed on the Good Friday Agreement by Fianna Fáil, the party's commitment, in the long term, to a united Ireland is clear. The Minister for Foreign Affairs, Dermot Ahern, asserted that the Good Friday Agreement presents a framework for unity.[25] John O'Donoghue stressed the party's continued desire for a united Ireland.[26] Also discussing the possibility of a united Ireland, the Government Chief Whip, Tom Kitt, stated: 'Will I see a united Ireland? That's a hard question to answer but you say to yourself that there's an evolutionary thing happening here that I would say "yes we're moving in a particular direction".'[27] As well as a continued advocacy of reunification, the issue of Northern Ireland generally remains central to Fianna Fáil. Northern Ireland and the economy are the two main priority issues for the party.[28] Defending the party's record in government, Seamus Brennan pointed to its successes with the economy and the peace process.[29] Noel Treacy emphasized the importance of the issue of Northern Ireland as central to the party. In his view, 'It's deep-rooted, it's engrained in our ethos, our mentality, our psyche, our culture, our political philosophy, our idealism. Everything to do with Fianna Fáil is about a republican island of Ireland.'[30] Mary O'Rourke stated that the issue relates to the very ethos of the party[31] and Frank Fahey referred to the issue of Northern Ireland as 'fundamental to our being. We are the republican party and central to our whole existence is creating a united Ireland but doing it by consent.'[32] An illustration of how important the issue of Northern Ireland is for Fianna Fáil is best seen in the party's informal agreement with the Progressive Democrats prior to going into government with them in 1997 that the Progressive Democrats would not, through language or otherwise, interfere with the peace process.[33]

The long-term goal for Fianna Fáil is clearly a united Ireland. On a short-term basis Fianna Fáil is committed to the implementation of the Good Friday Agreement and the peace process. Since all parties in the Republic share the same short-term and long-term goals in relation to Northern Ireland, the issue does not dominate election campaigns. When the issue of Northern Ireland is raised, it is generally within the context of debate about Sinn Féin's suitability for government in the Republic and support for the peace process. The political parties do not compete over a policy on Northern Ireland since they have a shared one through their support for the peace process. Instead they contest the title of who can best manage the peace process and Fianna Fáil has repeatedly argued that, because of its track record, it is the best party to do this.

The peace process was continually faced with crises throughout 2005, but these problems have not upset Fianna Fáil's overall approach to the peace process. The Minister for Justice, Equality and Law Reform, Michael McDowell, has, in his severe criticism of the Sinn Féin connection with criminality, made it appear as though the Irish government's approach to Sinn Féin and the peace process has altered. But this is not the case. Bertie Ahern and Fianna Fáil's commitment to a peace process including Sinn Fein remains paramount. John O'Donoghue said that, while the government's attitude towards Sinn Féin was altered in the wake of the Northern Bank robbery, its attitude towards the peace process did not change.[34] The party has been very careful not to criticize Sinn Féin's part in the peace process. For example, in stating the party's reasons for rejecting Sinn Féin as a potential coalition partner, Ahern highlighted Sinn Féin's economic policies rather than its continued connection with the IRA. This has been done so as to avoid criticizing a peace process which Fianna Fáil seeks to promote, but also because the party believes that elements of its voter base do not approve of its senior members being critical of Sinn Féin.[35] Thus, criticism of Sinn Féin is not in the political or electoral interests of Fianna Fáil. Instead Fianna Fáil has been happy to allow the Progressive Democrats and Michael McDowell, in particular, to do this for them in order to put pressure on the IRA. This is convenient because such criticisms of Sinn Féin are acceptable to Progressive Democrats supporters but not to Fianna Fáil supporters.

While the Northern Bank robbery and the continued debates about IRA criminality did not alter the Irish government's belief that a commitment to a peace process inclusive of Sinn Féin is the correct approach, it did affect the consensus about the peace process that had existed in the Republic since the 1994 ceasefire. The peace process and cross-party support for the Good Friday Agreement have meant that a level of bipartisanship has been established. This has necessitated that all parties modify their approaches in embracing the principles which are at the core of the peace process. The discourse surrounding the Good Friday Agreement and the peace process has come to define a new paradigm of language and policy formation in relation to Northern Ireland for all the parties in the Republic. This has been periodically broken around election time and in recent times has been severely fractured. The dialogue relating to the peace process in the Republic throughout much of the first half of 2005 centred around criticisms of IRA criminality and, in the case of many opposition members, the peace process itself. IRA decommissioning in September 2005 ensured that cross-party commitment to the peace process survived the challenges posed to it earlier in the year.

David Trimble has spoken of the challenge that the 'adoption by the Republican Movement of a different political approach' has posed for unionists.[36] This book has pointed to the way in which this decision by the republican movement in the 1980s impacted upon the Fianna Fáil party as well as upon politics in the Republic of Ireland. The relationship between Fianna Fáil and Sinn Féin has not only configured Fianna Fáil's record on Northern Ireland but it has also represented the core development of the peace process. In highlighting the centrality of this point, the book has encouraged a broader approach to understanding the peace process that looks beyond the internal dynamics of Northern Ireland. The changing relationship between Fianna Fáil and Sinn Féin has come to characterize the peace process and this has impacted on politics in the Republic, North–South and Anglo-Irish relations in a way which had not been fully acknowledged. The peace process has not only effected a change in Fianna Fáil's approach to Northern Ireland but it has also altered that of all the other parties.

While the peace process has not radically affected Fianna Fáil's core ideology, the party has lost the distinctive value that the historical adherence to traditional republican rhetoric afforded it. The electoral divide between the political parties in the Republic has been altered through the construction of this new cross-party commitment to the peace process and Fianna Fáil now seeks to draw its distinctive value and base its dominance on its record on the peace process. It does so by arguing that it is the only party equipped to manage the Northern Ireland issue effectively. The introduction of Sinn Féin into that mix has also been a notable implication of the peace process for electoral politics in the Republic. Such modifications to electoral politics in the Republic illustrate the implications of the peace process not only for Fianna Fáil policy and language on Northern Ireland but also for the status which the party assumes within Irish politics.

NOTES

1. Interview with Conor Lenihan, 16 Nov. 2005.
2. Interview with Tom Kitt, 12 Jan. 2006.
3. Albert Reynolds said both parties had reached agreement on the peaceful removal of Britain from Ireland. Interview with Albert Reynolds, 8 Aug. 2003.
4. *The Irish Times* 22 Oct. 2003.
5. Ibid.
6. *Dáil Éireann Debates* Vol. 449, Col. 1354, 22 Feb. 1995.
7. See McGarry, J. 'Civic Nationalism and the Agreement', in J. McGarry (ed), *Northern Ireland and the Divided World: Northern Ireland conflict and the Good Friday Agreement in comparative perspective* (Oxford: Oxford University Press, 2001), p. 112.
8. Bertie Ahern, *Northern Ireland–Building the peace*, 16 May 2002, available at http://www.fiannafail.ie/archive_article.php4?id=661; accessed August 2003.
9. Ibid.
10. See, for example, the Joint statement by President Bush and Prime Minister Tony Blair and Taoiseach Bertie Ahern, 8 April 2003, available at http://www.fiannafail.ie/archive_article.php4?id=1433; accessed August 2003.
11. *The Irish Times* 14 April 2003.
12. See, for example, the coverage in both *The Irish Times* and the *Irish Independent* 11 April 2003. The coverage underlines the view of the two governments as partners in the peace process.
13. For example, Lyons, F.S.L. *Ireland since the Famine* (London: Fontana Press, 1985), p. 539.
14. Minister for Foreign Affairs, Brian Cowen, '*Clarity; Courage; Change*', speaking at the Annual John Hume Lecture, MacGill Summer School, 20 July 2003, available at http://www.gov.ie/iveagh/information/display.asp?ID=1245; accessed August 2003.
15. Bertie Ahern, *Northern Ireland–Building the peace*, 16 May 2002, available at http://www.fiannafail.ie/archive_article.php4?id=661.
16. Interview with Conor Lenihan, 16 Nov. 2005.

17. Gareth Ivory has referred to a 'one nation, two states, or in our case, two jurisdictions' doctrine. Ivory, G. 'Revisions in Nationalist Discourse among Irish Political Parties', *Irish Political Studies*, 14 (1999), p. 99.
18. O'Brien, C.C. *Passion and Cunning: Essays on nationalism, terrorism and revolution* (New York: Touchstone, 1989), p. 196.
19. English, R. '"Paying no heed to Public Clamor": Irish republican solipsism in the 1930s', *Irish Political Studies*, XXVIII, 112 (November 1993), pp. 426–39.
20. Interview with Martin Ferris, 12 June 2003.
21. Interview with John O'Donoghue, 7 Feb. 2006.
22. Interview with Tom Kitt, 12 Jan. 2006.
23. The Belfast (Good Friday) Agreement states that the aim of both of these institutions is to deal with 'the totality of relationships' pertaining to the two islands. The British–Irish Council was established to 'promote the harmonious and mutually beneficial development of the totality of relationships among the people of these islands'. *Agreement Reached in the Multi-Party Negotiations*, pp. 12–13.
24. See *Dáil Éireann Debates*, Private Members' Business, Irish Unification Motion, Vol. 609, Nos. 1 and 2, 2, 3 Nov. 2005.
25. *Irish Independent* 8 May 2002.
26. Interview with John O'Donoghue, 7 Feb. 2006.
27. Interview with Tom Kitt, 12 Jan. 2006. Tom Kitt stressed this would not happen without the safeguards in place for unionists.
28. This is confirmed by candidate survey data from the 2002 General Election, See Gillian Lutz, K. 'Irish Party Competition in the New Millennium: Change of plus ça change?, *Irish Political Studies*, 18, 2 (Winter 2003).
29. Seamus Brennan, Questions and Answers, RTÉ 1, 20 Feb. 2006.
30. Interview with Noel Treacy, 1 Dec. 2005.
31. Interview with Mary O'Rourke, 15 Nov. 2005.
32. Interview with Frank Fahey, 13 Dec. 2005.
33. Interview with Conor Lenihan, 16 Nov. 2005.
34. Interview with John O'Donoghue, 7 Feb. 2006.
35. Interview with Conor Lenihan, 16 Nov. 2005.
36. Trimble, D. 'Engaging Reality' speech at Ulster Young Unionist conference 3 Oct. 1998, reprinted in Trimble, D. *To Raise up a New Northern Ireland: Articles and Speeches 1998–2000* (Belfast: The Belfast Press, 2001), p. 41.

Dramatis Personae

Adams, Gerry: born in Belfast in 1948; interned in 1972 and from 1973–7; elected Sinn Féin President in 1983 and MP for West Belfast in the same year; involved in talks with SDLP in 1988 and with John Hume in 1992; member of the Sinn Féin delegation at the Forum for Peace and Reconciliation in 1994; elected MLA in 1998.

Ahern, Bertie: elected to the Dáil as Fianna Fáil TD in 1977; appointed as Assistant Government Whip in 1980; Minister of State at the Department of the Taoiseach and of Defence and Government Chief Whip, 1982; Minister for Labour in Haughey's government in 1987; promoted to Minister for Finance, 1991; succeeded Albert Reynolds as leader in November 1994; became Taoiseach in the Fianna Fáil/Progressive Democrats coalition in June 1997; retained this position after the general election of 2002.

Ahern, Dermot: elected as Fianna Fáil TD in 1987; Minister of State at the Department of the Taoiseach, November 1991–February 1992; Minister for Social, Community and Family Affairs, June 1997–June 2002; Minister for Communications, Marine and Natural Resources from June 2002 until 2004 when he was appointed Minster for Foreign Affairs.

Blair, Tony: born 6th May 1953; elected as Labour Party MP for Sedgefield in 1983; became leader of the Labour Party in 1994 and British Prime Minister in 1997 following a landslide win in the general election of that year; re-elected in 2001 and 2005.

Blaney, Neil: first elected as a Fianna Fáil TD in a by-election in the constituency of Donegal North-East in 1948; appointed Minister for Posts and Telegraphs, 1957; Minister for Local Government, 1958–66; appointed as Minister for Agriculture in 1967; dismissed from government in 1970 as a result of accusations about his involvement in the illegal importation of arms for the IRA, the Arms Crisis; expelled from Fianna Fáil in 1971; continued as Independent Fianna Fáil TD until his retirement in 1994; Member of European Parliament, 1979–84, 1989–94.

Boland, Kevin: born 1917 son of Gerald Boland, a participant in the 1916 Easter Rising; elected to the Dáil in 1957; resigned from the cabinet in 1970 in sympathy with Charles Haughey and Neil Blaney, who had been sacked by Jack Lynch; formed a new party, Aontacht Éireann, or Irish Unity, but lost his seat in the next election.

Bruton, John: elected as Fine Gael TD in 1969; Parliamentary Secretary to the Minister for Education, 1973–7; Minister for Finance, 1981, 1986; Minister for Industry, Trade, Commerce and tourism, 1982; elected leader of Fine Gael, 1990; became Taoiseach in December 1994 in the 'Rainbow Coalition' involving Fine Gael, Labour and Democratic Left; deposed from leadership, 2001.

Corish, Brendan: leader of The Labour Party (Ireland), 1960–77.

Cosgrave, Liam: leader of Fine Gael, 1965–77; Taoiseach in a Fine Gael/Labour Party Coalition 1973–77.

Currie, Austin: born in Co. Tyrone in 1939; Stormont MP for East Tyrone, 1964–72; active participant in the Northern Ireland civil rights movement, 1968–9; founding member of SDLP in 1970; member of the Northern Ireland Assembly, 1973–5; Chief Whip of SDLP, 1974; elected to the Dáil in 1989 as Fine Gael TD; Fine Gael Presidential candidate, 1990; Minister of State at the Departments of Education, Justice and Health, 1994–7; lost his Dáil seat in 2002.

De Valera, Eamon: Irish Volunteer commandant at Easter Rising 1916; elected as Sinn Féin MP and President of Sinn Féin in 1917; opposed the Anglo-Irish Treaty in 1921; elected as Sinn Féin TD in 1923; founded Fianna Fáil in 1926; led Fianna Fáil into government in 1932; Taoiseach 1937–48, 1951–4, 1957–9; President of Ireland 1959–73.

Doherty, Pat: born in Glasgow of Donegal parents; returned to Donegal in 1968; Sinn Féin vice-president since 1988; headed the Sinn Féin delegation to the Forum for Peace and Reconciliation in 1994; stood for Dáil election in the Donegal North-East constituency in 1989 and in the Connacht/Ulster constituency in the EU elections in 1989 and 1994; elected to the Northern Ireland Assembly in 1998; elected as Westminster MP in 2001 for West Tyrone.

Fahey, Frank: elected to the Dáil as Fianna Fáil TD for Galway West in February 1982; Minister for the Marine and Natural Resources, 2000–2; appointed Minister of State at the Department of Justice, Equality and Law Reform in 2002.

Ferris, Martin: elected as Sinn Féin TD for Kerry North in 2002; between 1984 and 1994 he served a ten year prison sentence for his part in an attempt to import arms into the Republic of Ireland; in 2005 he was named by the Minster for Justice, Equality and Law Reform, Michael McDowell, as a member of the IRA Army Council.

FitzGerald, Garret: appointed as Fine Gael senator in 1965; elected as TD in 1969; Minister for Foreign Affairs, 1973–7; leader of Fine Gael, 1977–87; Taoiseach, 1981–2, 1982–7.

Harney, Mary: elected as Fianna Fáil TD for Dublin South West in 1982; founder member of the Progressive Democrats in 1986; in October 1993 she succeeded Desmond O'Malley as the leader of the Progressive Democrats; became Tánaiste in 1997 and again in 2002; stepped down as Tánaiste and party leader in 2006.

Haughey, Charles: elected to the Dáil as Fianna Fáil TD in 1957; Minister for Justice, 1961–4; Minister for Agriculture, 1964–6; Minister for Finance, 1966–70; dismissed from government in May 1970 for suspected involvement in the importation of arms for use by the IRA, the Arms Crisis; acquitted of the charge of conspiracy to import arms, October 1970; restored to government when appointed Minister for Health and Social Welfare by Jack Lynch in 1977; leader of Fianna Fáil, 1979–92; Taoiseach, 1979–81, 1982, 1987–92.

Hillery, Patrick: elected as Fianna Fáil TD for Clare in 1951; Minister for Foreign Affairs, 1969–73; President of Ireland for two terms, 1976–90.

Hume, John: elected to Stormont as nationalist MP in 1969; founding member of the SDLP in 1970; appointed leader of the party in 1979; elected as MP in 1983; involved in controversial talks with the Sinn Féin leader in 1988 and again in 1992; joint winner of the Nobel Peace Prize in 1999 for his role in the Northern Ireland peace process.

Kenny, Enda: elected as Fine Gael TD for Mayo West in 1975; succeeded Michael Noonan as leader of Fine Gael in June 2002.

Kitt, Tom: first elected as Fianna Fáil TD for Dublin South in 1987; appointed as Minister of State at the Departments of the Taoiseach and Defence, Government Chief Whip, in 2004.

Lemass, Seán: Irish Volunteer involved in the Easter Rising 1916; member of anti-Treaty IRA 1922–3; elected as Sinn Féin TD in 1924; founding member of Fianna Fáil in 1926; Tánaiste 1945–8, 1951–4, 1957–9; Taoiseach 1959–66.

Lenihan, Brian: elected Fianna Fáil TD for Roscommon/Leitrim in 1961; 1964–8 Minister for Justice; 1968–9 Minister for Education; 1969–73, Minister for Transport and Power; Minster for Foreign Affairs, 1973, 1979–81, 1987–990; Tánaiste, 1987–90.

Lynch, Jack: born in Cork in 1917; elected as Fianna Fáil TD in 1948; appointed as Parliamentary Secretary to the government and to the Minister for Lands by de Valera in 1951; Minister for Education, 1957–9; Minister for Industry and Commerce, 1959–65; Minister for Finance, 1965–6; Taoiseach, 1966–73, 1977–9.

Major, John: first elected as Conservative MP for Huntingdonshire in 1979; became Foreign Secretary in July 1989 and then Chancellor of the Exchequer in October 1989; succeeded Margaret Thatcher as leader of the Conservative Party on 27 November 1990, Prime Minister of the United Kingdom, 28th November 1990–2nd May 1997.

Mansergh, Martin: entered the Department of Foreign Affairs as a civil servant in 1974, promoted to First Secretary, 1977; special advisor, in particular, on issues relating to Northern Ireland, to Fianna Fáil leaders, Charles Haughey, Albert Reynolds and Bertie Ahern; involved in talks with Sinn Féin and church intermediaries prior to the first and second IRA ceasefires; involved in the drafting of the Downing Street Declaration in 1993 and in the negotiations leading to the Good Friday Agreement in 1998; elected as Fianna Fáil senator on the Agricultural Panel in July 2002.

McCartney, Robert: joined the UUP in 1981; elected to the Northern Ireland Assembly, 1982–6 for North Down; expelled from the UUP in 1987; elected to Westminster as UK Unionist in 1995 but lost his seat in 2001; elected as an MLA in 1998.

McDowell, Michael: grandson of Eoin MacNeill, co-founder of the Gaelic League and founder of the Irish Volunteers; barrister at law since 1974; elected as Progressive Democrats' TD for Dublin South-East in 1987; Attorney General, 1999–2002; President of the Progressive Democrats since February 2002; became Minister for Justice, Equality and Law Reform in 2002; became Tánaiste and leader of Progressive Democrats in 2006.

McGuinness, Martin: born in Derry in 1950; joined the IRA in 1970, becoming a leading figure and Chief of Staff in the late 1970s; elected as Sinn Féin MP in 1997 and MLA in 1998; appointed Northern Ireland Minister for Education in 1999.

McLaughlin, Mitchel: elected to the Derry City Council for Sinn Féin in 1985; party talks negotiator, 1996–8; elected member of the Northern Ireland Assembly in 1998.

Molyneaux, James: UUP MP for South Antrim, 1970–1983 and for the Lagan Valley, 1983–97; leader of the UUP, 1979–95; returned to the Northern Ireland Assembly for South Antrim, 1982–6; stood down as leader in 1995.

O'Brien, Conor Cruise: achieved distinction at international level as a diplomat at the Department of Foreign Affairs; returned to Ireland in the late 1960s and was elected as a Labour Party TD in 1969; appointed Minister for Posts and Telegraphs, 1973–7; a renowned academic, broadcaster and writer.

O'Donoghue, John: first elected as Fianna Fail TD for Kerry South in 1987; Minister for Justice, Equality and Law Reform, 1997–2002; appointed Minister for Arts, Sport and Tourism in 2002.

O'Malley, Desmond: elected as Fianna Fáil TD in 1967; succeeded Michael Moran as Minister for Justice in 1970, when Lynch sacked Moran on health grounds in the midst of the Arms Crisis; split from Fianna Fáil in 1985 to form the Progressive Democrats, owing to his personal antipathy of Charles Haughey and, in particular, his decision to oppose the Anglo-Irish Agreement; entered coalition with Fianna Fáil in 1989.

O'Neill, Terence: leader of the Unionist Party and Prime Minister of Northern Ireland, March 1963–May 1969.

O'Rourke, Mary: Fianna Fáil TD, November 1982–2002; deputy leader of Fianna Fáil, 1994–2002; became leader of Fianna Fáil in the Senate in 2002.

Ó Snodaigh, Aengus: elected as Sinn Féin TD for Dublin South Central in 2002.

Paisley, Ian: DUP leader and founder; MP, MEP and MLA for North Antrim; leader of the Free Presbyterian Church.

Quinn, Ruairi: Labour Party TD for Dublin South-East; first elected to the Dáil in 1977; Minister for Finance, 1994–7; deputy leader of the Labour Party, 1990–7; leader of the Labour Party, 1997–2002.

Reid, Alex: a Tipperary-born Redemptorist priest based in West Belfast's Clonard Monastery; had been involved as an intermediary in republican feuds during the 1970s; trusted by republicans, particularly by Adams.

Reynolds, Albert: elected as Fianna Fáil TD in 1977; appointed Minister for Posts and Telegraphs in Haughey's administration in 1979; Minister for Industry and Energy, 1982, 1987; appointed as Minister for Finance in 1988; sacked from government in 1991 after a failed bid to oust Haughey as leader; became leader in 1992 until 1994; Taoiseach, 1992–4.

Spring, Dick: elected as Labour Party TD in 1981 and became a junior minister in the government; succeeded Michael O'Leary as leader of the Labour Party in 1982; Tánaiste and Minister for the Environment in 1982 coalition with Fine Gael; Tánaiste and Minister for Foreign Affairs, 1992–4 in coalition with Fianna Fáil; retained these posts during the 'Rainbow Coalition' of Fine Gael, Labour and Democratic Left, 1994–7; lost his Dáil seat in 2002 to Sinn Féin's Martin Ferris in the constituency of Kerry North.

Thatcher, Margaret: first elected as Conservative MP for Finchley in 1959; became leader of the Conservative Party in February 1975; Prime Minister of the United Kingdom, May 1979–November 1990.

Treacy, Noel: first elected as Fianna Fáil TD for Galway East in May 1982; appointed Minister of State at the Department of the Taoiseach and Foreign Affairs in 2004.

Trimble, David: elected as UUP MP in 1990; elected to the Northern Ireland Assembly in 1998; appointed First Minister in 1999; joint winner of the Nobel peace prize in 1999; leader of the UUP from 1995 until June 2005, when he was succeeded by Sir Reg Empey.

Chronology

1st February 1967

The Northern Ireland Civil Rights Association (NICRA) was formed. The Civil Rights Movement called for a number of reforms including 'one man, one vote', an end to gerrymandering of electoral boundaries, an end to perceived discrimination in the allocation of public sector housing, the repeal of the Special Powers Act and the disbandment of the 'B-Specials' (Ulster Special Constabulary).

24th August 1968

The Campaign for Social Justice (CSJ), NICRA and a number of other groups held the first civil rights march in Northern Ireland, from Coalisland to Dungannon.

5th October 1968

The Royal Ulster Constabulary (RUC) stopped a civil rights march in Derry which had been organized by members of the Derry Housing Action Committee (DHAC) and supported by NICRA. The RUC broke up the march by baton-charging the crowd, injuring many people. This was followed by two days of serious rioting in Derry between the Catholic residents of the city and the RUC.

12th August 1969

Serious rioting erupted in Derry in the aftermath of an Apprentice Boys parade close to the Bogside area. The RUC entered the Bogside and the subsequent 'Battle of the Bogside' between the RUC and Bogside residents lasted for two days.

13th August 1969

As rioting spread across Northern Ireland, Taoiseach Jack Lynch, in a television address on RTÉ, said that 'the Irish government can no longer stand by'. He announced that 'field hospitals' would be set up in border areas.

28th December 1969

The IRA split into the Provisional IRA and the Official IRA.

21st August 1970

The Social, Democratic and Labour Party (SDLP) was established with Gerry Fitt as leader and John Hume as deputy leader.

9th August 1971

Internment was introduced in an attempt to resolve the security problems. Some 342 people were immediately interned. Over the next forty-eight hours violence and protests against internment resulted in seventeen deaths.

30th January 1972

'Bloody Sunday': fourteen people were killed and thirteen injured when British paratroopers opened fire on a section of a NICRA-organized march in Derry. It is a matter of contention whether or not the soldiers came under fire first. The soldiers claimed to have come under sustained attack by gunfire and bombs. No soldiers were injured, however, and no guns or bombs were recovered at the scene of the shooting.

2nd February 1972

The British embassy in Dublin was burnt down during protests following Bloody Sunday.

24th March 1972

In an attempt to take control of security in Northern Ireland the British Prime Minister, Edward Heath, announced that the Stormont parliament was to be prorogued. Direct rule from Westminster was imposed on Northern Ireland on 30th March 1972.

1st December 1972

Two people were killed and 127 injured when two car bombs exploded in the centre of Dublin.

28th February 1973

Fianna Fáil lost power in the General Election in the Republic of Ireland. Liam Cosgrave replaced Jack Lynch as Taoiseach and led a Fine Gael and Labour Party coalition. Jack Lynch remained as leader of Fianna Fáil.

6–9th December 1973

The British Prime Minister, Edward Heath, the Taoiseach, Liam Cosgrave, and representatives of the Ulster Unionist Party (UUP), the SDLP, and the Alliance Party of Northern Ireland (APNI) met in Sunningdale, England. The participants issued an agreed communiqué on 9th December 1973.

16th June 1977

In the general Election in the Republic of Ireland Fianna Fáil was returned to power with Jack Lynch as Taoiseach.

7–11th December 1979

Charles Haughey replaced Jack Lynch as leader of Fianna Fáil on 7th December 1979 and became Taoiseach on 11th December 1979.

1st March–3rd October 1981

H-Block Hunger Strikes: Bobby Sands, then leader of the IRA in the Maze Prison, started a hunger strike demanding the reintroduction of political status for republican prisoners. The strike lasted until 3rd October 1981 and ten republican prisoners died on hunger strike.

11th June 1981

In the general election in the Republic of Ireland Garret FitzGerald (Fine Gael) became Taoiseach and Michael O'Leary (the Labour Party) became Tánaiste. The H-Block candidates won two seats depriving Fianna Fáil of an overall majority.

18th February 1982

Fianna Fáil returned to power with Charles Haughey as Taoiseach.

24th November 1982

In the second general election of that year Fine Gael, under Garret FitzGerald, regained power and the Labour Party's new leader, Dick Spring, became Tánaiste.

30th May 1983

The New Ireland Forum met for the first time in Dublin Castle. The Forum consisted of eight members of Fine Gael, nine members of Fianna Fáil, five members of the Labour Party and five members of the SDLP. The UUP, the Democratic Unionist Party (DUP), and the APNI were invited but declined to attend. Sinn Féin was excluded because of its failure to reject violence. The New Ireland Forum report was published on 2nd May 1984 and it set out three possible options for the future of Northern Ireland: join with the Republic in a United Ireland; joint authority by the Republic of Ireland and Britain; a federal arrangement.

15th November 1985

The Taoiseach, Garret FitzGerald, and the British Prime Minister, Margaret Thatcher, signed the Anglo-Irish Agreement at Hillsborough, Co. Down. The Agreement gave the Irish government a consultative role in matters relating to Northern Ireland. On 21st November 1985 Fianna Fáil voted against the agreement in a Dáil. The agreement was passed by eighty-eight votes to seventy-five.

11th January 1988

The SDLP leader, John Hume, met the leader of Sinn Féin, Gerry Adams.

March and June 1988

An Irish delegation including Martin Mansergh, advisor to Charles Haughey, and Fianna Fáil TD, Dermot Ahern, met with Sinn Féin's Gerry Adams, Mitchel McLaughlin and Pat Doherty.

25–26th March 1991

The UUP, the SDLP, the DUP and the APNI all agreed to the arrangements for political talks on the future of Northern Ireland. The Secretary of State, Peter Brooke, stated that the talks (which became known as the Brooke/Mayhew talks) would involve a three-strand process: Strand One (relationships within Northern Ireland); Strand Two (relations between Northern Ireland and the Republic of Ireland); and Strand Three (relations between the British and Irish governments).

17th June 1991

The Brooke/Mayhew talks began when the four main political parties met at Stormont, Belfast to discuss the future of Northern Ireland.

3rd July 1991

The political talks ended when Peter Brooke announced that he was bringing this stage of the talks to a close.

29th April 1992

The political talks under the guidance of the new Secretary of State, Patrick Mayhew, were recommenced at Stormont with the four main political parties attending.

10th November 1992

Unionists withdrew from the Brooke/Mayhew talks and the process was brought to a close.

15th December 1993

The Taoiseach, Albert Reynolds, and the British Prime Minister, John Major, issued a joint statement that became known as the Downing Street Declaration.

31st August 1994

The IRA announced a complete cessation of military activities as of midnight, 31 August 1994.

13th October 1994

Loyalist paramilitary organizations called a ceasefire.

15th December 1995

John Bruton, leader of Fine Gael, became Taoiseach. He led a coalition government of Fine Gael, the Labour Party and Democratic Left known as the Rainbow Coalition. Albert Reynolds' Fianna Fáil/the Labour Party government had collapsed due to controversy relating to the appointment of the Attorney General, Harry Whelehan, and the attempted extradition of a paedophile Catholic priest, Father Brendan Smyth.

19th December 1995

Bertie Ahern replaced Albert Reynolds as leader of Fianna Fáil.

22nd February 1995

The Taoiseach, John Bruton, and the British Prime Minister, John Major, launched the framework documents, 'A New Framework For Agreement' and 'A Framework For Accountable Government In Northern Ireland'.

9th February 1996

The IRA ceasefire came to an end when it exploded a large bomb at Canary Wharf in London, killing two people.

10th June 1996

All-party negotiations began in Stormont, Belfast. Sinn Féin was refused entry to the talks due to the collapse of the IRA ceasefire.

1st May 1997

In the General Election in the United Kingdom the Labour Party won and entered government with Tony Blair as Prime Minister.

6th June 1997

In a general election in the Republic a coalition of Fianna Fáil, the Progressive Democrats and a number of independents came to power with Bertie Ahern as Taoiseach.

20th July 1997

The IRA renewed its ceasefire at 12.00pm.

15th September 1997

Sinn Féin attended the political talks at Stromont, Belfast. The UUP, the Progressive Unionist Party (PUP), and the Ulster Democratic Party (UDP) joined the talks on 17th September 1997. The DUP and the United Kingdom Unionist Party (UKUP) did not attend.

10th April 1998

The British and Irish governments and the political parties involved in the talks at Stormont reached agreement. The Belfast or Good Friday Agreement was the result of two years of substantive talks.

1st July 1998

Those elected to the Northern Ireland Assembly took their places in the new Assembly at Stormont. David Trimble, leader of the UUP, was elected First Minister Designate of the new assembly and Seamus

Mallon, the deputy leader of the SDLP, as Deputy First Minister Designate.

17th May 2002

Fianna Fáil and the Progressive Democrats were returned to power in the general election. Bertie Ahern was again appointed Taoiseach. Sinn Féin increased its number of seats from one to five.

14th October 2002

The Secretary of State, John Reid, suspended the Northern Ireland Assembly and direct rule from Westminster was restored. The assembly had already been subject to a number of temporary suspensions in 2000. This latest suspension came after Sinn Féin's offices at Stormont were raided by police amidst allegations of spying by republicans.

26th November 2003

Elections to the Northern Ireland Assembly took place. The DUP and Sinn Fein emerged as the largest unionist and nationalist parties respectively.

21st December 2004

£26.5m was stolen from the Northern Bank in Belfast city centre. The IRA said it was not involved in the bank robbery but the British and Irish governments accepted the judgement of Hugh Orde, the Chief Constable of the Police Service of Northern Ireland (PSNI), that the robbery was carried out by the IRA.

30th January 2005

IRA members were believed to be involved in the killing of Robert McCartney, stabbed to death near a Belfast bar. Mr McCartney's sisters subsequently led a high-profile campaign calling for his killers to be brought to justice.

28th July 2005

The IRA formally committed itself to pursue exclusively peaceful means and ordered an end to its armed campaign.

6th May 2005

The DUP won nine seats in the United Kingdom general election. The UUP leader, David Trimble, was defeated in the Upper Bann constituency and subsequently stood down as leader and was replaced by Sir Reg Empey. Sinn Féin became the biggest nationalist party at Westminster, having won five seats.

26th September 2005

The chairman of the arms decommissioning body, General John de Chastelain, reported that the IRA had put all of its weapons beyond use. Father Alex Reid and Reverend Harold Good witnessed the act of decommissioning.

SELECT BIBLIOGRAPHY

NATIONAL ARCHIVES OF IRELAND:

Departments of the Taoiseach and Foreign Affairs, File Nos.
99/1/284, 2000/6/657, 2000/6/658, 2001/6/515, 2001/6/520,
2001/8/6, 2001/8/7, 2001/8/10, 2002/8/487, 2002/8/489,
2002/8/251, 2002/8/252, 2003/13/7, 2003/13/6, 2003/13/16,
2003/16/461, 2003/17/30

FIANNA FÁIL ARCHIVES, UNIVERSITY COLLEGE, DUBLIN:

File Nos. P176/944, P176/775, P176/764, P176/785, P176/790,
P176/781, P176/842, P176/847, P176/851

PUBLIC RECORDS OFFICE OF NORTHERN IRELAND:

File No. CAB/9U/5/2

GOVERNMENT PUBLICATIONS:

Dáil Éireann Reports
Seanád Éireann Reports

BOOKS, ARTICLES, PARTY PUBLICATIONS:

Adams, G. *The Politics of Irish Freedom* (Kerry: Brandon Book
  Publishers, 1986).
——, *Before the Dawn: An autobiography* (London: Mandarin
  Paperbacks, 1996).
——, *Hope and History: Making peace in Ireland* (Kerry: Brandon,
  2003).
Agreement Reached in the Multi-Party Negotiations, Belfast, April 1998.

Ahern, B. *Northern Ireland–Building the peace*, 16 May 2002, avail-
able at http://www.fiannafail/archive_article.php4?id=661 accessed
Aug. 2003.
——, *Joint Statement by President Bush and Prime Minister Tony Blair
and Taoiseach Bertie Ahern*, 8 April 2003, available at
http://www.cain.ulst.ac.uk/events/peace/docs/bi080403.htm
accessed 15 March 2006.
Arnold, B. *What Kind of Country? Modern Irish politics 1968–1983*
(London: Jonathan Cape, 1984).
——, *Haughey: His life and unlucky deeds* (London: HarperCollins
publishers, 1994).
——, *Jack Lynch: Hero in crisis* (Dublin: Merlin Publishing, 2001).
Arthur, P. 'The Brooke Initiative', *Irish Political Studies*, 7 (1992), pp.
111–5.
——, 'The Anglo-Irish Joint Declaration: Towards a lasting peace',
Government and Opposition, 29, 2 (1994), pp. 218–30.
——, 'Anglo-Irish Relations and Constitutional Policy', in P. Mitchell
and R. Wilford (eds), *Politics in Northern Ireland* (Oxford:
Westview Press and PSAI, 1999).
——, *Special Relationships: Britain, Ireland and the Northern Ireland
problem* (Belfast: The Blackstaff Press, 2000).
Augusteijn, J. 'Political Violence and Democracy: An analysis of the
tensions within Irish republican strategy, 1914–2002', *Irish
Political Studies*, 18, 1 (Summer 2003), pp. 1–26.
Bean, K. 'Defining Republicanism: Shifting discourses of new nation-
alism and post-republicanism', in M. Elliott (ed), *The Long Road to
Peace in Northern Ireland. Peace lectures from the Institute of Irish
Studies at Liverpool University* (Liverpool: Liverpool University
press, 2002).
Bew, P. and Gillespie, G. *Northern Ireland: A chronology of the
Troubles 1968–1993* (Dublin: Gill and Macmillan, 1993).
——, *Northern Ireland: A chronology of the Troubles, 1968––1999*
(Dublin: Gill and Macmillan, 1999).
Bew, P., Hazelkorn, E. and Patterson, H. *The Dynamics of Irish
Politics* (London: Lawrence and Wishart, 1989).
Bew, P., and Patterson, H. *Seán Lemass and the Making of Modern
Ireland 1945–66* (Dublin: Gill and Macmillan, 1982).
Bew, P., Patterson, H. and Teague, P. *Between War and Peace: The
political future of Northern Ireland* (London: Wishart and
Lawrence, 1997).
Bloomfield, D. *Political Dialogue in Northern Ireland: The Brooke*

initiative, 1989–92 (London: Macmillan Press, 1998).

Bloomfield, D. *Developing Dialogue in Northern Ireland: The Mayhew Talks, 1992* (Hampshire: Palgrave, 2001).

Bourke, R. *Peace in Ireland: The war of ideas* (London: Pimlico, 2003).

Bowman, J. *De Valera and the Ulster Question, 1917–1973* (Oxford: Clarendon Press, 1982).

Boyce, D.G. '"Can Anyone Here Imagine": Southern Irish political parties and the Northern Ireland problem', in B. Barton and P.J. Roche (eds), *The Northern Ireland Question: Myth and reality* (Aldershot: Ashgate, 1991), pp. 173–99.

Boyce, D.G. and O'Day, A. (eds), *The Making of Modern Irish History: Revisionism and the revisionist controversy* (London and New York: Routledge, 1996).

Brady, C. (ed), *Interpreting Irish History: The debate on historical revisionism* (Dublin: Irish Academic Press, 1994).

Browne, N. *Against the Tide* (Dublin: Gill and Macmillan, 1986).

Burke, J. 'On Walzer's Hermeneutics of Justice, Gadamer's Criterion of Openness and Northern Ireland's Belfast Agreement', *Irish Political Studies*, 14 (1999), pp. 1–22.

Cadogan Group. *Northern Limits: The boundaries of the attainable in Northern Ireland politics* (Belfast: Cadogan Group, 1992).

Callaghan, J.A. *House Divided: The Northern Ireland dilemma* (London: Collins & Co. Ltd, 1972).

Chubb, B. *The Government and Politics of Ireland* (Stanford: Stanford University Press, 1982).

——, *The Politics of the Irish Constitution* (Dublin: Institute of Public Administration, 1991).

Clarke, L. and Johnston, K. *Martin McGuinness: From guns to government* (Edinburgh: Mainstream Press, 2001).

Coakley, J. 'Conclusion: New strains of unionism and nationalism', in J. Coakley (ed), *Changing Shades of Orange and Green: Redefining the Union and the Nation in contemporary Ireland, Perspectives in British–Irish Studies* (Dublin: University College Dublin Press, 2002).

Cochrane, F. 'Any Takers? The isolation of Northern Ireland', *Political Studies*, XLII (1994), pp. 378–95.

Cochrane, F. 'The isolation of Northern Ireland', *Political Studies*, XLIII (1995), pp. 506–8.

Cochrane, F. *Unionist Politics and the Politics of Unionism since the Anglo-Irish Agreement* (Cork: Cork University Press, 1997).

Collins, S. *The Power Game: Ireland under Fianna Fáil* (Dublin: The O'Brien Press, 2001).

Connolly, M. and Loughlin, J. 'Reflections on the Anglo-Irish Agreement', *Government and Opposition*, 21 (1986), pp. 146–60.

Couto, R.A. 'The Third Sector and Civil Society: The case of the "Yes" campaign in Northern Ireland', *Voluntas: International Journal of Voluntary and non-profit organisations*, 12, 3 (Sept. 2001), pp. 221–38.

Cowen, B. Minister for Foreign Affairs, *Clarity; Courage; Change*, speaking at the Annual John Hume Lecture, MacGill Summer School, 20 July 2003, available at http://www.gov.ie/iveagh/information/display.asp?ID=1245 accessed Aug. 2003.

Cox, M. 'Bringing in the "International": The IRA ceasefire and the end of the Cold War', *International Affairs*, 93.4 (1997).

——, 'Thinking "globally" about Peace in Northern Ireland', *Politics*, 18.1 (1998).

——, 'Northern Ireland after the Cold War', in M. Cox, A. Guelke, and F. Stephen (eds), *A Farewell to Arms? From 'long war' to long peace in Northern Ireland* (Manchester: Manchester University Press, 2000).

Cox, W.H. 'Who Wants a United Ireland?', *Government and Opposition*, 20, 1 (Winter 1985).

——, 'Public Opinion and the Anglo–Irish Agreement', *Government and Opposition*, 22 (1987), pp. 336–58.

Crossman, R. *The Diaries of a Cabinet Minister: Volume three, Secretary of State for Social Services 1968–70* (London: Hamish Hamilton and Jonathan Cape, 1977).

Cunningham, M. *British Government Policy in Northern Ireland 1969–2000* (Manchester: Manchester University Press, 2001).

Daly, E. *Mister, Are You a Priest?* (Dublin: Four Courts Press, 2001).

De Bréadún, D. *Far Side of Revenge: Making peace in Northern Ireland* (Cork: The Collins Press, 2001).

Delaney, E. *Accidental Diplomat: My years in the Irish foreign service, 1987–1995* (Dublin: New Island, 2001).

Dixon, P. 'Internationalization and Unionist Isolation: A response to Fergal Cochrane', *Political Studies*, XLIII (1995), pp. 497–505.

——, *Northern Ireland: The politics of war and peace* (Hampshire: Palgrave, 2001).

Duignan, S. *One Spin on the Merry-Go-Round* (Dublin: Blackwater Press, 1996).

Dunphy, R. *The Making of Fianna Fáil Power in Ireland, 1923–1948*

(Oxford: Clarendon Press, 1995).

Dwyer, T.R. *Michael Collins and the Treaty: His differences with de Valera* (Dublin and Cork: The Mercier Press, 1981).

——, 'Eamon de Valera and the Partition Question', in J.P. O'Carroll and J.A. Murphy (eds), *De Valera and his Times* (Cork: Cork University Press, 1983).

——, *Nice Fellow: A biography of Jack Lynch* (Cork and Dublin: Mercier Press, 2001).

——, *Short Fellow: A biography of C. J. Haughey* (Dublin: Marino, 2001).

Edwards, O.D. *Eamon De Valera: Political portraits* (Cardiff: GRC Books, 1987).

Edwards, R.D. *The Faithful Tribe: The loyal institution* (London: HarperCollins Publishers, 2000).

——, *Patrick Pearse: The triumph of failure* (Dublin: Poolbeg Press, 1990), 1st Edition (London: Victor Gollancz, 1977).

English, R. '"Paying No Heed to Public Clamor": Irish republican solipsism in the 1930s', *Irish Historical Studies,* XXVIII, 112 (Nov. 1993), pp. 426–39.

——, 'The State and Northern Ireland', in R. English and C. Townshend (eds), *The State* (London: Routledge, 1997).

——, *Ernie O'Malley: IRA intellectual* (Oxford: Clarendon Press, 1998).

——, *Armed Struggle: A history of the IRA* (Oxford: Macmillan, 2003).

Fanning, R. *Independent Ireland* (Dublin: Helicon, 1983).

——, 'Anglo-Irish Relations: Partition and the British dimension in historical perspective', *Irish Studies in International Affairs,* 2, 1 (1985), pp. 1–20.

——, 'Playing It Cool: The response of the British and Irish governments to the crisis in Northern Ireland, 1968–9', *Irish Studies in International Affairs,* 12 (2001).

Farrell, B. *Seán Lemass* (Dublin: Gill and Macmillan, 1991).

Farren, S. 'The SDLP and the Roots of the Good Friday Agreement', in M. Cox, A. Guelke and F. Stephen (eds), *A Farewell to Arms? From 'long war' to long peace in Northern Ireland* (Manchester: Manchester University Press, 2000).

Farrington, C. 'Ulster Unionist Political Divisions in the Late Twentieth Century', *Irish Political Studies,* 16 (2001), pp. 49–72.

——, *Ulster Unionism and the Peace Process in Northern Ireland* (Basingstoke: Palgrave Macmillan, 2006).

Faulkner, P. *As I Saw It: Reviewing over 30 Years of Fianna Fáil and Irish Politics* (Dublin: Wolfhound Press, 2005).

Feeney, B. *Sinn Féin: A hundred turbulent years* (Dublin: O'Brien Press, 2002).

Finlay, F. *Snakes and Ladders* (Dublin: New Island Books, 1998).

FitzGerald, G. *Towards a New Ireland* (Dublin: Gill and Macmillan, 1972).

——, *All in a Life: An autobiography* (Dublin: Gill and Macmillan, 1992).

——, *Reflections on the Irish State* (Dublin: Irish Academic Press, 2003).

Fitzpatrick, D. 'De Valera in 1917: The undoing of the Easter Rising', in J. O'Carroll and J.A. Murphy (eds), *De Valera and his Times* (Cork: Cork University Press, 1983).

——, *The Two Irelands 1912–1939* (Oxford: Oxford University Press, 1998).

Foster, J.W. 'The Downing Street Declaration (1993)', in J.W. Foster (ed), *The Idea of the Union: Statements and critiques of the Union of Great Britain and Northern Ireland* (Canada, Belcouver Press, 1995).

Gallagher, M. 'Do Ulster Unionists Have a Right to Self-Determination?', *Irish Political Studies*, 5 (1990), pp. 11–30.

Garvin, T. *1922: The birth of Irish democracy* (Dublin: Gill and Macmillan, 1996).

Garvin, T. 'Patriots and Republicans: An Irish evolution', in W. Crotty and D.E. Schmitt (eds), *Ireland and the Politics of Change* (London and New York: Longman, 1998).

——, 'The Fading of Traditional Nationalism in the Republic of Ireland', in J. Coakley (ed), *Changing Shades of Orange and Green: Redefining the Union and the Nation in contemporary Ireland, Perspectives in British–Irish Studies* (Dublin: University College, Dublin Press, 2002).

Gillian Lutz, K. 'Irish Party Competition in the New Millennium: Change or plus ça change?, *Irish Political Studies*, 18, 2 (Winter 2003).

Goodall, D. 'Actually It's All Working out Almost according to Plan', *Parliamentary Brief*, 5, 6 (May/June 1998).

——, 'Hillsborough to Belfast: Is this the final lap?', in M. Elliott (ed), *The Long Road to Peace in Northern Ireland: Peace lectures from the Institute of Irish Studies at Liverpool University* (Liverpool: University Press, 2002).

Guelke, A. 'British Policy and International Dimensions of the Northern Ireland Conflict', *Regional Politics and Policy: An international journal*, 1, 2 (1991), pp. 140–60.

——, 'International and North/South issues', in W. Crotty and D.E. Schmitt (eds), *Ireland and the Politics of Change* (London and New York: Longman, 1998).

Hanley, B. *The IRA 1926–36* (Dublin: Four Courts Press, 2002).

Harkness, D. *Northern Ireland Since 1920* (Dublin: Helicon Limited, 1983).

Hauswedell, C. and Brown, K. *Brief 22 Burying the Hatchet: The decommissioning of paramilitary arms in Northern Ireland* (Bonn International Center for Conversion, INCORE, no date).

Hayes, B.C. and McAllister, I. 'British and Irish Public Opinion towards the Northern Ireland Problem', *Irish Political Studies*, 11 (1996), pp. 61–82.

'Hearts and Minds', BBC1 Northern Ireland, 12 June 2003.

Hennessey, T. *The Northern Ireland Peace Process: Ending the Troubles?* (Dublin: Gill and Macmillan, 2000).

Hopkinson, M. *Green Against Green: The Irish Civil War* (Dublin: Gill and Macmillan, 1988).

Horgan, J. *Seán Lemass: The enigmatic patriot* (Dublin: Gill and Macmillan, 1997).

Horowitz, D.L. 'The Northern Ireland Agreement: Clear, consociational, and risky', in J. McGarry (ed), *Northern Ireland and the Divided World: Northern Ireland conflict and the Good Friday Agreement in comparative perspective* (Oxford: Oxford University Press, 2001).

Hume, J. *Personal Views: Politics, peace and reconciliation in Ireland* (Dublin: Town House, 1996).

Irwin, C. *The People's Peace Process in Northern Ireland* (Hampshire: Palgrave Macmillan, 2002).

Ivory, G. 'Constitutional Republicanism, and the Issue of Consent 1980–1996', *Éire-Ireland* (Summer/Fall 1997), pp. 93–116.

——, 'Revisions in nationalist discourse among Irish political parties', *Irish Political Studies*, 14 (1999), pp. 84–103.

Keena, C. *Haughey's Millions: Charlie's money trail* (Dublin: Gill and Macmillan, 2001).

Kennedy, D. *The Widening Gulf: Northern attitudes to the independent Irish state, 1919-49* (Belfast: The Blackstaff Press, 1988).

Kennedy, M. *Division and Consensus: The politics of cross-border relations in Ireland, 1925–1969* (Dublin: Institute of Public Administration, 2000).

Keogh, D. *The Vatican, The Bishops and Irish Politics, 1919–39* (Cambridge: Cambridge University Press, 1986).

—, *Twentieth Century Ireland: Nation and state* (Dublin: Gill and Macmillan, 1994).

Kissane, B. *Explaining Irish Democracy* (Dublin: University College Dublin Press, 2002).

Laffan, M. *The Partition of Ireland, 1911–1925* (Dundalk: Dundalgan Press, Historical Association of Ireland, 1994).

Laver, M., Mair, P. and Sinnott, R. (eds), *How Ireland Voted: The Irish general election 1987* (Dublin: Poolbeg and PSAI Press, 1987).

Lee, J.J. and Ó Tuathaigh, G. *The Age of de Valera* (Dublin: Ward River Press in association with RTÉ, 1982).

—, *Ireland 1912–1985: Politics and society* (Cambridge: Cambridge University Press, 1989).

Longford, Earl of and O'Neill, T.P. *Eamon de Valera* (Dublin: Gill and Macmillan, 1970).

Lynch, J. *Speeches and Statements on Irish Unity, Northern Ireland, Anglo-Irish Relations, August 1969–October 1971* (Dublin: Government Information Bureau, 1971).

Lyons, F.S.L. *Culture and Anarchy in Ireland, 1890–1939* (Oxford: Clarendon Press, 1979).

—, *Ireland since the Famine* (London: Fontana Press, 1985).

MacArdle, D. *The Irish Republic* (London: Victor Gollancz Ltd, 1938).

MacDermott, E. *Clann na Poblachta* (Cork: Cork University Press, 1998).

MacGinty, R. and Darby, J. *Guns and Government: The management of the Northern Ireland peace process* (Hampshire: Palgrave, 2002).

Mair, P. 'Breaking the Nationalist Mould: The Irish Republic and the Anglo-Irish Agreement', in P. Teague (ed), *Beyond the Rhetoric: Politics, economics and social policy in Northern Ireland* (London: Lawrence and Wishart, 1987).

Major, J. *An Autobiography* (London: HarperCollins, 2000).

Mallie, E. and McKittrick, D. *Endgame: The search for peace in Northern Ireland* (Belfast: Blackstaff Press, 1994).

—, and McKittrick, D. *The Fight for Peace: The secret story behind the Irish peace process* (London: Heinemann, 1996).

—, and McKittrick, D. *Endgame in Ireland* (London: Hodder and Stoughton, 2001).

Mansergh, M. (ed), *The Spirit of the Nation: Speeches by C.J. Haughey 1957–1987* (Cork and Dublin: Mercier Press, 1986).

—, 'The Background to the Irish Peace Process', in M. Cox, A.

Guelke, and F. Stephen (eds), *A Farewell to Arms? From 'long war' to long peace in Northern Ireland* (Manchester: Manchester University Press, 2000).

——, 'Mountain-Climbing Irish Style: The hidden challenges of the peace process', in M. Elliott (ed), *The Long Road to Peace in Northern Ireland. Peace lectures from the Institute of Irish Studies at Liverpool University* (Liverpool: Liverpool University Press, 2002).

Marsh, M. and Mitchell, P. (eds), *How Ireland Voted 1997* (Oxford: Westview Press and PSAI Press, 1999).

Maume, P. 'The Ancient Constitution: Arthur Griffith and his intellectual legacy to Sinn Féin', *Irish Political Studies*, 10 (1995), pp. 123–37.

McCartney, R. *The Unionist Case*, submitted to the Taoiseach, Garret FitzGerald and the leader of the opposition, Charles J. Haughey in 1981, unpublished.

——, *Reflections on Liberty, Democracy and the Union* (Dublin: Maunsel and Co., 2001).

——, 'The McCartney report on Consent' (Belfast: UK/Unionist Party, 1997) as reproduced in R. McCartney, *Reflections on Liberty, Democracy and the Union* (Dublin: Maunsel and Co., 2001).

——, 'The McCartney report on the Framework Documents' (Belfast: UK/Unionist Party, 1997) as reproduced in McCartney, Robert, *Reflections on Liberty, Democracy and the Union* (Dublin: Maunsel and Co., 2001).

McDonald, H. *Trimble* (London: Bloomsbury, 2000).

McGarry, J. and O'Leary, B. *Explaining Northern Ireland: Broken Images* (Oxford: Blackwell Publishers, 1995).

——, *The Politics of Antagonism: Understanding Northern Ireland* (London: The Athlone Press, 1996).

McGarry, J. 'Civic Nationalism and the Agreement', in J. McGarry (ed), *Northern Ireland and the Divided World: Northern Ireland conflict and the Good Friday Agreement in comparative perspective* (Oxford: Oxford University Press, 2001).

Meehan, E. 'Europe and the Europeanisation of the Irish Question', in M. Cox, A. Guelke and F. Stephen, *A Farewell to Arms? From 'long war' to long peace in Northern Ireland* (Manchester: Manchester University Press, 2000).

Mitchell, G. *Making Peace: The inside story of the making of the Good Friday Agreement* (London: William Heinemann, 1999).

Mitchell, P. 'Futures', in P. Mitchell and R. Wilford (eds), *Politics in Northern Ireland* (Oxford: Westview Press and PSAI, 1999).

Moloney, E. *A Secret History of the IRA* (London: Penguin Press, 2002).

Moynihan, M. *Speeches and Statements by Eamon de Valera 1918–73* (Dublin: Gill and Macmillan, 1980).

Mulholland, M. *Northern Ireland at the Crossroads: Ulster Unionism in the O'Neill years 1960–9* (Basingstoke: Macmillan, 2000).

Multi-party Talks, Submissions to Strand Two, 1997–8.

——, Submissions to Strand Two, *Address on behalf of Irish Government by Mr John O'Donoghue TD, Minister for Justice, Equality and Law Reform,* 7 Oct. 1997.

——, *Nature, Form and Extent of New Arrangements–Irish Governments,* 24 Oct. 1997.

Murphy, J.A. *Ireland in the Twentieth Century* (Dublin: Gill and Macmillan, 1981).

Murray, G. *John Hume and the SDLP: Impact and survival in Northern Ireland* (Dublin: Irish Academic Press, 1998).

New Ireland Forum Report (The) 2 May 1984 (Dublin: Stationery Office, 1984).

Northern Ireland Information Service, *Statement by Prime Minister, Tony Blair on Northern Ireland,* Sept. 16 1994.

O'Brien, C.C. *States of Ireland* (London: Hutchinson & Co publishers, 1972).

——, *Passion and Cunning: Essays on nationalism, terrorism and revolution* (New York: Touchstone, 1989).

——, *Ancestral Voices: Religion and nationalism in Ireland* (Dublin: Poolbeg Press, 1994).

O'Brien, J. *The Arms Trial* (Dublin: Gill and Macmillan, 2000).

——, *The Modern Prince: Charles J. Haughey and the quest for power* (Dublin: Merlin Publishing, 2002).

Ó Dochartaigh, N. *From Civil Rights to Armalites: Derry and the birth of the Irish Troubles* (Cork: Cork University Press, 1997).

O'Doherty, M. *The Trouble with Guns: Republican strategy and the Provisional IRA* (Belfast: The Blackstaff Press, 1998).

O'Donnell, C. 'Fianna Fáil and Sinn Féin: The 1988 Talks Reappraised', *Irish Political Studies,* 18, 2 (Winter 2003), pp. 60–81.

——, 'Pan-nationalism: Explaining the Irish Government's role in the Northern Ireland peace process, 1992–1998', *Contemporary British History,* 21, 2 (June 2007), pp. 223–45.

O'Duffy, B. 'British and Irish Conflict Regulation from Sunningdale to Belfast Part I: Tracing the status of contesting sovereigns, 1968–1974', *Nations and Nationalism*, 5, 4 (1999), pp. 523–42.

——, 'British and Irish Conflict Regulation from Sunningdale to Belfast, Part II: Playing for a draw, 1985–1999', *Nations and Nationalism*, 6, 3 (2000), pp. 399-435.

O'Halloran, C. *Partition and Limits of Irish Nationalism: An ideology under stress* (Dublin: Gill and Macmillan, 1987).

O'Leary, B. 'Comparative Political Science and the British–Irish Agreement', in J. McGarry (ed), *Northern Ireland and the Divided World: Northern Ireland conflict and the Good Friday Agreement in comparative perspective* (Oxford: Oxford University Press, 2001).

O'Malley, P. *The Uncivil Wars* (Belfast: The Blackstaff Press, 1983).

O'Toole, F. *The Lie of the Land: Irish identities* (Dublin: New Island Books, 1998).

Paisley, I. *Ulster Democratic Unionist Party's Opening Statement at the Second Plenary Meeting of Strand Two*, Lancaster House, London, July 7 1992.

Paths to a Political Settlement in Ireland: Policy papers submitted to the forum for peace and reconciliation (Belfast: Blackstaff Press, 1995).

Patterson, H. *The Politics of Illusion: A political history of the IRA* (London: Serif, 1997).

——, 'Seán Lemass and the Ulster question, 1959–1965', *Journal of Contemporary History*, 34, 1 (1999), pp. 145–59.

——, *Ireland since 1939* (Oxford: Oxford University Press, 2002).

Peck, J. *Dublin from Downing Street* (Dublin: Gill and Macmillan, 1978).

Prager, J. *Building Democracy in Ireland: Political order and cultural integration in a newly independent nation* (Cambridge: Cambridge University Press, 1986).

Rafter, K. 'Priests and Peace: The role of the Redemptorist Order in the Northern Ireland peace process', *Etudes Irlandaises*, Printemps, 28.1 (2003), pp. 159–76.

Raymond, R.J. 'De Valera, Lemass and Irish Economic Development 1933–1948', in J.P. O'Carroll and J.A. Murphy (eds), *De Valera and his Times* (Cork: Cork University Press, 1983).

Regan, J.M. *The Irish Counter-Revolution 1921–1936: Treatyite politics and the settlement in Independent Ireland* (Dublin: Gill and Macmillan, 1999).

Robinson, P.D. *The Union Under Fire: United Ireland framework revealed* (Belfast: Peter D. Robinson, 1995).

Rose, P. *How the Troubles Came to Northern Ireland* (Hampshire: Palgrave, 2001).

Rowan, B. *The Armed Peace: Life and death after the ceasefires* (Edinburgh and London: Mainstream Publishing, 2003).

RTÉ, 'RTÉ Election 2002', 18 May 2002.

——, 'The Week in Politics', 19 May 2002.

Ruane, J. and Todd, J. *The Dynamics of Conflict in Northern Ireland: Power, conflict and emancipation* (Cambridge: Cambridge University Press, 1996).

——, 'Peace Processes and Communalism in Northern Ireland', in W. Crotty and D.E. Schmitt (eds), *Ireland and the Politics of Change* (London and New York: Longman, 1998).

——, 'Irish Nationalism and the Conflict in Northern Ireland', in D. Millar (ed.), *Rethinking Northern Ireland* (London and New York: Longman, 1998).

——, 'The Belfast Agreement: Context, content, consequences', in J. Ruane and J. Todd (eds), *After the Good Friday Agreement: Analysing political change in Northern Ireland* (Dublin: University College Dublin Press, 1999).

Ryan, T. *Dick Spring: A safe pair of hands* (Dublin: Blackwater Press, 1993).

Sinn Féin, *Sinn Féin Yesterday and Today* (Dublin: Sinn Féin, 1971).

——, *Towards a Lasting Peace in Ireland* (Dublin: Sinn Féin, 1994), also available at http://sinnfein.ie/pdf/TowardsLasting_Peace.pdf accessed 15 March 2006.

Skelly, J.M. 'Appeasement in Our Time: Conor Cruise O'Brien and the peace process in Northern Ireland', *Irish Studies in International Affairs*, 10 (1999), pp. 221–36.

Smith, J. *Making the Peace in Ireland* (Edinburgh and London: Pearson Education Ltd, 2002).

Social Democratic and Labour Party, *Agreed Statement from John Hume and Gerry Adams* (Belfast: SDLP, 25 Sept. 1993).

Staunton, E. *The Nationalists of Northern Ireland, 1918–1973* (Dublin: The Columba Press, 2001).

Tonge, J. 'The Origins and Development of the Peace Process', in C. Gilligan and J. Tongue (eds), *Peace or War? Understanding the peace process in Northern Ireland* (Aldershot: Ashgate, 1997).

Townshend, C. *Political Violence in Ireland: Government and resistance since 1848* (Oxford: Clarendon Press, 1983).

——, *Ireland: The Twentieth Century* (London: Arnold, 1998).

Trimble, D. *To Raise up a New Northern Ireland: Articles and speeches 1998-2000* (Belfast: The Belfast Press, 2001).

Ulster Unionist Party, *Opening Statement at the Second Plenary Meeting of Strand Two*, Lancaster House, London, July 7 1992.

——, 'A Response to the Government of the Irish Republic', *Submission to the Plenary Meeting on Strand Two at Parliament Buildings*, Belfast, Friday 24 July 1992.

——, *Response to Frameworks for the Future*, available at http://www.uup.org/current/fraMr.esp.html accessed Aug. 2003.

Whelan, K. and Masterson, E. *Bertie Ahern: Taoiseach and peacemaker* (Edinburgh: Blackwater Press, 1998).

Whyte, J.H. *Church and State in Modern Ireland, 1923–1970* (Dublin: Gill and Macmillan, 1971).

——, *Interpreting Northern Ireland* (Oxford: Clarendon Paperbacks, 1990).

Wilson, A.J. *Irish America and the Ulster conflict, 1968–1995* (Belfast: Blackstaff Press, 1995).

Zartman, I.W. 'The Timing of Peace Initiatives: Hurting stalemates and ripe moments', in J. Darby and R. MacGinty (eds), *Contemporary Peacemaking: Conflict, violence and peace processes* (Hampshire: Palgrave Macmillan, 2003).

NEWSPAPERS:

An Phoblacht/Republican News
Andersonstown News
Belfast Telegraph
Connacht Tribune
Daily Ireland
Daily Mail
Derry Journal
Economist
Guardian
Independent
Irish Independent
Irish Independent Weekly Review
Irish News
Irish Press
Newsletter
New Ulster Defender

Saturday *Times*
Sun
Sunday *Business Post*
Sunday *Independent*
Sunday *News*
Sunday *Observer*
Sunday *Press*
Sunday *Times*
Sunday *Tribune*
The Irish Times
Time
Times

INTERVIEWS:

Dermot Ahern, Fianna Fáil Minister, 1 Nov. 2002
Martin Ferris, Sinn Féin TD, 12 June 2003
Frank Fahey, Fianna Fáil Minister of State, 13 Dec. 2005 and correspondence 4 Jan. 2006
Tom Kitt, Fianna Fáil Minister of State, 12 Jan. 2006
Conor Lenihan, Fianna Fáil Minister of State, 16 Nov. 2005
Martin Mansergh, Fianna Fáil Senator, 12 Dec. 2002
John O'Donoghue, Fianna Fáil Minister, 7 Feb. 2006
Mary O'Rourke, Fianna Fáil Senator, 15 Nov. 2005
Aengus Ó Snodaigh, Sinn Féin TD, 12 June 2003
Albert Reynolds, Former Fianna Fáil Taoiseach, 8 Aug. 2003
Noel Treacy, Fianna Fáil Minister of State, 1 Dec. 2005

Index